Reading Hemingway's *The Old Man and the Sea*

READING HEMINGWAY SERIES
MARK CIRINO, EDITOR
ROBERT W. LEWIS, FOUNDING EDITOR

Reading Hemingway's *The Sun Also Rises*
   H. R. Stoneback

Reading Hemingway's *Men Without Women*
   Joseph M. Flora

Reading Hemingway's *Across the River and into the Trees*
   Mark Cirino

Reading Hemingway's *To Have and Have Not*
   Kirk Curnutt

Reading Hemingway's *The Old Man and the Sea*
   Bickford Sylvester, Larry Grimes, and Peter L. Hays

Reading Hemingway's
The Old Man and the Sea

GLOSSARY AND COMMENTARY

Bickford Sylvester, Larry Grimes, and Peter L. Hays

The Kent State University Press

KENT, OHIO

© 2018 by The Kent State University Press, Kent, Ohio 44242
All rights reserved
Library of Congress Catalog Card Number 2018008753
ISBN 978-1-60635-342-4
Manufactured in the United States of America

LIBRARY OF CONGRESS CATALOGING-IN-PUBLICATION DATA
Names: Sylvester, Bickford, 1925- author. | Grimes, Larry E. (Larry Edward), 1942- author. | Hays, Peter L., 1938- author.
Title: Reading Hemingway's The old man and the sea : glossary and commentary / Bickford Sylvester, Larry Grimes, and Peter L. Hays.
Description: Kent, Ohio : The Kent State University Press, [2018] | Series: Reading Hemingway series ; 5 | Includes bibliographical references and index.
Identifiers: LCCN 2018008753 | ISBN 9781606353424 (pbk. : alk. paper)
Subjects: LCSH: Hemingway, Ernest, 1899-1961. Old man and the sea.
Classification: LCC PS3515.E37 O5294 2018 | DDC 813/.52--dc23
LC record available at https://lccn.loc.gov/2018008753

22 21 20 19 18   5 4 3 2 1

Dedicated to
Bruce L. Grenberg
by his colleague and friend
Bickford Sylvester

CONTENTS

Preface   ix

Acknowledgments   xi

Introduction to *The Old Man and the Sea*   xiii

Abbreviations for the Works of Ernest Hemingway Used in This Book   xxvii

Series Note   xxix

Pages 5 through 27   3

Pages 28 through 43   44

Pages 44 through 53   63

Pages 54 through 77   71

Pages 78 through 96   86

Pages 97 through 106   96

Pages 107 through 119   104

Pages 120 through 127   112

Works Cited   119

Index   127

PREFACE

This is a book by three hands. Most of it was written by Bickford Sylvester, longtime Hemingway scholar, who died on 24 July 2014. Bick was a World War II veteran, musician, soccer enthusiast, and—significant for this book—deep-sea fisherman and salmon guide in Alaska, British Columbia, Canada, and northwest Washington state where he lived. He sailed the open ocean, as Santiago did; he knew currents and wind patterns; and he knew fish—but salmon, not marlin. His research into *The Old Man and the Sea* began long ago for his 1966 articles in *PMLA* and *Modern Fiction Studies*, continued through his contribution to Scott Donaldson's *Cambridge Companion to Ernest Hemingway* (1996), and lasted until shortly before his death, with the publication of *Hemingway, Cuba, and the Cuban Works* (2014), which had to be completed by Larry Grimes. A generous scholar, Bick often put his own work aside to help others, as he did when he shelved work on this book to edit Morris Buske's book *Hemingway's Education: A Re-examination* (Mellen, 2007), after Buske's death. Throughout his work, Bick was supported by his wife, helpmate, and chief proofreader, Barbara. Before his own death, Bick asked Peter Hays and Larry Grimes to finish his work, and we have, to the best of our abilities.

The Old Man and the Sea mentions Santiago's "hard-braided" line (15:5). The three hands pulling these annotations together sometimes tugged in slightly different directions, but we have striven to construct a seamless text and an informative one, a hard-braided one. We have also worked to weave together various strains of interpretation. First, there is the factual base of wind and water that Bick knew, fishing and fishes, which we all researched and got wonderful help from university types, a Cuban journalist, *Wikipedia,* and even Sea World biologists. Next is the various allusions and symbols, the Christian being most apparent: saints' names—James (Santiago), Peter, and Martin—and references to the Passion of Christ. There are also obvious references to baseball, and a detailed knowledge of the game both dates the novella and explains other aspects. Less obvious are the allusions to the Afro-Cuban religion that we know as Santeria, that Santiago also acknowledges, perhaps practices, and that Hemingway includes in his novella. There also seem to be references to Friedrich Nietzsche and his philosophy of the autonomous individual, as well as references to the Grail myth and the Fisher King. Finally, and pervasively, there is a theme of what might be called mysticism or, perhaps, ecological awareness together with a sense of one's purpose in that ecology: Santiago bonds with certain aspects of nature early on—the white peaks of mountains in the Canaries and the lions he sees playing on the beaches of Africa. He identifies with creatures in the ocean, particularly the marlin that he paradoxically respects and kills. Those paradoxes play throughout the work, sometimes pulling in different directions (like the three contributors to this book): Christianity against Santeria, Christianity against Nietzscheism and against nature red in tooth and claw, where one may be imbued with love for all things but still kill to live, where we have to recognize limits to our compassion and charity. But Christianity itself has its internal paradoxes, such as a three-person God or a death that confers life.

Paradoxes are part of *The Old Man and the Sea*. Mysteries are not solved. And in not doing so, Hemingway has captured life with its myriad influences and, as seen by others, multiple meanings. His novella inspired millions of readers and innumerable interpretations. We cannot say one interpretation is the only correct one, for many are possible. What we have tried to do is provide the facts of the ocean, the marlin and the sharks, and Cuban fishing, and to identify as many of the possible allusions and connections as we could. Interpretation, as always in Hemingway, is up to the reader, as catching the fish is up to the person holding the line, hard-braided, from many different strands and sources.

ACKNOWLEDGMENTS

First, and most important of all, we thank our wives—Carol Grimes and Myrna Hays—whose love and support made our research, writing, and editing possible as we undertook the challenge of completing the work of our friend and colleague Bick Sylvester, who spent much of his life on *The Old Man and the Sea* and at least the last twenty years of his life on this book, which is largely his. Also owed thanks is Bick's wife, helpmeet, and proofreader, Dr. Barbara Sylvester.

We also wish to acknowledge the invaluable help of Raúl Villarreal, Ismael León Almeida, Dr. D. Duane Cummins, the audiovisual archivists who curate the Hemingway Collection at the John F. Kennedy Presidential Library and Museum in Boston, and Jeffrey and Nancy Seglin, who provided generous hospitality to wandering scholars. We especially wish to thank Duane Raver for his painting of the marlin and Kay Smith for her cover painting.

We are grateful for the many specialists—on everything from arm wrestling to heart conditions, from marine biology to ophthalmology—who provided expertise as it was needed. Finally, we acknowledge the Edward A. Dickson Award (University of California, Davis) for making publication of the color images possible.

Fig. 1. Hemingway and Carlos in 1936 with a blue marlin, the type of fish Santiago catches. (Courtesy Ernest Hemingway Collection. John F. Kennedy Library and Museum, Boston)

INTRODUCTION TO

THE OLD MAN AND THE SEA

The seed for *The Old Man and the Sea* was planted long before the book was written out fully. In Hemingway's essay "On the Blue Water: A Gulf Stream Letter," published in *Esquire* in 1936, he recounts a story told to him by his boat pilot, Carlos Gutiérrez. It begins,

> Another time an old man fishing alone in a skiff out of Cabañas hooked a great marlin that, on the heavy sashcord handline, pulled the skiff far out to sea. Two days later the old man was picked up by fishermen sixty miles to the eastward, the head and forward part of the marlin lashed alongside. What was left of the fish, less than half, weighed eight hundred pounds. (*BL* 239)

The remainder of the account describes the shark attack and the old man's condition when rescued. The long paragraph provides the narrative outline of the action in *The Old Man and the Sea*. Figure 1 pictures Hemingway and Carlos in 1936 with a blue marlin.

The story Carlos told occurred much earlier than 1936. According to Cuban Hemingway specialist Mary Cruz, such a story was printed in *La Habana Elegante*, 28 June 1891. The article on marlin fishing in the Gulf Stream, written by famous Cuban novelist Ramón Meza, details the daily routine of simple fishermen like Santiago. What Meza describes anticipates details in Gutiérrez's story, much as Gutiérrez's story forecasts *The Old Man and the Sea*. What is most striking about Meza's article is that what some have seen to be a romanticized exceptionalism depicted in Santiago was the common experience of those who ventured out in fishing skiffs. Meza writes, "Man must employ all his experience and skill in that struggle where he is the weakest because he is out of his element. . . . The line must be let out and pulled in in brief and precise instances. . . . When the fisherman manages to pull the fish close to the boat, the danger increases. . . . [T]he fisherman makes sure to kill it by stabbing it with his harpoon. A bitter struggle ensues, often in the dark of night" (Cruz 168–70, translated by Mary Delpino). According to Cruz, Hemingway told a story lived many times over by Cuban fishermen, one that may have taken on a certain formulaic shape by the time Gutiérrez told it to the author. Hemingway's retelling grows the narrative from its roots in the daily round, from its shape as a folk/fishing story into a finely crafted, numinous fiction rich in possible interpretations, and builds from several separate yet intersecting genres, including the big-fish-that-got-away stories, a manual for early billfishing off the Cuban coast, a naturalist's guide to the Gulf Stream, a fable (beast, religious, modern), a tragedy (Greek, Christian, modern), an existentialist novel (Sisyphus, Übermensch, knight of faith), an example of literary naturalism, and a saint's tale (St. James, St. Francis).

A photograph taken by Hemingway while fishing in the Gulf Stream in 1932 may also be preparatory to *The Old Man and the Sea* (see page 19, Figure 7, which shows Cuban fishermen landing a shark). Although the picture is of fishermen with a shark rather than a marlin, it records accurately the construction of the fishing skiff, provides a sense of scale between large fish and small boat, as another provides a clear view of a patched sail that, "furled, . . . looked like the flag of permanent defeat" (*OMS* 9:13–14).

More than the germ of a story grew from Hemingway's own encounter with the Gulf Stream in the 1930s. He constantly increased his knowledge of the Stream itself and received his thousands of hours on it with great pleasure and deep sustenance. Both the knowledge Hemingway accumulated about all life in the "Great Blue River," as he called it, and the deep joy he experienced fishing in it contributed both to the speed with which he would later compose the novella and the powerful experience it gave to his readers. No one has calculated the hours Hemingway spent fishing in the Gulf from 1932 to 1952, but certainly it was several thousand. During that time, he took delight in the sport of big-game fishing, at which he was extremely capable, but he also found great pleasure in studying life in the Gulf Stream as a serious amateur naturalist. Perhaps the best evidence of his serious study comes from his work with Charles Cadwalader, director of the Natural History Museum of Philadelphia, whom Hemingway invited onboard his boat the *Pilar,* along with ichthyologist Henry Fowler, to record catches and describe them (Baker, *Life* 264; Ott 36–40). Evidence of his mastery as a big-game fisherman comes from his recorded catches and victories in fishing tournaments. Bridging his passion as a fisherman and his concerns as a naturalist is his founding and becoming vice-president of the International Gamefish Association (Ott 55). His fishing logs bear testimony to both his passion as a fisherman and his knowledge as a naturalist. The pictures in Figures 2 and 3, both from 1934, show Hemingway with caught marlin, with Carlos Gutíerrez in Figure 3, holding the marlin's fin, and Joe Russell, owner of the *Anita,* which Hemingway rented before he owned the *Pilar,* in both pictures on the other side of the beam in tie, jacket, and cap.

In his insightful study of Hemingway's fishing logs, Mark Ott quotes entries that directly prefigure lines in *The Old Man and the Sea*. Two entries for 14 July 1934, from the *Anita* log illustrate this well. Commenting on the behavior of two marlin, Hemingway writes, "pair when we find them/male rush boat and refuse/to leave

Left: Fig. 2. Hemingway with silver marlin on dock. In both photos, Joe Russell, owner of the *Anita,* which Hemingway rented before he owned the *Pilar,* stands on the other side of the beam in tie, jacket, and cap, 1934. (Courtesy Ernest Hemingway Collection. John F. Kennedy Library and Museum, Boston)

Below: Fig. 3. Hemingway with silver marlin on dock with Carlos Gutiérrez holding the fin, 1934. (Courtesy Ernest Hemingway Collection. John F. Kennedy Library and Museum, Boston)

when female hooked" (Ott 12–13). In *The Old Man and the Sea* (49:10–50:1–2) Santiago recalls a similar event. In the logs, Hemingway also comments on the sex life of loggerhead turtles (Ott 23), something Santiago calls "strange" in *The Old Man and the Sea* (36:23–37:1). In the *Anita* log, we read, "Carlos had one [marlin]/could not get/into boat and sharks bit off all/except head and [shoulders?]" (Ott 13). This observation anticipates the destruction of Santiago's marlin by the sharks. Ott also quotes from the memoir of Arnold Samuelson, who kept Hemingway's log. Samuelson recounts an incident that happened when Hemingway and his crew tied up at the small town of Cabañas. There, Ott recounts, quoting Samuelson, a "market fisherman gave E. H. the sword of an 800 pound marlin that had towed his skiff three miles out to sea before he could kill it" (45). This material from 1934 suggests that Hemingway's acquaintance with the rudiments of his great fishing story were placed in his imagination long before he shaped them into *The Old Man and the Sea* and committed them to print. In a letter dated 7 February 1939, Hemingway tells his editor Maxwell Perkins that among the long works he plans to write is one about "the old commercial fisherman who fought the swordfish all alone in his skiff . . . and the sharks finally eating it after he had it along side." Hemingway goes on to say that he plans to have Carlos Gutíerrez on his skiff "so as to get it all right" (*SL* 479). Clearly, during the 1930s, Hemingway thought often about what would become *The Old Man and the Sea*, though it would take another decade for it to become a book.

Biographers Carlos Baker (*Life* 488–90) and Michael Reynolds (*Final Years* 235–38) both speculate that the arrival of Adriana Ivancich at his Cuban home, the *Finca*, on 28 October 1950 ended a period of deep "black ass," Hemingway's name for the depression that beset him, which had descended on Hemingway earlier that year as he dealt with marital troubles caused by his obsession with Ivancich, negative critical reviews of *Across the River and into the Trees*, and blowback from the Lillian Ross "Portrait" in the *New Yorker*, as well as possible underlying physical and mental conditions. Several weeks of intense work on the "sea book" followed shortly after Ivancich's arrival. Baker and Reynolds also agree that the manuscript of *The Old Man and the Sea*, originally intended to be a section of the "sea book," was written in eight extremely productive weeks from early January through mid-February 1951. Burwell writes of four parts to the sea book (52); Baker, of three, with *The Old Man and the Sea* being the part entitled "The Sea in Being" (*Life* 488–89). In a July 1951 letter to Charles Scribner, Hemingway dropped the "Sea in Being" title and for the first time referred to the novella as "the old man and the sea" (*Life* 494*).* The following year, in a letter of 4/7 March 1952 to his then-current editor Wallace Myers at Scribner's, Hemingway chronicles his efforts toward securing an appropriate publication of the manuscript, including reference to his rejection of an offer from *Cosmopolitan* and to Hollywood producer Leland Hayward's February suggestion that he secure a contract for publication in *Life* magazine and as a Book-of-the-Month selection. Hemingway would follow through on Hayward's suggestions. Near the conclusion of this letter, Hemingway reflects briefly on the composition of *The Old Man and the Sea,* saying that he has read it about twenty times "besides reading all of it from the beginning each day I wrote it. Not sure there is much I would change" (*SL* 759).

The novella had its original place in a sprawling and never fully realized project derived from Hemingway's World War II experiences and envisioned as a land, air, and sea trilogy. According to Rose Marie Burwell who has provided a detailed study of the manuscripts, Hemingway began this larger work in 1946. The other three parts of the "sea book" were published posthumously as *Islands in the Stream;* the land portion became *Across the River and into the Trees;* and the air portion never materialized. In manuscript, Hemingway first used the title "The Sea in Being" for the *The Old Man and the Sea* section of the "sea book," as yet unwritten. Burwell suggests that, as originally conceived, *The Old Man and the Sea* was a work written by Roger Davis, a protagonist in the "Bimini" section of the "sea book," and would have been presented as such had it not been excised for stand-alone publication (59–61). Further, she connects *The Old Man and the Sea* with the "Miami" section of the "sea work" (also excised) and notes its echoes of the shark attack in the "Bimini" section. While Burwell's description of the place of *The Old Man and the Sea* in the larger "sea work" ur-text is helpful, her suggestion that the story takes place in 1936 (52, 58) does not square with the published text of *The Old Man and the Sea*—especially baseball references to Joe DiMaggio's 1949 and 1950 seasons. As Hemingway told Wallace Meyer, "he had learned enough in twenty-five years [since writing *The Sun Also Rises*] so that he didn't have to rewrite *The Old Man* at all" (Baker, *Life* 500). There is no manuscript evidence to suggest any other designation for the novella beyond "The Sea in Being" until it is finally given the title *The Old Man and the Sea.*

Hemingway carefully selected the titles for his stories and novels. In *The Paris Review* interview with George Plimpton, Hemingway says, "I make a list of titles *after* I've finished the story or book, sometimes as many as a hundred" ("Interview" 235; emphasis in original). While the number may be exaggerated, the practice of thoughtfully selecting titles from a long list was his common practice. The most noted case is *A Farewell to Arms.* Manuscript material shows that he considered thirty-four titles for that novel before settling on one (Oldsey 11–34).

The selection of the title, like the completion of the novella itself, seems to have come about quickly during the near-manic writing days of 1950–51. Hemingway did not turn to the King James Bible as he often did, where he might have selected a title such as "Leviathan on a Fish Hook" (Job 41:1); nor did he turn to a favorite anthology, *The Oxford Book of English Verse;* or to Shakespeare where, in *Hamlet,* we read about kings, fish, and worms; or to Izaak Walton's *Compleat Angler,* which sat on a shelf in his library. The title suggested for the novella appears to have come from Hemingway's daily critical rereading of the manuscript and to have grown easily and organically from the narrative itself. It may, however, also have roots in myth and folklore from as far back as his high school days in Oak Park, Illinois.

Tale type G311 in the Stith Thompson *Motif Index of Folk Literature* is the old man of the sea. Also, the Greek mythological figure Nereus, a sea deity and grandfather of Achilles, appears six times in the *Iliad,* unnamed, but called, rather, "the old man of the sea," the title Edith Hamilton bestows on him in her mythological dictionary. Quoting Hesiod's *Theogony* (ll. 234–36), she describes Nereus as "a trusty god and gentle, who thinks just and kindly thoughts and never lies" (38). Hemingway had a copy of the *Iliad* in his library, read excerpts in high school, and, according to Michael Reynolds, read the epic poem again in 1929 (*Hemingway's Reading* 26).

Oldsey suggests that Hemingway's titles provide "thematic thrusts and narrative emphasis," and so they do (16). The early references to what would become *The Old Man and the Sea* direct attention to "the sea in being" rather than "the fish as marlin." At no point does it appear that Hemingway thought about titling the novella "The Old Man and the Fish" or "The Old Man and the Marlin." A cautionary note is sounded in the title choice—don't overread the contest between Santiago and the marlin and don't underread the larger ontological, ecological, and transcendental contest/agon between an old man and the sea. There is throughout the novella a concern with Being-Itself and the place of humankind within all that is, as well as with the relation of all that is, including small birds, turtles, and sharks, to humankind.

The title Hemingway selected does not name Santiago. Instead, a more generic phrase is chosen. We are not reading *Santiago and the Sea* or *Santiago and the Fish/Marlin*. Readers should not forget that Santiago's age shapes his behaviors and his reflections as well as his place in "the sea of being." In 1950, according to CDC data, the average life span for a white male in the United States was 66.5, for an African male, 59.1 (https://www.cdc.gov/nchs/data/hus/2010/022.pdf). If one takes these data into consideration and translate them either to Hemingway, whose health was troubling, or to Santiago, who is a poor, aging Cuban fisherman, then the phrase "old man" points toward ways of being and doing shaped by some certainty that death is only a decade away. Limits are a major theme in the novella. Death sets the harshest of boundaries. The title selection suggests several themes in relation to limits and boundaries: How restrictive are they? What happens when one trespasses? What can one do when too far out? How should one act at the edge of it all? What is the sum of a person when the full measure of a life is taken? How does one evaluate the worth of life over and against the limits? Old-folk questions. Perhaps the wise reflections of Santiago are a gift to readers, unless Santiago is more fool than saint. As Oldsey suggests, the title Hemingway selected does indeed provide "thematic thrusts and narrative emphasis," thrusts and emphases that push the reader toward questions that make the sum of the novella greater than its parts.

If holographic manuscripts or early typescripts of *The Old Man and the Sea* were available, there might be a better understanding of the title; however, the only manuscript version of the novella presently available is Item EH 90, a typescript of the work with penciled revisions, in the Hemingway Collection at the John Fitzgerald Kennedy Library and Museum in Boston. Most of the revisions are minor copyediting changes, corrected spellings, insertion of omitted words, and such. The revisions were made in January/February 1951 and probably represent Hemingway's last significant changes in the manuscript, although slight variations between the typescript and the published work suggest some further editing, most likely as the galley was proofed.

Several additions in the typescript are quite significant. Those additions suggest that Hemingway shifted from writer to perceptive and critical reader as he reworked the manuscript. These additions function much like couplets at the end of a well-crafted sonnet—sometimes bringing dramatic closure to an action or thought, sometimes providing important clarification of an episode or reflection, sometimes offering deep meditation on the moment at hand. Often a minor change has a major impact, as when Hemingway added the phrase "by himself" to "alone" when referring to Santiago's habit of talking aloud (EH 90, 27; *OMS* 39:8–11), thus emphasizing the old man's isolation and individuation during his agon. Or the simple change of "From out here" to "This far out" (EH 90, 29; *OMS* 41:22), reinforcing the "too far out" theme that runs through the novella. Among the additions are lines such as "I do not care who kills who" (*OMS* 92:17–18), "Fishing kills me exactly as it keeps me alive" (*OMS* 106:6–7), and "finally and without remedy" (*OMS* 119:9–10).

Below is a list of the most significant additions to the text added in the manuscript. The left-hand column indicates where the addition is located in *The Old Man and the Sea*, while following the addition is its placement in the EH 90 typescript:

22:12	, the father, was playing	(EH 90, 12)
22:20	*Jota* for J.	(EH 90, 12)
46:22–23	I wish I could see him only once to know what I have against me.	(EH 90, 33)
48:2–5	It would be wonderful to do this with a radio. Then he thought, think of it always. Think of what you are doing. You must do nothing stupid.	(EH 90, 34)
50:4–5	He was beautiful, the old man remembered, and he had stayed.	(EH 90, 35)
50:19	Beyond all people in the world.	(EH 90, 36)
54:12–13	It was the yellow Gulf weed that made so much phosphorescence in the night.	(EH 90, 40)
69:17–21	The walls were painted bright blue and were of wood and the lamps threw their shadows against them. The negro's shadow was huge and it moved on the wall as the breeze moved the lamps.	(EH 90, 57)

87:2–3	Now I must convince him and then I must kill him.	(EH 90, 69)
92:17–18	I do not care who kills who.	(EH 90, 75)
94:12–13	and he could not see well.	(EH 90, 77)
106:6–8	Fishing kills me exactly as it keeps me alive. The boy keeps me alive, he thought. I must not deceive myself too much.	(EH 90, 90)
112:1–3	showing first life-size, then smaller, then tiny. That always fascinated the old man. But he did not even watch it now.	(EH 90, 96)
119:9–10	finally and without remedy	(EH 90, 104)

The Old Man and the Sea was well received upon publication both in the 1 September 1952 *Life* magazine—it sold over five million copies in two days—and in hard copy a few days later, winning Hemingway the Pulitzer Prize in 1952 and pushing forward his award of the Nobel Prize in 1954. Robert O. Stephens compiled a selection of thirty-one early reviews of *The Old Man and the Sea*. Of the thirty-one reviews only five were qualified or negative in their evaluation of the work (338–71). Many used the word "classic" when describing it. The novella was applauded as proof that Hemingway had recovered fully from the failure most thought *Across the River and into the Trees* had been. Many placed it in the tradition of Herman Melville's great American novel *Moby-Dick*. Its character as a parable, its tragic sense, its lean, clear prose style, its profound exploration of the relation of humanity to nature, its religious and moral depth were all singled out for praise. Many saw it as the apex of the Hemingway canon. A few dissenters saw *The Old Man and the Sea* as a rehash of earlier work, his own and others, as so stripped down as to be little more than a fishing story, as not completely serious.

Three of the early commentators accused Hemingway of imitating his own early style in *The Old Man and the Sea*. Leslie Fiedler did so in *End to Innocence* (1955, 4; repeated in *Waiting for the End*, 10), and Delmore Schwartz did so in *The Partisan Review* (reprinted in Meyers, *Critical Heritage* 415). Dwight MacDonald said in an *Encounter* piece of January 1962 that "Hemingway had begun to parody himself in *The Old Man and the Sea* . . . [using] a slack, fake biblical style" (121). Even more shrill in his condemnation was Phillip Toynbee, who said that *The Old Man and the Sea* was "meretricious from beginning to end. . . . [T]he archaic false simplicities of its style are insufferable. . . . [The sentimentality is flagrant and outrageous and . . . the myth is tediously enforced" (87). It is true that the style of *The Old Man and the Sea* is simpler than that of *For Whom the Bell Tolls* and *Across the River and into the Trees*. But, in those works, the protagonists are educated, deeply self-reflexive men, given to an introspection that demands a style capable of handling their thoughts and the complicated situations in which we find them. Santiago, in contrast, is a simple, uneducated man, little given to philosophizing, much more concerned with the physical tasks at hand. What these commentators fail to recognize is that

Hemingway chose a style—in all these works—appropriate for the protagonists' thoughts and actions. Their criticisms are as if one would criticize Paul Cézanne for using a brush stroke or a color he had previously used.

Hemingway himself engaged in this early conversation about *The Old Man and the Sea* in interviews, letters, and, it seems, in his Nobel Prize address in 1954. His response was twofold. On the one hand he maintained, in a letter to Bernard Berenson, dated 13 September 1952, that "there isn't any symbolysm [sic]. The sea is the sea. The old man is an old man. The boy is a boy and the fish is a fish. The sharks are all sharks no better and no worse. All the symbolism people say is shit. What goes beyond is what you see beyond when you know" (*SL*, 780). This attitude he seems to confirm in remarks Lillian Ross recalls in the afterword of her *Portrait*: "He had fun with the way some highbrow critics discussed the 'symbolism' in the story. 'Down here [Cuba] nobody sees symbolism in it at all,' he said. 'They think it is about la puta mar and an old man and a fish and sharks just the way I wrote it" (Kindle Afterword, np.)

On the other hand, he does suggest that parabolic, allegoric, and figurative elements are placed in the text. For example, in a 14 July 1954 letter to Robert Morgan Brown, Hemingway wrote, "[Y]ou know about Santiago and you know his name was no accident." In *The Paris Review* interview with George Plimpton, he backs away from the absolute claim that there is no symbolism in his work, saying, "I suppose there are symbols since critics keep finding them. If you do not mind I dislike talking about them and being questioned about them" (229). In the afterword to Lillian Ross's *Portrait*, Hemingway's reflection on writing in his Nobel Prize speech suggests that he understood *The Old Man and the Sea* to contain a "parable" about writing itself. The story of the old man is the very type of writer Hemingway describes in that speech: "Writing, at its best, is a lonely life. . . . [The writer] does his work alone and if he is a good enough writer he must face eternity, or the lack of it, each day. . . . [A] writer is driven far out past where he can go, out to where no one can help him." Ross, again in her afterword, provides Hemingway's reflection on *The Old Man and the Sea,* which seems to confirm this way of reading the novella: "I've tried to go past the best of whatever I could do best and see how far you could concentrate on the prose. . . . But I tried to do it without making any break in a straight simple story. . . . [W]hen you have a book, you should keep your mouth shut and not say any thing you know about it."

With the publication of Philip Young's *Ernest Hemingway* (1952) and Carlos Baker's *Hemingway: The Writer as Artist* (1952), careful scholarly commentary on *The Old Man and the Sea* began. Providing a capstone summary of that first round of scholarship, Wirt Williams suggests that the "cardinal interpretations" formulated by this early scholarship "were the naturalistic tragedy, the Christian tragedy, the parable of art and the artist, and even the autobiographical mode" (173). Two anthologies from that period bring together an excellent sampling of critical perspective on the book during this period: Carlos Baker's *Ernest Hemingway: Critiques of Four Major Novels* (1962) and Katherine T. Jobes's *Twentieth-Century Interpretation of* The Old Man and the Sea (1968). A look at selected essays from these volumes provides a good summary of critical views from the period. Baker, in his assessment of *The Old Man and the Sea,* explores the tragic dimensions of the story and says that the ending of the contest between man and nature "is not necessarily a Christian victory. Yet it is clear that Hemingway has enhanced the native power of his tragic parable by enlisting the further power of Christian symbolism" (*Critiques* 171). While Baker diminishes the tragic dimension of the work by carefully analyzing Christian elements, Clinton Burhans provides a darker reading of the story that explores the nature and limits of Santiago's heroism in a violent and capricious universe, one that tilts toward a harsh, naturalistic nihilism. However, Burhans, in his much anthologized essay, argues that Hemingway's Santiago affirms and exemplifies in his terrible struggle the oldest human values: "courage, love, humility, solidarity and independence . . . an essentially tragic vision" (Baker, *Critiques* 155). Melvin Backman says of Santiago that we have in him "a blending of two motifs—the matador and the crucified." Backman points out parallels between the old man and the matador figure but stresses differences, most notably that between the "artificial setting of the bullfight" and the natural setting of the old man fishing on the Gulf Stream (142). This natural setting, according to Backman, places Santiago in a universe that is "neither hostile nor beneficent, but mysteriously just" (ibid.). With that distinction drawn, moving the story away from the tragic naturalism identified by Burhans, Backman focuses on parallels between Santiago and the crucified Christ. Given this Christic and natural backdrop, Backman's conclusion is that "the final effect is that of a triumph which is invested not with the violent ritualized quality of the bullfights . . . but with a warm autumnal glow" (143). For Leo Gurko, *The Old Man and the Sea* marks a movement in Hemingway's works from "the confinements of society to the challenges of Nature" (Jobes 70). Nature, for Gurko, is seen as a universe that is "changeless and bare of divinity, [where] everyone has his fixed role to play" (65). That role can be played out in lesser or greater (that is, heroic) ways. In this world, as Gurko reads it, a

> sense of brotherhood and love . . . in which everyone is killing or being killed, binds together the creatures of Nature, establishes between them a unity and an emotion which transcends the destructive pattern in which they are caught. In the eternal round, each living thing, man and animal, acts out its destiny according to the drives of its species, and in the process becomes part of the profound harmony of the natural universe. (65)

Gurko suggests that *The Old Man and the Sea* identifies two orders in every species in the natural world: the greater and the lesser. Santiago is clearly an example of "the greater" among his species—a hero. By "hero," Gurko means one who dares more than others, takes greater risks with death and defeat (Jobes 66). With the great ones, "the greatness of experience and the inevitability of the loss are bound up together" (ibid.). Within this framework, Gurko sees Santiago stand out among Hemingway protagonists as truly heroic: a man alone exerting himself beyond the limits and confines of society in a full, and ultimately tragic, struggle with nature. Gurko's reading steps outside the bounds of naturalism and offers a perspective that calls to mind the ideas of Friedrich Nietzsche.

In "Hemingway's Extended Vision," Bickford Sylvester rejects the view that Hemingway affirms "an inscrutable natural order in which, ultimately, man can play no part" (Jobes 81). Rather, Sylvester argues, *The Old Man and the Sea* "reveals Hemingway's successful achievement at last of a coherent metaphysical scheme—of a philosophical naturalism which . . . embraces the realm of human affairs and gives transcendent meaning to harsh inevitabilities" (ibid.). Like Gurko, Sylvester sees Santiago as heroic, as a champion. But his heroic behavior is of a different and paradoxical order. The sea, Sylvester notes, "bestows her greatest favors on those who make their own conditions" (Jobes 85). Santiago confronts the sea on his own terms, engaging in what Sylvester sees as a "fundamental natural principle of harmonious opposition," resulting in a series of thematic oxymorons: "compassionate violence, comfortable pain, life in death, aged strength, and victorious defeat" (ibid.). Looking through the prism of paradoxes, Sylvester concludes that "as a champion [Santiago] has contributed to the order of the universe . . . relaxing the tension of life even though he has felt his death in him" (Jobes 92). Though Sylvester recognizes a tragic element in the story of the old man and the marlin, he thinks that Santiago's exceptional, heroic, and paradoxical actions are "valuable as the only means whereby each species is permitted its contribution to the systematic tension of the universe" (ibid.).

In the 1960s, John Killinger situated the novella in the existential tradition of Albert Camus, Jean-Paul Sartre, and Friedrich Nietzsche. Richard Hovey extended the autobiographical/psychoanalytic approach in his book *Hemingway: The Inward Terrain*, focusing on the Oedipal complex and arguing that Eros triumphs over Thanatos in the short novel. Philip Young provided a reassessment of *The Old Man and the Sea* in his 1966 edition of *Ernest Hemingway: A Reconsideration*, an update of his 1952 book. Young's commentary on the novella itself (121–33) includes an interesting note in which he suggests that Anselmo Hernández has a legitimate claim to being a/the model for Santiago (124). However, Carlos Gutiérrez, Hemingway's mate on the *Anita* who told him the story of the old man and the fish, and Gregorio Fuentes, a Canary Islander who served as mate and cook on the *Pilar* for many years, seem to be part of the greater mix in the compound character that is Santiago.

Young praises the novella in the original edition of his book (1952): "[T]his short novel is beyond any question a triumph" (125). But in an afterword written in the

Fig. 4. Gregorio Fuentes, age 100, with Dr. D. Duane Cummins in Fuentes's home in 2000. (Courtesy D. Cummins.)

later edition (1966), he backs away from his early praise, stating that he "would greatly tone down the praise.... The feeling is now that although the tale is here and there exciting it is itself drawn out a little too far.... Hemingway was now trading on and no longer inventing the style that made him famous" (274). Here he sets a tone that dulled scholarly interest in the work for several years.

In the 1990s, scholarly attention again returned to the novella. The first such book, one of severe criticism after the comments that condemned Hemingway for imitating his own early style, came from contrarian critic Gerry Brenner in *The Old Man and the Sea: The Story of a Common Man* (1991). As his title indicates, Brenner wanted to minimize any elevating myth or tragedy connected to Santiago and to portray him as ordinary and, in Brenner's psychologically oriented view, afflicted with sexism, repression, feminism, and latent homosexuality.

While praising much of the poetry-like quality of Hemingway's prose (68–70), Brenner criticizes the stylistic ineptness of lines like "The great Sisler's father was never poor, and he, the father, was playing in the Big Leagues when he was my age" (*OMS* 22:11–14; Brenner 78), never realizing that Hemingway is calling attention to the vague pronoun reference to provide a clue to Manolin's actual age. Would Santiago share a beer with a ten-year old (*OMS* 11:3–5, 20:2–3, and 20:15—two beers and two sets of knives and forks), or would the proprietor of the Terrace restaurant offer a young child a drink (123:12)?

As an environmentalist, Brenner wants Santiago to engage in catch-and-release fishing, never minding that Santiago depends on caught fish for his livelihood. In most of his explications, Brenner ignores the economical, or severely minimalizes it, as in the following: "Santiago cannot think his way out of a cash consciousness to recognize that his profession disables him from coming to a serene harmony with his natural surroundings" (66). Actually, Santiago's hand-held line and craft fishing are much less likely to deplete endangered fish stocks than the multiple-hook rigs from which Santiago separates himself (29:23–24), a distinction the novella makes that Brenner ignores.

Except for noting that Santiago has a saint's name (Brenner 32) and has been likened to Christ (37–38), Brenner focuses instead on Santiago's calling the fish "brother" and then alludes to the Cain and Abel story of the Old Testament to accuse Santiago of fratricide (36). The narrator says that Santiago puts his wife's picture on a shelf under his one other shirt "because it made him too lonely to see it" (16:5). Disregarding this explanation, Brenner insists it is "an aggressive repudiation of the gender whom she represents in his mind" (84). Similarly, Santiago's calling the Portuguese man-of-war jellyfish a "whore" (*OMS* 35:22) is a "blatant case of Santiago's sexist aggression" (Brenner 82). And that primitive Santiago thinks that "the moon affects [the sea] as it does a woman" (*OMS* 30:7–8) is part of this "litany of sexist aggressions" (84). Despite this sexism, Santiago, in Brenner's view, is feminized, and "the battle with the marlin is psychologically vital to the feminized Santiago: it provides him with the ordeal he requires and punishes him for his latent homosexual desire for Manolin's companionship (96). Manolin's memory of Santiago's clubbing to death a green fish Brenner turns into "Manolin cowering in abject fear in the boat's bow, terror stricken at the sudden emergence of Santiago as a man of murderous potential, a man whose violent behavior could someday, if provoked, turn on him" (81). "Cowering," "abject fear," "terror stricken," and "murderous" are Brenner's words, not those of Manolin or the narrator of the novella. Of course, in Brenner's environmental eye, killing fish even without clubbing them is murder, and this whole passage reeks of rabid exaggeration and misreading, as does much of his book.

Another ecology-minded critic is Glen Love, who feels that "Hemingway's work demonstrates . . . ascendancy of human will over the abiding earth" (203) and "a tendency to war against the earth" by killing animals (ibid.). Specifically of *The Old Man and the Sea,* Love says Santiago is a "tragic hero, indisputably affirming the spirit of man in conflict with natural laws. . . . [His] sense of the nobility of nature proves inadequate and unequal to his pride" (206); that is, while Santiago values the marlin, his pride demands that he conquer and kill it. Such a reading considers the sea creatures Santiago encounters only as they benefit or harm him. It ignores, as Brenner also does, the economic: that Santiago fishes to eat and also to feed others. It also ignores his respect for the mako shark. And, finally, it asks of an uneducated Cuban fisherman in 1950 a knowledge of the worldwide food chain and how Portuguese man-of-war jelly fish and *galano* sharks fit into it, at a time when few except biologists were concerned with the problem.

Years earlier, Hemingway's son Gregory, in a quote used by both Jeffrey Meyers and Kenneth Lynn in their biographies, called *The Old Man and the Sea* "as sickly a bucket of sentimental slop as was ever scrubbed off the bar-room floor" (Ernest quoted the criticism in a letter to his middle son, Patrick, 26 November 1952, so Gregory must have written soon after the book came out [Meyers, *Biography* 481, 615n7; Lynn 563]. The son describes his rage in the opening pages of *Papa: A Personal Memoir* (1976), when he beat a man so severely—"broke . . . his nose, knocked out two of his front teeth, and half of his ear was hanging loosely from the side of his head" (2)—that he was afraid the man might choke on his own blood. Caught cross-dressing in a Los Angeles theater in September 1951, Gregory was jailed. When Pauline, Ernest's second wife and Gregory's mother, called Ernest to tell him what had happened on the night of the thirtieth, they quarreled heatedly, with Ernest saying, "[S]ee how you brought him up!" The quarrel incited the enlarged tumor on Pauline's adrenal gland to release more adrenaline into her blood stream, causing dangerously high blood pressure, a burst blood vessel, shock, and death. Ernest blamed Gregory, and they argued through correspondence until Ernest's suicide. Thus, Gregory's dismissive comment can be put down as part of his anger toward his father, although another critic, Edwin Muir, in a review of the book, also commented on the unusual show for Hemingway of sentimentality in the novella (7).

Kelli Larson provides an annotated bibliography of that scholarship from 1988 to 2013 (263–326), much of which has been incorporated into this book. As Hemingway wrote, "What goes beyond is what you see beyond *when you know*" (SL 780; emphasis added). We have endeavored to help readers go beyond a surface reading of *The Old Man and the Sea,* thrilling and sad as that reading is, by providing the what-you-know to go beyond. He also wrote, "You can be sure that there is much more there than will be read at any first reading" ("Interview" 230). In that same interview, elaborating on his iceberg principle of writing, Hemingway states, "[A]ll the stories I know from the fishing village I leave out. But the knowledge [of them] is what makes the under-water part of the iceberg" (236). It also makes this novella both complicated and weighty. Most of the facts, the underwater, are here, although we would not claim that all of them are. But we hope that readers will enjoy the exploration, over- and underwater, so appropriate to this book.

ABBREVIATIONS FOR THE WORKS OF ERNEST HEMINGWAY USED IN THIS BOOK

ARIT	*Across the River and into the Trees.* Scribner's, 1950.
AMF	*A Moveable Feast.* Scribner's, 1964.
BL	*By-Line: Ernest Hemingway: Selected Articles and Dispatches from Four Decades.* Edited by William White. Scribner's, 1967.
DIA	*Death in the Afternoon.* Scribner's, 1932.
FTA	*A Farewell to Arms.* Scribner's, 1929.
FWBT	*For Whom the Bell Tolls.* Scribner's, 1940.
GHOA	*Green Hills of Africa.* Scribner's, 1935.
GOE	*The Garden of Eden.* Scribner's, 1986.
IIS	*Islands in the Stream.* Scribner's, 1970.
MF	*A Moveable Feast.* Scribner's, 1964.
OMS	*The Old Man and the Sea.* Scribner's, 1952.
SAR	*The Sun Also Rises.* Scribner's, 1926.
SL	*Ernest Hemingway: Selected Letters, 1917–1961.* Edited by Carlos Baker. Scribner's, 1981.
SS	*The Short Stories of Ernest Hemingway.* 1938. Scribner's, 1995.
THHN	*To Have and Have Not.* Scribner's, 1937.

SERIES NOTE

All page references in this volume are keyed to the page and line numbers of the Scribner's paperback edition of the novella published in 1995 (and subsequently reprinted). Chapter 1 begins on page 9, and the final words appear on page 127. There are no chapters designated in the text. Line numbers begin with the first line on each page.

Annotations are given a page and line number, separated by a colon. A reference to the third line on page 17, for instance, would be 17:3. A reference to the first three lines of page 40 would be 40:1–3.

When citing, we have appropriated the standard abbreviations for Hemingway texts used by the *Hemingway Review,* in concert with the Hemingway Letters Project, available online at https://hemingwaysociety.org/abbreviations-works-ernest-hemingway.

Reading *The Old Man and the Sea*

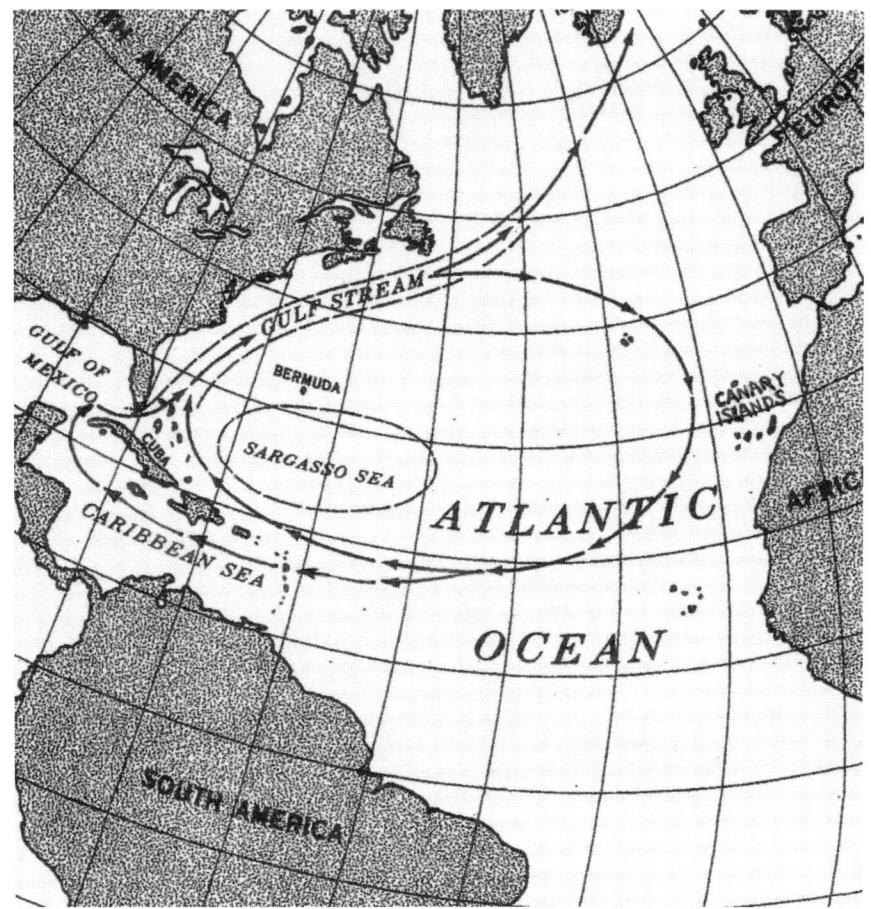

Fig. 5. The Gulf Stream. (Courtesy NOAA)

PAGES 5 THROUGH 27

5 Dedication: Hemingway dedicated *The Old Man and the Sea* to his longtime publisher, Charlie Scribner—actually, Charles Scribner III (1890–1952)—who took control of Charles Scribner's Sons publishing house in 1932—and Max Perkins (1884–1947), his longtime editor. Both were confidants and personal friends, then deceased. Scribner had died in February 1952, months before the publication of the novella; Perkins had persuaded the conservative firm of Scribner's to publish Hemingway's irreverent satire *Torrents of Spring* in 1926 in order to get Hemingway and *The Sun Also Rises* and was Hemingway's friend until his death.

9:2 Gulf Stream: The popular, if scientifically inaccurate term for the vast, clockwise, perpetually rotating system of currents circling the North Atlantic, carrying warm, high-saline water, rich in plankton and the food chain of sea life that begins with these tiny organisms (35:7). The main part of the Stream's flow passes above the eastern half of Cuba's north coast and up the North American coast. But a portion of the water from the main flow is diverted southward, carried under and around Cuba and up into the Gulf of Mexico by what amounts to a side system of the Atlantic circle. From the Gulf, the Gulf Stream water in this side series of currents is turned back eastward through the Florida Strait between Florida and northwestern Cuba, then up the Florida coast to merge with the main flow north of the Bahamas. (See Figure 5.) The old man fishes in this side system's final current (the Florida Current), as it flows off Havana, still carrying a portion of North Atlantic water that will shortly rejoin the great circle forever passing, and symbolically connecting, North America, Europe, and the Canary Islands off Africa with Cuba.

Thus, the oceanographic details of the Stream contribute to a pattern of circularity with thematic implications later in the narrative (see entries 24:19, 25:8, 25:13–14, and especially 94:6). For this and other reasons, the Gulf Stream serves as a microcosm of the sea, which, in turn, represents nature's cosmic order in this novella (entry 10:7). And many navigational details of the book's plot depend on the fact that the Stream's current runs eastward where the action at sea occurs (entry 45:2–3). Hemingway celebrates the Gulf Stream in *Green Hills of Africa* (149–50) in a very long sentence that flows like the Stream itself. He regularly fished its waters, from Key West, Cuba, and Bimini, buying a thirty-eight-foot boat, which he named *Pilar,* in 1934. Many of his excursions on the sea found their way into his fiction— *To Have and Have Not, The Old Man and the Sea,* and *Islands in the Stream*—often after having been first noted in the *Pilar's* sea logs. For the definitive study of Hemingway and the Gulf Stream, see Mark Ott's *A Sea of Change.*

9:2 **Eighty-four days:** Such a long number of fishing days to go without taking a large fish indicates great confidence to keep trying. Santiago has caught smaller fish on his trolling line, enough to feed himself and to use for bait, but never one large enough to bring to market. Except for the local record of eighty-seven days, set earlier by the old man himself (17:24), eighty-four days is longer than anyone has gone in the story without catching a fish or in popular literature about fishing, for that matter. The adventure writer Zane Grey (like Hemingway, a sports-fishing enthusiast) had written of going eighty-three days himself without a fish in 1928, proclaiming, "There is a record that will stand" (Broadus 152). But there is another reason for Hemingway's choice of the number eighty-four (entries 16:20 and 17:1–2), one equally emphasizing the old man's characterization as a champion, *El Campeón* (70:2), whose accomplishments and capabilities are singular and outsized. Eighty-four also has baseball significance and will be referenced later at 17:1–2.

9:4 **forty**: The number forty is widely applied in scripture to represent unusual duration. In the Old Testament, for example, the rain of the Deluge fell for forty days; another forty passed before Noah opened the window of the ark; Moses was forty days on the mount; Elijah was fed by ravens for forty days; the Israelites wandered for forty years in the wilderness. In the New Testament, Christ fasted for forty days in the desert, preached for forty months, and remained in the tomb for forty hours; there were forty days between Christ's resurrection and ascension.

9:6 **salao:** A contraction of *salado* (the *d* in past participles is dropped in Latin American Spanish). Pronounced "sa-LAH-oh," the word literally means "salted" or "briny," but the figurative Central American definition is "hapless." Both literally and figuratively, then, the term fits an ocean fisherman who seems deserted by luck. (But see entries 10:20, 10:24, 11:1–2.)

9:10 **skiff:** In this case, a narrow wooden rowboat with a small sail. The old man's skiff is sixteen feet long, or two feet shorter than the eighteen-foot marlin he will hook and capture (122:23). See Figure 6.

9:11 **coiled lines:** Heavy, hand-held fishing lines important to the plot (entry 15:4–5).

9:11 **gaff:** A strong, sharp-pointed iron hook attached to a wooden shaft. The hook is driven into a fish to secure it in the water beside a boat and pull it on board.

9:11–12 **either . . . or:** The boy helps the man carry "either" the lines "or" the gaff, harpoon, and the sail furled around the mast. See also entry 15:4–5.

9:12 **harpoon:** A heavy spear attached to a light rope coiled in the boat, with its other end fastened to the bow (front end) of the boat (91:9–11). When a large, uncontrollable fish—caught on one of the hand lines—has been played nearly to exhaustion and passes near the boat, the fisherman throws or drives the harpoon into the fish. The harpoon's spearhead has a barb, a pointed part projecting backward from the tip, so that, once the tip is driven into flesh, the barb resists extraction and the harpoon cannot easily be pulled loose. The fish, losing blood, either dies at once or expends its final energy pulling against the boat.

9:14 **flag of permanent defeat:** Tied lengthwise along the mast rather than stretched out to reveal its triangular shape, the sail resembles a drooping, white, hand-held flag like those traditionally signaling surrender ("permanent defeat"), as the old man carries it back to his shack after a luckless day.

Fig. 6. Cuban fishing skiff. Note the tattered sail. Photo by Ernest Hemingway. (Courtesy Ernest Hemingway Collection. John F. Kennedy Library and Museum, Boston)

9:17 **benevolent:** The supposedly benign rash caused by the tropical sunlight reflected by the sea is here called a "cancer," technically a contradiction in terms. (Of course, if the condition is keratosis, it can eventually develop into a form of skin cancer.) Hemingway conspicuously uses "benevolent" rather than "benign," the standard term for a tumor that is not malignant.

The two words have essentially the same dictionary meanings. But in any reference to medical affairs, "benign" has become associated solely with the absence of disease, while "benevolent" is free to convey its associations with charity: the bestowal of favors. Hemingway's arresting choice of words, therefore, suggests something about the old man's relationship with the forces of nature: even his "cancer" is presented as a kindness, a gift of sun and sea.

Put another way, even the gift has a price. It is perhaps relevant that Hemingway repeatedly called his own chronic facial rash a "benign sun cancer," despite the objections of his irritated Cuban doctor, who pointed out the contradiction in terms. S. Kip Farrington Jr., a friend and fishing companion of Hemingway's in Bimini and Cuba, was probably echoing Hemingway's own self-diagnosis, when he called Hemingway's condition "skin cancer" (37). Jeffrey Meyers lists skin cancer as an ailment afflicting Hemingway (but with a question mark; see *Biography* 574), as does A. E. Hotchner, again echoing Hemingway (156). Most likely, the skin ailment afflicting Hemingway was seborrheic dermatitis, which can cause a rash and patches of flaky skin. In the novella, this use of "benign skin cancer" is the first in a pattern of various paradoxes defining nature's challenging relation to her favored creatures. (See entry 94:22–23 for a list and discussion of these major paradoxes.)

10:3–5 **deep-creased scars . . . fishless desert:** As if produced by a geological process of abrasion that takes ages to accomplish. By this set of associations, the old man himself is seen as an ancient natural form. As for the seemingly redundant "fishless desert," there once were fish in the oceans that covered what are now the driest spots on earth, but that was ages ago. To one of less faith than Santiago, the sea might be said to have become for the old man as infertile (without fish) as a desert and for seemingly as long. The drought imagery insistently echoes that of T. S. Eliot's celebrated poem *The Waste Land* (V.11.331–38 esp.). This echo, early in the novella, prefigures a developing parallel between Santiago's social and spiritual role in the book and that of the mythical Fisher King in Eliot's poem of 1922. (See entry 125:2.)

10:7 **same color as the sea:** The blue of the old man's eyes is revealed in a way stressing his kinship with the ocean, particularly with the blue Gulf Stream (35:5), the locus of natural order in the narrative. The color serves the same purpose in portrayals of confident, assertive, natural creatures celebrated later in the novella as central to nature's order (96:20–21, 100:16). The association of a youthfully indomitable "outlook" with kinship to nature is extensively developed in Santiago's characterization (for example, entries 25:2–3, 25:8, 25:14, 25:15–16, 25:16). Blue eyes also indicate that Santiago is unlikely to be an ethnic Cuban but rather a Canary Islander, a descendant of its original blue-eyed Guanche inhabitants. Jeffrey Herlihy-Mera states that Santiago's blue eyes indeed mark him as a Spanish Canarian and, thus, an expatriate in Cuba (much as Jake Barnes is an expatriate in France in *The Sun Also Rises* and Robert Jordan is in Spain in *For Whom the Bell Tolls*). In 1950, according to Herlihy-Mera, there was still antipathy between native Cubans and those of Spanish origin or descent; thus, the scorn Santiago receives (11:7) may not be just for his temporary failure as a fisherman but also for his Spanish origins. Santiago is, therefore, exceptional in his surroundings: by his age, his unluckiness, his eye color and ethnic origin, and his dedication to the natural order (Herlihy [-Mera], "'Eyes the Same Color as the Sea,'" 25–44).

10:9 **Santiago:** Spanish for "Saint James," with whom the old man is compared in many ways. Saint James was the brother of John the Divine. He and John, fishermen who lived in Galilee, were mending nets with their father in a fishing boat when called by Jesus to follow him (Matt. 4:21-22) and become "fishers of men." James was the first disciple to die for the Christian faith. His reputation as a defender of Christianity prompted the growth of a medieval cult that believed his remains (relics) had been mysteriously brought by a small boat from Jerusalem to Compostela in northwestern Spain (entry 16:2). From the tenth to the sixteenth century, Compostela was a principal destination of pilgrimages by these believers, and such pilgrimages continue today. This novella will draw a parallel between the journey of these pilgrims in search of mystical fulfillment and the voyage Santiago makes in his skiff (entry 98:21–23). For background, see entries 16:2 and 25:8.

10:10–11 **I could go with you:** The boy asserts his willingness to follow Santiago, as Saint James followed Christ, suggesting the master/disciple relationship and also preparing for the Fisher King/Perceval allusion.

10:11 **money:** The boy has caught and sold many fish with a fisherman his father has forced him to work for after making him stop fishing with the old man (10:21). The boy believes he may have earned enough money to satisfy his materialistic father (entry 29:23–24), who might now allow the boy to rejoin Santiago, for whom challenging accomplishments of craftsmanship are more important than a steady income (entry 14:11).

10:20 **doubted:** The boy has not gone with the other fisherman because he had any doubt that luck would favor the old man again and eventually let him find a big fish. The ensuing discussion of doubt versus faith (10:21–11:2) echoes Christ's affirmation to his disciples: "If you have faith and doubt not . . . it shall be done. And all things, whatsoever ye shall ask in prayer, *believing, ye shall receive*" (Matt. 21:21-22; emphasis added). This has psychological as well as spiritual implications in the characterization of these two true "fishermen" (11:5).

10:21 **a boy:** Apparently, a statement of the obvious. However, see entries 15:5 and 22:11–13.

10:23 **normal:** The old man acknowledges that the boy's obedience to his father is conventional and understandable. But see entry 22:11–13 for a crucial difference between this relationship in Cuba and that between a son and his father in North America or Europe.

10:24 **faith:** Here "faith" has two levels of meaning. The boy's father lacks confidence in the boy's judgment in choosing a fisherman to work for, as well as in Santiago's chance of further luck. But the boy also means that his father lacks a more fundamental confidence: his father mistrusts any life experience involving risk, luck, or destiny. In this regard, "faith" here and elsewhere in the novella has its traditional philosophical and/or religious meaning of trust in things beyond ratiocinative logic (see entry 10:20, for example).

11:1–2 **Haven't we:** In effect, "We share a special attitude toward luck setting us apart from many in our community. In stating this partly as a question, I am at once reminding you of our bond and asking you to reinforce my commitment." This early exchange on faith is the first reference to a complex stance toward destiny and natural order that evolves throughout the narrative and becomes part of the work's central theme. Subsequent entries will deal with this attitude as it is developed; for some examples of that development early in the narrative, see entries 10:20, 11:5, 13:7, 14:11, 14:24, 16:17–18, 16:20, 17:1–2, 25:14, 25:15–16, 25:16, and 32:23.

11:3–4 **the Terrace:** A restaurant and bar (La Terraza; see Color Plates 1 and 2) overlooking the harbor in Cojimar, ten miles east of central Havana. Cojimar is the community used as the model for Santiago's fishing village. The Terrace was a favorite gathering spot for fishermen before Castro's revolution.

11:5 **Between fishermen:** Words reflecting an intimacy based on shared values essential to the highest practice of their ancient trade. The old man's respect for the boy as his equal in this regard contrasts sharply with the attitude of the boy's father and the man the boy now works with (10:20, 14:11, 14:16, 14:24, 27:6–7, and 29:23–24). "Fishermen" also prepares us for later sections where we are reminded that Christ's original disciples were fishermen—Saints Peter, Andrew, James ("Santiago" in Spanish) and John—and that these fishermen then became "fishers of men." It also prepares us to see Manolin as Santiago's disciple.

11:6–7: **many of the fishermen made fun of the old man:** Why? It may simply be because of his lack of luck, that to the successful fishermen, he is a "loser." It may be because of his dedication to his craft, to test himself against large fish rather than settling for smaller, more easily caught prey, that they, as commercially minded fishermen, do. Or it may be, as Jeffrey Herlihy-Mera says, because Santiago is an outsider, a foreigner, a Canarian and not a Cuban, despite his many years in Cuba (entry 10:7). Hemingway does not specify why. As with other facets of the novella, it is up to the reader to determine.

11:11 **weather:** The weather is nearly always fair because it is now September (18:10–11). Although this is the hurricane season—at its peak in late August and September—the weather is uncommonly good most of the time during these months, yet can be disastrous when it is bad (61:6–9). The Atlantic marlin migrating past Havana at this time are often very large (entry 18:13), so that seeking the largest fish requires risking the most dangerous weather. For survival, one must be highly skilled at reading nature's signs of her approaching violence so as not to be lulled into complacency by the usually calm weather. For many other paradoxes defining nature's challenging relationship with her creatures (human and otherwise) in this work, see entries 9:17 and especially 94:22–23.

11:18–19 **shark factory on the other side:** Stressing the separation between the two processing centers on opposite sides of the "cove" (11:19) or, more accurately, the long, deep "harbour" (11:24) that shelters Cojimar on its western shore and the shark factory on its eastern shore. This is the first intimation in the novella of a division in the Cuban fishing industry. Because Santiago fishes for love of craft and quarry as well as for money, he will compete fiercely with his fish, as one natural creature with another. But the progressive young fishermen fishing for sharks hold themselves apart from nature. Motivated solely by money, they passively exploit the sea, using machinery to give them an advantage (entries 11:20, 29:23–24, and 30:3). Shark fishing had indeed been very profitable in the period before 1950, the date of the novella's action (entry 17:1–2). The oil extracted from their large livers (30:1) was sold in North America in the 1930s and 1940s as "cod liver oil," a popular vitamin A supplement. (See entry 29:24–30:1, and Farrington 28–34 for descriptions of this Cuban shark fishery written for Farrington's book by Perry W. Gilbert of Cornell and the Mote Marine Laboratory.) In 1944, shark livers sold for $14.25 a pound; in 1950, after the introduction of synthesized Vitamin A, shark livers sold for 10 cents a pound (Beegel, "Guide to Marine Life," 254; see also Beegel, "Santiago and the Eternal Feminine,"144, and "The Monster of Cojimar," 14–15).

11:20 **block and tackle:** Even on shore, shark fishermen use mechanical devices (entries 29:23–24, 30:3), while marlin fishermen lift and carry their catches with their own hands, on simple wooden planks (11:14)—although sharks and marlin both average several hundred pounds.

11:23 **wind:** Cojimar is located on the western side of the cove. The shark factory is on the east, and an east wind brings a foul smell toward Cojimar, the physical locus of vocational purity in the area. But on this day, there is very little of the stench (11:24–12:3) "because the wind [has] backed into the north" (12:1–2) and disappeared, leaving calm, good weather. (For the meteorological explanation of this reference to the wind, and for its implications for the plot, see entry 14:6.)

12:6 **years ago:** In dwelling upon the past, Santiago exhibits a tendency common among the elderly (12:8, 22:17, 22:18). But here (as often elsewhere) he is reliving uncommon moments of self-discovery encountered during sea voyages when he was the boy's age. See 22:14–16 and entries 24:20–21, 25:8, 25:14, and 25:16.

12:7 **sardines:** Not those packed in cans, but small, fresh fish similar to herring, commonly used as bait for fishing. Santiago will use them to fill in the small spaces left uncovered by larger bait fish on his big marlin hooks (31:5) and use them by themselves for middle-sized fish (34:4).

12:8 **baseball:** Santiago is telling the boy to enjoy his youth by playing a game that is a Cuban passion. (For more on baseball, see esp. entries 17:1–2 and 23:9.) Santiago knows that the boy is sometimes more interested in baseball than in the memories of long ago that he has just been daydreaming about (12:6)—and about which he realizes he sometimes tires the boy (22:17). This is evidence that "the old man is an old man" (*SL* 780)—a realistic, elderly person—despite his extraordinary physical and emotional formidability (entries 14:21 and 14:24). Evidence of his convincing humanity is important to our acceptance of Santiago as heroic rather than fantastic. His physical flaws—his spastic left hand (58:8–64:4) and other infirmities of aging—are not the only evidence of Santiago's mortal imperfection. The natural incompatibilities between Santiago and the boy are human frailties, typical of age and youth, that make both characters endearing, playful mortals, despite the unusual selflessness and sense of vocation they display in the narrative as a whole. Thus, we can relate to—and imagine ourselves emulating—these uncommon common people who nearly always behave as we behave only in our very best moments (see, for example, entries 20:8, 20:14, 22:17, and 22:18). (For an opposing interpretation of the old man's common characteristics, in a denigrating reading of his relationship to others and to nature, see Brenner throughout.)

12: 8–9 **Rogelio:** Not mentioned again, this character is one of several members of the community who appreciate and assist Santiago. The net will be a "cast net" (15:2). Flat and circular, such a net is thrown by hand over a school of small fish in shallow water and pulled in as its weighted edges sink around the fish and trap them.

12: 13 **already a man:** In buying Santiago a beer, the boy has taken part in a social ritual of adult males and is, therefore, "already" grown up. However, Santiago is also remarking upon the boy's mature sense of reciprocal responsibility; for a fuller perspective on this remark and all other early indications of the boy's chronological age, see entry 22:11–13. For his early social and moral maturity, see entry 12:23.

12:16 **green:** Lively, not yet exhausted. Santiago pulled a large fish on board when it still had the strength to damage the boat and possibly injure him and the boy. See next entry for discussion of this incident.

12:23 **blood . . . over me:** The blood trope in *The Old Man and the Sea*, introduced here, is complex and its significance varies from context to context. However, the various manifestations of the trope are united by an understanding that blood serves as a natural binding agent among persons, persons and groups, and between people and nature. Blood is our common bond, the stuff of our oneness.

As for extant comment on the blooding scene, there are two treatments. Peter Hays has discussed the Native American parallels between *The Old Man and the Sea* and Faulkner's "The Bear." And Susan Beegel ("Santiago and the Eternal Feminine" 141) has referred to the blood as symbolizing the ocean's giving birth to the boy. But the birth symbolism in this scene actually functions to stress rebirth: the boy's psychological and spiritual discovery of his true identity as a traditional fisherman, his first awareness of his role in nature's scheme as the future champion of Santiago's values.

The very early age of the boy at this his blooding/christening/consecration also reveals his nearly life-long orientation to the view of violence and eternal order as a mystery of nature. This lengthy tutelage provides readers with an "objective correlative"—a plausible cause—not only for the unanimity of core values between "the boy" and the old man, but for "the boy's" precocious, overall maturity, a maturity unusual even in young men. (For more on the boy's emotional and social maturity, see esp. entry 22:11–13).

In this first instance in *The Old Man and the Sea* of blood, though reminiscent of blooding rituals among hunters (compare Faulkner's "The Bear," 209–10), the blood splattered on the boy serves less as a rite of passage into manhood than it does as a sign and affirmation of this vocation: fisherman. It is more consecration or ordination (as setting aside) than initiation. It unites him with Santiago at an ontological level: they *are* fishermen. Santiago will reflect on vocation as an ontological category on two occasions (40:2–3, 50:22–23). He and the boy are, thus, set apart from those for whom fishing is simply a job. The imagery through which the boy recalls the blooding event suggests both anointing oil and baptismal immersion: "the sweet blood smell all over me." The emphasis on smell anticipates later passages in which blood is present as "scent" rather than as liquid. It is notable that almost the same the words "the sweet smell of blood," are also associated with Lt. Henry with his initiation into paradoxical realities of his violent world (*FTA* 59). Apparently, the sweetish odor of blood (in this context, a paradox in itself: precious blood leaving the body but still conjuring the sense of sweetness) is persistent in Hemingway's personal imagination, very probably impressed there by the trauma of his own wounding at almost nineteen.

Finally, it should be noted the "application" of the blood comes not from the touch of Santiago's hand but from his violent clubbing of the fish. Blood and violence are united in this trope. Readers who take into account the blood allusion in *The Old Man and the Sea* (Christian, American Indian, Afro-Cuban, and even more ancient rites) will see in this passage a unification of violence and compassion, a mysterious paradox of nature affirmed in both pagan and Christian cultures. The scene, thus, reinforces the book's larger themes. In the novella, this paradoxical relationship (with its suggestion that boon can be bane, bane can be boon) is the first in a pattern of various paradoxes defining nature's challenging relation to her favored creatures. (See entry 94:22–23 for a list and discussion of these major contraries, as William Blake might have called them.)

Santiago lives by precisely this paradoxical vision. Together with the Christian mysteries, acceptance of these contraries, including the hunter's role in nature's mysterious order, is the basis of the faith, humility, and equanimity he and the boy share. See especially 11:1–2 and 11:5; both are Christian allusions.

13:7 **gamble:** If the boy were Santiago's own son, Santiago would let him share the financial risk of going many days without any fish: the two would be fishing in waters where there were fewer marlin, but there would be a greater chance of taking a very large one (entry 14:11). Gambling is prominent in Cuban culture, and the connection between gambling, luck, faith, and catching fish is made often in the novella. See 10:14, 13:9, and especially entry 17:1–2.

13:8 **father's and your mother's:** See 10:21. See also entries 15:5 and 22:11–13.

13:21 I **would:** Even steal, if necessary, to help Santiago.

14:3–4 **this current:** A brisk one. Although sometimes slowing to a standstill and occasionally reversing its flow, the Florida Current runs eastward off Havana at various speeds, normally up to four miles per hour. Santiago has observed that fish feed, and therefore take bait, more readily when the current is fast, as it is this day and as he has reason to believe it will be the next day, for he knows (entry 14:6) that the trade winds from the east will not be blowing against the current to slow it down (email from Dean Churchill). When Hemingway started marlin fishing in 1932, he observed that marlin off Havana "ran" (appeared and fed) when the current in the stream picked up (*SL* 390, 392). In the two letters just cited, Hemingway was observing May fish on an annual feeding migration, so that they would, in any case, be more voracious than the September fish Santiago seeks (entry 18:13). But at any time of the year, marlin do tend to feed heavily during a brisk current, as do many ocean fish.

14:6 wind shifts: Santiago's knowledge of local weather patterns tells him that the present calm weather will continue, allowing him to go farther out than usual the next day. He also knows that, after he has drifted to the east with the current as he fishes (see below), the eastern trade wind should pick up and help him sail back westward to Cojimar.

Two wind systems dominate in this part of the Florida Strait. There are the land breezes blowing to the north in the mornings, as the land's residual warmth at night pushes the trade winds blowing from east to west on the water in the afternoons and evenings, aided by building warmth in the sunbathed ocean as the sun moves westward. But starting in September, a third wind system frequently complicates that pattern; cold fronts often move south from the United States. These cooler fronts carry gentle breezes, "but after they pass they leave relatively cool, dry air with little wind and good visibility that holds out the trade winds and leaves a day or so of calm seas, before the dominant trades push in again" (email from Churchill). When noticing the mild weather and the lack of odor from the shark factory to the east this evening (11:23–12:1), Santiago had apparently remembered a counterclockwise movement of the wind sometime earlier that told him such a front had moved through. The usual midday breeze from the east (the trade wind) had been gradually pushed back and replaced by a breeze from the north.

Technically called "backing," this phenomenon has already been named in the narrative (12:2) and its effects illustrated (11:23–12:3). But Hemingway has left it up to readers either to know or to learn what the term means and what it has told Santiago: that a cold front has just moved through and that the next day will still be flat and nearly windless, so that he will be able to row farther out than usual. The only appreciable wind will be the offshore, morning land breeze. Unopposed by the customary trade wind, the land breeze will begin earlier than usual (25:5–6), in time to be helpfully behind him as he goes out in the predawn hours. He also knows that, once he starts drifting and rowing to the east with the current as he fishes (30:20–21), he will be able to go farther and fish a larger section of water than usual. For he will not encounter the usual head wind, and accompanying small waves, to slow him down; the calm following the front will keep the trade winds away until evening, at least. Then, as the calm after the front weakens, he expects the trade wind to push in again from the east and help him sail back westward to Cojimar.

Santiago's knowledge that the weather will be entirely in his favor is important. That knowledge will add to other key reasons for the extraordinary confidence he has, later in the evening, in his good luck the next day. (See entries 16:20 and esp. 17.1.)

14:7 **before . . . light:** Fish feeding partly by sight are hungry by morning and feed heavily at the very first light even though they may be in the darkness of the depths. A disciplined fisherman will have his lines in the water at that time.

14:11 **too far out:** The words "too far," later in the narrative (116:16, 120:15), will have a complex meaning for Santiago. But here "too" simply means "very" distant from land and implies "in excess of" the distance the boy's very cautious new employer considers safe. "He," the new man, is not confident at sea, as Santiago and the boy are (entry 13:7). As a gesture of disrespect for this man's lack of the trust, faith, and hope they live by (27:5–7, entries 10:24 and 11:1–2), the boy and Santiago avoid speaking his name, referring to him only as "he" or "him" (27:7). Fishing far out in the Stream for large fish means giving up more numerous though smaller fish in the safer yet more productive water closer to land (entry 28:19), within or at the edge of the coastal shelf. The new fisherman settles for fish of moderate size, assuring regular money, because he is not motivated in his work by pride in craftsmanship or love of the sea's challenges, as Santiago is. Nor would he trust either nature or chance to reward him if he pitted himself against the sea's dangers. For he is not confident (as Santiago is) that nature rewards such efforts. He would not understand Santiago's interest in fewer but more formidable fish and more challenging fishing conditions.

14:13 **bird working:** A seabird is diving to pick up small fish herded together and driven to the surface in a dense "bait ball" by somewhat larger fish feeding on them. These larger fish are fed on by marlin. So, experienced marlin fishermen watch for birds diving into bait balls (33:21–34:1, 37:21–38:2).

14:16 **almost blind:** This reference to the other fisherman's (the one with whom Manolin now fishes) impaired eyesight is also a reminder of the man's restricted mental and spiritual perspective. He cannot "see" beyond the safe, conventional, and material (entries 14:11, 14:24).

14:17 **strange:** Here the word is used in the usual way, to mean "odd"; for example, see 35:8. But see entries 14:21, 14:24, 35:8, and 98:21–23.

14:18 **turtle-ing:** Harvesting turtles for their tender meat, rich oil, and shells. Turtle harvesting has long been profitable for fishermen in the Caribbean and the Florida Straits, who sold them for export to the United States and Europe, where the meat is considered a delicacy.

14:18 **kills the eyes:** The most common method of hunting turtles was to drift in small boats, peering beneath the surface for turtles to harpoon, despite the damaging brilliance of tropical sunlight reflected constantly by the water into the eyes. But English ships exploring the Caribbean in the seventeenth and eighteenth centuries often employed native fishermen who used a more sophisticated technique. (See entry 14:24 for details of this method and for Hemingway's reason for leaving such information out of his narrative.)

14:19–20 **Mosquito Coast:** A vast, sparsely settled portion of Central America's east coast, shared by Honduras and Nicaragua. Its many turtles draw boats from nearby countries.

14:21 **strange:** Santiago's reference to himself as "strange" is more complex in this particular instance than in line 14:17; entry 14:24 includes a discussion of the difference. As elsewhere in this novella and in Hemingway's other works, for example, "The Snows of Kilimanjaro" (74), the word in all its forms generally means "numinous": surpassing human comprehension in an emotionally and spiritually elevating way. (Entry 98:21–23 discusses this work's central example; but for other important, thematically related examples, see entries 35:8 and 40:10–19).

14:24 **tricks:** This remark misleads readers (and the boy, as well) into assuming that Santiago is thinking solely of worksaving tricks to conserve his energy during his next voyage, but he is also thinking of the past. When he called himself "strange" a moment earlier (14:21), he had indeed meant crafty, experienced in "tricks of the trade" that few others know about. But he was thinking of one in particular, which would, in fact, make him appear to have a "strange" (supernormal) imperviousness to the sun's rays. And in line 14:24, he is still thinking of that insider's "trick," one he learned years ago on the turtle boats.

Readers investigating the history of turtle hunting can find that scattered groups of native fishermen in Central America had for centuries ingeniously used remoras (suckerfish) to capture turtles. The remora, a parasite, attaches itself to a larger creature like a shark or a turtle and eats the scraps drifting back when its host feeds. The native hunter suspended a remora in the water with a line tied to its tail. When the fish attached its suction-cup dorsal fin to a passing turtle, the hunter could feel the extra weight on his line and had only to follow his line to the remora and spear the turtle. He did not need to search with his eyes. Apparently, Santiago's resurrection of this technique saved his eyes from otherwise inevitable sun damage.

In this case, then, Santiago's appearance as "strange"—a natural rarity—is a deception, the result of an insider's device, or trick (see 66:11). For, as an old man (entry 12:8), he has many normal physical limitations, and he will, indeed, need tricks to supplement his resolution later in the narrative.

Yet Santiago chooses not to reveal this trick to the boy; and Hemingway himself chooses not to comment directly on either the potential cause of eye damage, on Santiago's trick for avoiding it, or on the reason for the old man's reticence. Readers must first of all notice these implied, unanswered questions and search beyond Hemingway's text for their answers. The "turtle-ing" exchange is an early example in this narrative of Hemingway's modernist expectation (like James Joyce's, for example) that it is up to his readers to account for every detail, including topical customs and other literal facts of the plot that he leaves for readers to fill in by their own investigations.

Hemingway's comment on "tricks" goes beyond those employed by Santiago, the master angler, to include those who have mastered the craft of fiction. The device was not Hemingway's invention; it was one characteristic of the modernist movement of which he was a part. A commentator on the pioneering modernist W. B. Yeats has noticed that Yeats's poems give readers "clues" to the "homework" they will "have to do" to become "really adequately prepared" for his works (Unterecker 174).

Here, readers need to find out why Hemingway raises the particular questions mentioned above, questions he does not answer in any explicit way. For example, as a native to this fishing community, the boy can be assumed to know that the sun is what causes damage to the eyes (entry 14:18); so the cause itself would not necessarily be named in his conversation with Santiago. But the boy's remark (14:19–20) clearly implies his doubt about how Santiago's eyesight managed to survive the sun's usual damage. And Santiago's evasive rejoinder that he is "a strange old man" (14:21) is hardly an answer of any direct use to readers, who need to know what Santiago means. Yet readers who gloss over such conspicuous omissions in Hemingway's narratives are ignoring one of his characteristic ways of nudging them to stop and work out the missing information for themselves. In this case, Hemingway leaves out so much that most readers will not follow him—an excess he had long been aware of (*AMF* 75).

Still, the "trick" in question is discussed in encyclopedia entries on turtle hunting. And readers who have found out about the sun and the remoras can fully understand why Santiago responds to the boy's earnest, practical question merely by referring enigmatically to his "strange," or special, capabilities. For, without violating the code he shares with the boy, Santiago cannot say openly that he relied solely on a common practice in the trade, rather than on extraordinary physiological capability and a clever insider's secret. The two customarily avoid directly mentioning their limitations. Throughout the narrative, both man and boy speak and act, instead, *as if* they will inevitably achieve practical success, even when they know they cannot. That is a "fiction" that Carlos Baker in another context called an "informed illusion" (*Writer as Artist* 273); both entries for 16:17–18, for example). The two characters use this "fiction" to help sustain the special faith they need to make the extreme sacrifices demanded of champions—as that theme develops later in the narrative (entries 45:8, 93:15–17 or 121:19, for example).

This sophisticated pretense is notably beyond the "vision" of the fisherman the boy now works for (entry 14:11 and 14:16); that contrast is part of the subtext of references to eyesight. Accordingly, Santiago abandons this psychological discipline only reluctantly, speaking of his reliance on "tricks" only to reassure the boy, whose second question (14:22–23) openly implies doubt, a severe violation of their code, although motivated by loving concern.

These subtleties on faith, doubt, and vision are accessible, then, only to readers who have pursued the dangling questions on turtle hunting, despite Hemingway's attempt to divert their attention forward to associate "tricks" with the coming trip rather than back to the unfinished business in the dialogue.

In fact, the diversion is part of this entire, artistically calculated puzzle Hemingway designed to be solved only by especially persistent readers. The hurdles and rewards in such passages are Hemingway's way of challenging his readers to achieve whatever degree of emotional, intellectual, and spiritual satisfaction each is willing to wrest from the narrative by his or her own initiative. And within *The Old Man and the Sea,* the unanswered questions in this early passage prepare vigilant readers for subsequent interpretive challenges and research demands that are even harder to notice than these are, yet are crucial to the facts of the plot. (See especially entry 17:1–2 and related entries on the dates of the novella's action. See also entries 15:5, 22:11–13, and others, on the length of Santiago's fishing lines and on the boy's age.)

This early challenge can also serve to sensitize readers to the sophisticated pretense between Santiago and the boy that becomes centrally important at the novella's end (entries 16:17–18, 124:2, and 124:7, as well as lines 126:3–13). (For other aspects of Santiago's continuing, unusual vision, see entry 17:1.)

The omissions of relevant fact, the homework required of readers, is part of what Hemingway referred to, and critics call, his "iceberg theory": that only one-eighth of the story is visible. As Hemingway said in his *Paris Review* interview,

> I always try to write on the principle of the iceberg. There is seven-eighth of it underwater for every part that shows. . . .
>
> *The Old Man and the Sea* could have been over a thousand pages long and had every character in the village in it and all the processes of how they made their living, were born, educated, bore children, etc. That is done excellently and well by other writers. . . . So I have tried to learn to do something else. First I have tried to eliminate everything unnecessary to conveying experience to the reader so that after he or she has read something it will become a part of his or her experience and seem actually to have happened. (235–36)

But to get the full experience, we have to do the homework that Hemingway asks of us; we have to recognize the iceberg and not be content with the merely visible. And if we do so, we become imbued in the story and emotionally involved. It becomes part of our experience.

15:4–5 **man carried the mast:** And the boy took all the rest of the equipment (15:4–6). The suggestion is that the old man has become worn down by his eighty-four days at sea and that the boy is ready and willing to take on even more of his mentor's burden than he has before. For the ultimate significance of this shifting balance in the literal and symbolic burden the two carry, see entry 125:2; see also Sylvester, "The Cuban Context," esp. 256–62.

15:5 **hard-braided:** A description of Santiago's "brown," handheld fishing lines, made of "good Catalan *cardel*" (51:18; properly "cordel," Spanish for "cord"). Many may have read "hand-braided" for the "hard-braided" actually on the page probably because "hand-braided" would seem more appropriate, given Santiago's pervasive association in the narrative with hand-made rather than manufactured items and with hands-on procedures. (See, for example, entries 11:18–19, 11:20, 30:3, and 30:20–21.) But "hard-braided" appears consistently in each of the known drafts of the book (email from James Roth), as well as in the setting copy at the Berg Library. And there is no known evidence to suggest an inadvertent error by Hemingway here. So we must conclude that "hard-braided" is what he wrote.

These lines are kept in a box to preserve the coils that allow the lines to pay out rapidly, without tangling, when a large fish runs. Lines also take up the least amount of space when coiled. And the old man uses a great deal of line for a small boat: 660 fathoms (see 30:22–31:1, 31:18–21, 44:5–8, and 51:11–17), or about three-quarters of a mile. Even factory-coiled, this length of a line having only the diameter of a regular pencil fills a 30x15x15-inch box, and could not be kept anywhere nearly that compact after daily use. A box large enough to hold that much used line of the diameter described is a remarkable bulk for a boy of any age—or even a powerful man—to carry, especially in view of its weight. Yet this boy somehow carries considerably more than 130 pounds of line, in addition to the gaff and harpoon (15:4–6; also see entry 15:4–5). A 660-fathom length of braided nylon "ground line" 9/32nds of an inch in diameter—the thickness of a standard yellow pencil—weighs nearly 130 pounds. And Santiago's line is larger, the thickness of "a big pencil" (31:16; see this entry for the symbolism implied by this comparison). Moreover, according to a technical consultant at one of the largest American manufacturers (email from Chuck Smith), Santiago's braided Spanish *cardel* is probably made of linen, weighing slightly more than the modern synthetics. Also, when wet (12:21), linen line (rare now) absorbs water and becomes both heavier and bulkier than the less-absorbent, synthetic modern lines (Smith). So the boy's burden is about 140 pounds. An explanation of this important, apparently incredible feat emerges later in the narrative (see entry 22.11–13).

As for the length of line Santiago uses (and, hence, the weight and bulk), the total stated above (660 fathoms, about three-quarters of a mile) is nowhere given directly in the text. Readers must compute it for themselves. In the relevant page references cited above, there are two separate sets of figures, located pages apart. Readers are thereby challenged to work out both totals for a double check. And to do so requires taking into account a third, limited set of figures (44:5–8) and also allowing for exactly what Santiago does with each of the four lines he sets out. See entries 14:24, 17:1–2, and 22:11–13 for similar challenges to readers to become responsible for ascertaining other facts of the plot.

15:7 **stern:** the whole back end of the boat, here meaning not "under" the boat, but under a seat or small deck across the back of this particular boat, where Santiago stores perishables while at sea (39:2–3, 57:16). Gulls (and people) cannot see the bait there.

15:9–10 **No one would steal . . . but:** Santiago's mixture here of caution and faith is repeated (15:12–14). It reflects his realistic yet positive acceptance of good and evil

Fig. 7. Cuban fishermen landing a shark. Usually two men fished on each skiff. (Courtesy Ernest Hemingway Collection. John F. Kennedy Library and Museum, Boston)

in humanity and the natural universe. That acceptance includes the human beings in one's community, Santiago's "good town" (115:7), although not all the townspeople sympathize with him (entries 11:6–7 and 29:23–24). This complex attitude is part of a thematically central, *cultivated* optimism on Santiago's part (see 16:17–18).

15:11 **dew was bad:** Both lines and sail are made of vegetable fiber, which mildews and rots unless periodically dried. So, these items must be taken inside every night. This potential damage is also Santiago's excuse for keeping his essential equipment from being stolen, even though he is reluctant to mistrust his neighbors (15:12–14; also see entry 15:9–10).

15:16 **open door:** Very likely an open doorway; many shacks in Cuban villages had doorless entrances. The inclusion of this detail calls further attention to Santiago's poverty and his commitment to trust (entry 15:9–10).

15:21 **guano:** Not bird dung in this case, but a Cuban term for American palm species, among them the royal palm, with tough, broad leaves. In 1950, a poor Cuban villager typically lived in a *bohio,* a one- or two-room shack made almost entirely of royal palm. The roof was thatched with the leaves (themselves called guano [pronounce goo-AH-no]), the walls were made of bark or boards cut from the trunk of the palm, and the floor was simply the bare ground. Beegel cites a similar structure ("Thor Heyerdahl's *Kon-Tiki*" 526).

16:1–7 **there was a picture . . . shirt:** The pictures in Santiago's shack function as graphic pointers toward different approaches to reading *The Old Man and the Sea.* The two pictures are described as "relics of his wife" (16:3). The choice of the word "relics" is significant since both pictures depict religious subjects. The first picture mentioned, the Sacred Heart of Jesus, is commonplace in homes of pious Catholics. This picture points toward a reading of the novella as Christian allegory, replete with Santiago's carrying a mast on his shoulder in the manner of Jesus bearing his cross (121:2), suggestions of Santiago's stigmata (10:3, 107:5–8), and Santiago's direct appeal to prayer (64:23–65:1–18; 87:16–19) and his constant engagement in the practice of unconscious prayer or mentioning God: 42:16, 20; 45:11, 53:18, 56:7, 60:4, 63:14, 66:5, 68:16, 85:8, 87:17.

The second picture is that of the Virgin of Cobre, patron saint of Cuba. In the Afro-Cuban religious traditions, the Virgin of Cobre is a mask for Oshún, the African *orisha* (child/emissary of the One God).

The emphasis in *The Old Man and the Sea* seems to be on the Afro-Cuban manifestation of the Virgin, especially if the time present in *The Old Man and the Sea* begins on September 12 as argued by Sylvester ("The Cuban Context" 247–248; see also entry 17:1–2 below). September 12 is the Santeria feast day for the Virgin of Cobre and marks the beginning of the pilgrimage to Santiago de Cuba and her shrine.

For Cuban readers, the picture of the Virgin of Cobre has specific content. She is painted as a mulatto and is placed above the image of a skiff manned by three fishermen (two Taino Indians and a young slave). See Color Plate 3.

According to tradition, a statue of the Virgin floated in the water near the fishermen, calming a stormy sea. That statue is enshrined in Santiago, Cuba, bringing *orisha* and the old man together linguistically in the name "Santiago." There is a slight trace of that traditional picture in the opening lines of *The Old Man and the Sea*: "He was an old man who fished alone in a skiff in the Gulf Stream." (9:1).

The third picture in Santiago's house is present as absence: "Once there had been a tinted photograph of his wife on the wall but he had taken it down because it made him too lonely to see it" (16:3–7). An emptiness, a loneliness, an absence seems to curse Santiago and haunts the old man throughout the story. This absence, this emptiness, corresponds to the dearth of fish, to the bad luck that has lasted for eighty-four days without a catch. At the heart of the novella is a quest to undo the curse, a quest to restore the feminine to Santiago's life. That quest and restoration lie at the heart of the study of Santiago's women. (For more on this quest and restoration, see Beegel, "Santiago and the Eternal Feminine," and Grimes, "Hemingway's Religious Odyssey.") The important women in Santiago's life are present as absence, trace, symbol, and force. They sustain his struggle and emerge as transforming presences in the midst of great loss.

16:2 **Virgin of Cobre:** Cobre, a small town in the eastern province of Oriente, is the site of the sanctuary of Our Lady of Charity, a small statue of the Virgin Mary. The shrine is actually located in Santiago del Prado, a suburb of El Cobre, which itself is near the city of Santiago, Cuba's second-largest city. In 1916, Pope Benedict XV declared the Virgin the principal patroness of Cuba (Herbermann 516). The statue, like the Sacred Heart, emphasizes the loving nature of the Virgin. Perhaps, like many Cubans, Santiago's wife once made a pilgrimage to the distant shrine and brought back this picture (entry 16:3). At any rate, images of the statue were found in most Cuban houses.

According to legend, this statue of the Virgin Mary was floating on a wooden board off the coast of eastern Cuba in 1628 when it was found by two Indians and a slave boy in a rowboat (*Enciclopedia Universal* 1090). William Caxton reports the legend that the body of Saint James (Santiago) also originally appeared floating on the sea, in a small boat off the coast of Spain near Compostela, where it was said to have found its way from the Holy Land, even though the boat had no rudder and no sail (Starkie 15). The relics (bodily remains) supposedly then disappeared to be rediscovered in the ninth century (ibid., 16–17). Thus, the legend of the patroness of Cuba in this respect parallels, in the Spanish New World, the legend of Santiago in old Spain. And these parallel earlier legends find a twentieth-century parallel in the Cuban Santiago's experience at sea later in this novella, where the three parallels function thematically and artistically in the narrative's structure (entries 10:9, 98:21–23, and 122:2).

For a good introduction to the Virgin of Cobre, see DeRojas, especially 133–42.

16:3 **relics:** a play on words. The two pictures (one of the statue that is a relic) are themselves relics, in that they are objects remaining from his wife's life that remind Santiago of her. See Grimes, "Lions on the Beach," especially 59.

16:9 **yellow rice:** The picture that Santiago's wife brought back from the shrine of Our Lady of Charity at Cobre (see above) would picture the Virgin in yellow robes above the boat of fishermen. Yellow is associated with both the Virgin and her Santeria counterpart, the *orisha* Oshún, and will figure prominently throughout the rest of the work: 28:18, 35:16, 54:10, 72:12, 98:4, 106:23. Yellow is often used to describe the Sargasso weed (35:16), although most scientific descriptions of the algae call it brown. In the context of Afro-Cuban religion, Hemingway's choice of yellow makes sense. It reinforces Oshún's constant presence in the text, ever present in the sea. The most telling evocation of yellow as Oshún's color and presence comes in this passage: "they passed a great island of Sargasso weed that heaved and swung in the light sea as though the ocean were making love to something under the blanket" (72:9–12).

16:17–18 **sold it:** The cast net (entry 12:8) was sold to buy food for Santiago.

16:17–18 **fiction:** They understand each other because this kind of dialogue is their regular practice. They frequently speak in a code that lets them refer only obliquely to a hurtful fact or a practical limitation on their desires (entry 14:24). If stated directly, any reminder that the net is gone or that there is, in fact, no rice or fish today might inhibit their commitment to a truth beyond mere fact. That higher truth for them is that there is a naturally sanctioned purpose in living and fishing as correctly as possible, regardless of practical results (entry 14:24) and personal cost (entry 93:15–17). This dialogue prepares us for their closing dialogue (124:1–125:11), which includes the indirect revelation of an important possibility for the plot (entry 125:20–21).

16:20 **Eighty-five:** This number seems lucky to Santiago partly because it is the number of the next day he will be trying for a fish: no matter how long he has been unsuccessful, a fisherman with "resolution" (23:21) must maintain his faith in continued effort. And it is psychologically advantageous, of course, to focus on the next day, the attempt immediately at hand—to "play them one game at a time," as the sports cliché goes. But Santiago's "faith" in his eighty-fifth attempt will very shortly be reinforced by literal, topical information (entry 17:1–2).

16:22 **dressed out:** Gutted, its tail and head removed, and otherwise trimmed down to marketable meat. A fish would have to weigh over 1,500 pounds to weigh over a thousand pounds after being thus prepared (see entry 97:5–6).

17:1 **yesterday's paper:** We should note that, in 1950 (before the Castro revolution stressing widespread literacy), this poor Cuban fisherman is literate—which is yet another dimension of his distinction in his community. And although he is portrayed (most agree) as at least in his seventies, he is shown here reading newsprint without using glasses—a biological improbability that cannot be entirely explained by his clever avoidance of sun damage during his turtle-hunting years (entry 14:24), for his freedom from that earlier occupational hazard could not have forestalled the normal effects of aging on his eyesight. Yet what appears to be a violation of medical reality is, in fact, not. Some people are born with monovision, one eye capable of distance vision and the other focused entirely on objects near at hand. Such people's sight—both near and far—does not change as distinctly with age as does "normal" vision. And those people are unaware that their vision is neurologically different from that of others, unless they are examined by an optometrist or ophthalmologist (Park email)—an unlikely event in Santiago's circumstances. Many, thus gifted, are only aware, as Santiago is, that they are in this regard unusual, an aspect, perhaps, of his strangeness. Therefore, Santiago's reading and distance vision is credible as an extraordinary but consistently observed medical phenomenon, rather than a violation of nature for the sake of artistic effect. There are advertent violations: the duration—but not the outcome—of the arm-wrestling scene, for example, and great marlin's gender; at that size, "he" is definitely a she (see entry 49:6).

17:1–2 **read the baseball:** Crabbed English to remind us that Spanish is being spoken. This is the first of several references to newspaper coverage of Major League pennant races (at first glance, either fictional or actual) portrayed as going on while the novella's action takes place. The references are so cleverly interspersed among other details in the dialogue between Santiago and the boy that the actual information these baseball comments disclose was not publicly recognized until Harold Hurley set these comments apart in sequence (77–93, 103–17). When we read them this way, we can more readily notice that the baseball references focus on Santiago's "study" of the news in his paper and provide, indirectly, a great many details about games and teams purportedly in the two pennant races of some given year. There are enough details to nudge alert readers to search through baseball coverage of the years immediately preceding composition of the novella (early 1951), on the chance that they might find the actual news Santiago will read. And close readers would look for matching details about games and teams reported on in September, since that is the month when Santiago and the boy are speaking (18:11).

Accepting this challenge, Hurley discovered that Santiago does, indeed, read about an actual victory, on Sunday, 10 September 1950, by his favorite team, the New York Yankees (17:11), led by his baseball idol, Joe DiMaggio. After being written off by commentators during a prolonged batting slump, DiMaggio had (in baseball parlance) a "statistically perfect game": four at-bats, four hits, four runs, and four runs-batted-in. In addition, DiMaggio's performance included a park-record three home runs in the unusually long home stadium of the Washington Senators, the opposing team, with his bat bringing home four of his team's eight runs in an eight-to-one win.

The spectacular details were reported in the papers of Monday, 11 September. They are now "yesterday's" papers to Santiago because they would not have been delivered to Cuba until the next day, Tuesday, if they were papers from the United States, but they may not have been. Cuban papers, such as *El Mundo* and *Diario de la Marina,* also published detailed accounts of American baseball and the pennant races, complete with pictures and box scores, for avid Cuban fans. Perico, at the bodega, may have saved a day-old Cuban paper for Santiago, possibly his own, knowing the old man's love of baseball. The University of Florida's Digital Library of the Caribbean retains a 12 September 1950 issue of *Diario de la Marina,* which has a headline announcing the Yankees leading the American League by half a game after a double victory over the Senators on the previous day, Monday, 11 September; the article also cites DiMaggio twice (18; Losch email). We have been unable to locate a paper from 11 September, but we can nevertheless place the action of the story in historical time: from Tuesday evening, 12 September, to Saturday afternoon, 15 September 1950.

And readers thus informed also know (as Santiago cannot) that DiMaggio's big game spurred him, during the rest of that week, to lead his formerly flagging team to a tie in the American League pennant race and to eventual victory in the World Series. This fact of the plot makes the coming, extraordinary performance at sea in the balance of that week by the champion fisherman, Santiago, coincide historically as well as fictionally with the week's monumental performance by the baseball champion (see also entry 62:21).

The chronological correspondence thereby anticipates and strengthens important thematic parallels between the two leaders as the novella develops. The aging, athletic baseball champion will overcome adversity to achieve the highest goal in his field of endeavor; in his fishing community, the aged champion fisherman will take the greatest fish he has ever seen, while representing the best qualities of humanity among the rest of the creatures and forces of nature (entries 37:3 and 70:2). Moreover, the date of the action, 1950, adds historical support and credibility to the work's later comments on changing cultural and commercial values in Cuba at that time. These changes become central thematically in later pages (entry 29:23–24). The 1950 date also puts the novella in the context of the Korean War and just five years past the end of World War II. Most important to the immediate facts of the plot, though, is that Santiago's knowledge of DiMaggio's big game (and its importance to the team's standing) provides the otherwise missing "objective correlative" (satisfactory motivation) for a sudden change in the old man's attitude that occurs while the boy is away getting his bait and supper. When the boy leaves, Santiago expresses sheer "faith" in DiMaggio's eventual resurgence to rescue his team (17:13–14). But when the boy returns, Santiago speaks after the fact: "It is the Yankees as I said" (21:11); "The great DiMaggio *is* himself again" (21:14–15; emphasis added). Clearly, Santiago knows something about the Yankees, something involving DiMaggio, that he had not known when the boy left, reminding the old man to "study" the baseball news (17:19). Yet only those readers who, in effect, study the actual baseball news of that day with Santiago can know what his new information is: that DiMaggio has recovered from his slump; the Yankees will win the pennant; Santiago's faith in star and team is confirmed. And, to Santiago, the other champion's recovery portends his own.

But, for Santiago, the clinching parallel between DiMaggio's resurgence and his own anticipated recovery is that DiMaggio's big game is directly associated with the number eighty-five. That added correlation is what has given the old man his certainty. The news accounts have told him not only that this victory was the Yankees' eighty-fourth of the season but that, if they win their next game, their eightyfifth, that victory would tie the Yankees with the Detroit Tigers for the lead in the pennant race. And eighty-five, of course, is the number of Santiago's next attempt to take a fish (17:21)—the very number he had mentioned three times to the boy as a lucky number (16:20, 17:20–22, 18:2,), before even knowing about either of the Yankees's games. We know that this numerical correlation has struck Santiago as almost magically reassuring, because his addiction to numerology (common in Cuba and among baseball enthusiasts everywhere) is so pointedly stressed in this scene alone.

Moreover, we are told indirectly that Santiago is sure this eighty-fifth victory has already taken place. For the Monday newspapers' accounts of DiMaggio's Sunday game (one of which Santiago had just read) also announced the Yankees's next games, forthcoming on Monday in a double-header against the notoriously weak Washington Senators. The revived Yankees could hardly have managed to lose both Monday games to a team like that, especially not with a first-place tie in the pennant race at stake. And the records show us that the fictional Santiago's certainty is borne out by history, as does the newspaper on file at the University of Florida's digital library: the Yankees beat the Senators twice that Monday.

Only if we are prompted to pursue research beyond the text, then, can we know what Santiago is ultimately talking about in his references to the Yankees, as he and the boy eat their supper. Only by such diligence can we know that it is the justification of his faith in the number eighty-five that accounts for Santiago's unexplained celebratory mood (21:11–12).

Of course, the number of Santiago's next contest with destiny coincides with the number of the Yankees' pull-even victory only because DiMaggio's resurgence led to an eighty-fourth win for his team, rather than to some earlier or later victory. And the correlation of an eighty-fourth victory with Santiago's eighty-fourth day of failure is inverse and negative, appearing to mock the old man—an implication that would be out of character for Santiago to miss. But, in this case, a correlation negative and illogical in itself has led, for Santiago, to a positive correlation (the eighty-fives)—a paradox we can assume to be additionally intriguing to him. For in the mystique of numerology that he subscribes to, no coincidence of any kind is ever accidental; nor is it susceptible to human logic. (For a numerological reading focused on Christian mysticism in the novella as a whole, see Strauch 208–18.)

Hemingway has arranged this particular interface of history and fiction to display the psychological complexities of numerology as part of a larger comment on the psychology of belief in this character's case (see entry 11:1–2). (For discussions of the way Hemingway communicates this information to readers intrigued enough to do the baseball research and does so without ever explicitly referring to DiMaggio's big game, see Hurley 77–93, 103–17; and Sylvester, "Cuban Context" 246–51.)

17:6 Perico: A familiar form of "Pedro," the Spanish form of "Peter," a name derived from the Greek for "stone." The fisherman Peter, one of Christ's twelve Apostles, is known as the "rock" upon which the Christian church was founded (Matt. 16:18). Perico is, like Rogelio (12:8–9), an otherwise undelineated character, presented as one of a cadre of young men in the village who are loyal to Santiago. "Perico" is also Spanish for parakeet and used, therefore, as a nickname for someone who chatters constantly or who has a large, beaked nose. See also Pedrico (124:8 and 126:10), whose name is another form of "Pedro," and Martin (20:6), other supporters, or disciples, of Santiago who bear the names of saints—as does Santiago himself (entry 10:9). Mandel has suggested that Perico may be a misspelling of Pedrico (*Reading Ernest Hemingway* 357). Cuban Spanish often drops a postvocalic *d*, which would make Pedrico Perico (Herlihy-Mera, "He Was Sort of a Joke, In Fact" 98, fn. 10).

17:6 **bodega:** Grocery store, often with a small bar.

17:7 **have the sardines:** The boy may cast for them with his employer's net, or he may buy them, possibly from his new employer (entry 27:6–7).

17:12 **the Indians of Cleveland:** A literally translated Spanish idiom. The Cleveland Indians won the World Series in 1948, dropped to third in 1949 and fourth in 1950, shortly before Hemingway composed this novella. But the team had still been a dangerous opponent during the 1950 season (entry 17:1–2).

17:14 **DiMaggio:** Joe DiMaggio (1914–99), son of a San Francisco fisherman, spent his entire, legendary career with the Yankees, a team that regarded him as its quiet leader. For Santiago, "He makes the difference" (21:17). See entry 17:1–2 for crucial details.

17:15 **Tigers of Detroit:** In 1950, the Detroit Tigers led the American League for much of the season and hung on against the resurgent Yankees until the last week of the playoffs. (See entry 17:1–2 for details).

17:17–18 **Cincinnati . . . Chicago:** Both the Cincinnati Red Sox and the Chicago White Sox finished sixth in 1950, so neither was a threat to any successful team; in fearing them, the boy is overly cautious. As for the Reds, moreover, they play in the *National League* and could hardly compete for the American League pennant. Santiago is gently chiding the excessiveness of his friend's concern about the Yankees' chances (entry 17:1–2). Jeffrey Herlihy [-Mera] suggests that, if Hemingway knew his baseball history, he would have known that the Reds, who were the first team to field Cuban players, was established in 1868, the same year that Cuba began its revolt against Spain, when Carlos Manuel de Céspedes spoke for independence at the shrine of the Virgin of Cobre near Santiago, Cuba ("Eyes the Same Color as the Sea" 38).

Whether there is a reference to communism in the line "Be careful or you will fear even the Reds of Cincinnati" to the anticommunist vehemence sweeping through the United States in 1950 and 1951, in part due to Senator Joseph McCarthy (R-Wisc.), is a matter of speculation only. McCarthy had attacked Hemingway's one-time friend from the Spanish Civil War, Gustavo Durán, in a Senate hearing in 1950; Hemingway had, however, insulted Durán in 1945 for not participating directly in World War II (Baker, *Life* 448). But, in May 1950, Hemingway wrote a letter to McCarthy offering to beat him up: "You can come down here and fight . . . an old character like me who . . . thinks you are a shit, Senator, and would knock you on your ass the best day you ever lived" (*SL* 693); the letter, however, may never have been mailed. But, in 1954, two years after the publication of *The Old Man and the Sea*, Hemingway wondered whether a .577-caliber bullet was the right treatment for Red-baiting Senator McCarthy (*BL* 450). However much we may see eternal themes in *The Old Man and the Sea*, it is important to realize that it is also a book of its time.

17:20–21 **terminal . . . eighty-five:** A terminal is a lottery ticket containing only the last three digits of a full lottery number—a number that, in its entirety, would have many digits. In this case, the terminal number would be 085 (see 16:20). A whole number (*una entero*) would cost more than a poor Cuban could afford (18:4–5). For the importance of the number eighty-five, see entry 17:1–2.

17:24 **eighty-seven:** Santiago's past "record" of the greatest number of days without fish of any local fishermen still holds. Santiago's adversities are as great as his victories (second entry 9:2). In this book, risk and gain are correlated in nature's scheme (9:17).

18:4 **sheet:** A sheet (*una hoja*), much like a sheet of postage stamps, containing ten random three-digit "pieces" of whole lottery numbers (see 17:20). This sheet would cost $2.50, as the novella states. Although the boy's dealer is not likely to have on hand a sheet with the desired terminal 085, the dealer can take an "order" for one (18:3).

18:10–11 **we are in:** In English, "it is" September, a literally translated Spanish idiom, *estamos en septiembre,* used for effect. Besides being a bit chilly in the evening, September is one of the hurricane months and, therefore, a dangerous time to fish (61:7–9, 11:11, and entry 18:13). Yet it is the time when the largest fish come (entry 18:13). In another context, knowing the month helps careful readers determine the exact dates of the novella's action, as explained at 17:1–2; September 12 is also the date of the work's opening scene, of DiMaggio's resurgence and the Yankees' winning week, and the Santeria pilgrimage to the shrine of the Virgin of Charity, Oshún, at Cobre.

18:13 **fisherman in May:** A metaphorical reminder for readers of Santiago's coming ordeal that it is much easier for a fisherman in the May of life to perform than it is for a fisherman in the September of his life, when he must rely on experience and concentration. Santiago, though, is thinking primarily of the hurricane threat in September (entry 18:10–11) and of the practical fact that, in his fishing waters at the time of the novella, marlin took bait far more readily when passing through in the spring than when passing through in the fall. As the waters warmed up in the spring, many migratory fish, including marlin, traveled east along the Florida Current. Moving through the Florida Strait in May and early June, they fed voraciously (entry 14:3–4) and spread out northward, we now know, in the main Gulf Stream off the Atlantic coast of Florida to feed throughout the summer. Scientists have established that most of these marlin had returned in the fall to the Gulf of Mexico, to spawn where they had been born, and had lost weight while wintering there. This explains why, in the novella, marlin in this area are portrayed as easily hooked at this time. Then, in the late summer and early autumn, these marlin—many now old, very large fish—repeated the annual cycle. Travelling back through the Strait and moving northwest when off of Havana, against the eastward current (see entry 9:2), they follow exactly the course Santiago's September marlin will take, once hooked (45:3). According to Eric Prince (email), this pattern may not be as consistent today because, from the mid-1950s on, overfishing modified many migratory patterns.

19:4 **barefooted:** An indication of the tropical climate and of the old man's material poverty. His lack of shoes recalls Christ's command to his disciples to "carry no purse; no bag, no sandals" (Luke 10:4) in their humble travels to spread his word.

As a similar sign of humility and deference, the Jews and the Romans used to remove their shoes in mourning.

19:10 **a long way away:** From dreams of "places" he visited during thematically important voyages to Africa in his youth (24:20–25:10) and/or of the lions he saw at one of those places (25:14, first entry).

19:16 **I have:** Kept on fishing without having anything to eat.

19:23 **black beans and rice.** Staple foods in the Caribbean region.

20:6 **Martin:** "Owner" of the Terrace and named for a saint, as are several of Santiago's supporters, or disciples (first entry for 17:6). Saint Martin is the patron saint of innkeepers and drunkards. Legend has it that he once gave half of his cloak to a beggar in midwinter; thus, he is an icon of generosity, like his namesake in the novella.

20:8–9 **don't need to thank him:** Seemingly a graceless remark. But it is not in the boy's character to be jealous or uncharitable, especially about others who are also helping the old man. Nor is the boy trying to protect the old man's pride; he knows that Santiago is too humble to be uncomfortable in thanking a benefactor. It is possible, therefore, that the boy has actually paid for the food on this particular day and does not want Santiago to find out by going to Martin to thank him. For we notice that the boy is curiously evasive (20:8–9) about Martin's role in this donation (20:12). It is likely that the boy is trying to avoid an outright lie, while still concealing the extent of his own contribution because, at some point, the fair and loving old man would no longer permit the boy to make sacrifices for him under any guise and would then go hungry and lose his strength. (See entry 20:14 for Santiago's response.)

At another level, the boy's statement reminds Santiago that just to be able to assist the old fisherman is all the reward Martin would want, since Martin is one of several in the community—it will emerge later in the story—who deeply respect Santiago for his integrity and fortitude (entry 29:23–24).

20:10 **belly meat:** This portion of a large fish is a delicacy in many cultures, although too striped with fat for most North Americans.

20:14 **He is very thoughtful for us:** A literal translation; the Spanish words for "thoughtful" (*pensativo* or *atento*) take the preposition "for." Santiago's comment should be considered in connection with entry 20:8–9. With tactful irony, using the masculine pronoun "he" that could apply either to Manolin or Martin, Santiago communicates his awareness that the boy, rather than Martin, may be the "thoughtful" one today. We cannot overlook the old man's pointed, further nudge a moment later: "*Your* stew is excellent" (21:9; emphasis added). Although Martin is, in fact, very kind to the pair (entry 20:6 and lines 123:5, 7–8, 12, and 16), Santiago suspects that the boy paid for the stew on this occasion. By letting the boy know his suspicion, the old man acknowledges and relieves the boy's discomfort, while simultaneously thanking the boy both for the stew (in case it is, in fact, not this time a gift from Martin) and for the boy's sensitivity, in any case.

Thus, like the earlier exchange discussed in entry 12:8, the boy's remark here (20:8–9) and the old man's subtle rejoinders (20:14 and 21:9) exemplify the extreme, highly cultivated delicacy with which these two recognize and honor each other's feelings. These ordinary members of the community become at the same time extraordinarily "civilized," because of the regard each has for the other's dedication to principles transcending material comfort or even survival. This aspect of their interplay stresses the refined sensibility beneath their outward simplicity and makes their natural aristocracy all the more powerful an affirmation of human potential.

20:15 **two beers:** Are both beers for Santiago? If not, would Martin have sent Manolin a beer if Manolin were only ten years old? See entry 22:12–13.

20:18 **Hatuey:** A popular Cuban beer of the period, brewed by the Modelo Beer Factory in Cotorro, a village near Hemingway's home outside Havana. The label carried the portrait of a native Indian chief (originally from Haiti) named Hatuey. Hatuey beer is also mentioned in *To Have and Have Not* (30). A few years after publication of *The Old Man and the Sea*, this brewery staged a lavish public ceremony to thank Hemingway. Hemingway cited this brand in the novella because Chief Hatuey was as indomitable as Santiago and the boy, and even more indomitable than Harry Morgan of *To Have and Have Not*: Hatuey led the first Cuban revolt against the conquistadors. And when captured, he chose to be burned at the stake rather than convert to Catholicism in exchange for his life. He had no wish, he said, to go to a heaven where he would meet more Spaniards (Fergusson 44–45).

21:4 **down the road:** It is unlikely that the tired old man has washed. Small Cuban villages commonly had only one well. For Santiago's polite fiction here, see second entry 16:17–18.

21:9 **Your:** Spoken ironically. The stew is supposedly Martin's gift (20:6), but Santiago suspects that the boy may well have paid for it (20:14).

21:11 **as I said:** See entry 17:1–2. Santiago had told the boy (17:13) to have faith in DiMaggio's recovery from the batting slump that has been holding the Yankees back in the American League pennant race. Now he has just learned from his newspaper that the Yankees's leader and pacesetter is hitting again. Therefore, Santiago is certain that the Yankees will win the pennant, just as he had predicted. (For details, see entries 21:14–15 and 17:1–2).

21:13 **lost today:** The boy implies that, despite Santiago's new certainty that the Yankees will win the pennant (17:1–2), the team was vulnerable on that day. The boy can only have learned of the team's loss from someone with a radio, whom he met while getting Santiago's bait (18:14) or while picking up supper at the Terrace (entry 17:1–2).

21:14–15 **himself again:** This "great" player is hitting with the consistency *and* power for which he is noted, so he will lead his team to ultimate victory, despite a loss here and there. DiMaggio had been hampered since early in the 1949 season by an aggravated bone spur on his heel. Like Santiago's weakened left hand (71:2–3), this is a reminder that even extraordinary human champions are mortal. Yet, despite his bone spur, DiMaggio has returned to form in a superb performance Santiago has just read about (entries 21:11, 21:17, and especially entry 17:1–2). DiMaggio, like Santiago, was also hampered by age; he retired at age thirty-seven in December 1951, one year after the events of the novella.

21:17 **makes the difference:** The presence of a truly great individual performer adds a crucial element to the Yankees's performances that cannot be attributed to teamwork or to their deep roster of players who are merely outstanding. This difference explains why Santiago believes the Yankees "cannot lose" (17:11; 17:13–14), even before he has other reasons for his confidence in the team (entry 17:1–2). Referring in this work to far more than sports teams, this concept applies to Santiago's role as well as to DiMaggio's. It applies as well to the leadership role of extraordinary individuals in nature's other species that Santiago will shortly contend with at sea. The importance of extraordinary ability combined with indomitable resolution is displayed by a marlin and a mako shark whose wills persist even in their death throes (94:6; 102:16–17).

21:18 **other league:** The National League, to which the Brooklyn Dodgers and the Philadelphia Phillies belonged.

21:19–20 **great drives . . . old park:** Dick Sisler played with the National League Philadelphia Phillies from 1948 to 1951. But, in 1945 and '46, he had played at the old Tropical Park in Havana, in what was called the Winter League—an off-season league that attracted many Major League players at the time. And in one two-day period, he hit four home runs there, including the first ball ever hit completely out of the park (Longmire 96–98; Barbour and Settelmeyer 281–87). Those hits at Tropical Park are certainly the "great drives in the old park" that Cuban fan Santiago is remembering. (Sisler later recalled that those hits "got a lot of ink" in Havana. It was at the height of this publicity that he met Hemingway there several times, and, when *The Old Man and the Sea* came out in 1952, Hemingway sent him an autographed copy [Sisler correspondence, November 1992].)

But the main topic of Santiago's dialogue with the boy is the 1950 National League pennant race, in progress as they speak on 12 September (entry 17:1–2). And they cannot know that, later in that season, in the National League final at famous "old" Ebbets Field in Brooklyn, Dick Sisler would hit a home run to win the game and the 1950 pennant for Philadelphia (see entry 17:1–2). Santiago and the boy can refer only to Sisler's earlier "drives" in Havana. However, from his vantage point in 1951, as he composed Santiago's tribute to Dick Sisler, Hemingway very probably alluded not only to the "great drives" in Havana but to this even more momentous drive in another "old" park, Ebbets Field. The latter was dramatic recent history that Hemingway could expect baseball-oriented readers to remember when the book appeared in 1952. Philadelphia had been enduring such a seemingly interminable run of bad luck in 1950 that some observers considered that victory at Ebbets Field to have been the team's most important game in thirty-five years. And it was Sisler who made "the difference," as Santiago says of DiMaggio with the Yankees. Thus, Santiago's implication that Dick Sisler possesses some of a champion's special qualities has two historical referents rather than one (entry 17:1–2), both meaningful to readers as steeped in baseball lore as Hemingway was.

However, for Dick Sisler, there were few such triumphs in his relatively short major league career. Following its pennant victory, his Philadelphia team was defeated in four games by the Yankees in the World Series that year (1950; see entry 17:1–2). And, in 1951, his last year, the club did not repeat its 1950 National League pennant victory.

Actually, it was Sisler's father, George, a hall-of-famer (entries 22:11–13), who truly deserved the boy's label, "The great Sisler" (22:11). "Oh, well, he was one of the greats," Dick remarked of his father (Sisler correspondence, November 1992). Even though George played for the weak Saint Louis Browns, he hit over .400 some years—thus having many "great drives" in "old Sportsman's Park" in Saint Louis (now Busch Stadium). Gifted with nearly incredible athletic ability, the elder Sisler is sometimes mentioned today as still the best first-baseman ever to play the game. We can see a reason, then, for the rather enigmatic presence in the novella of "the great Sisler's" even greater father (22:11–13). George Sisler's evocation is an instance of Hemingway's frequent practice of incorporating in one fictional character characteristics of two or more real-life models. In this case, George's consistent, dazzling talent and his son's seizure of a few moments to make history are combined in the champion "Dick," a fictional character bearing some of the qualities of two real Sislers.

22:11 **never poor:** George Sisler came from a prominent Ohio family. Socially, he and his son have less in common with Santiago and the boy than does DiMaggio. Yet, because Dick played in Cuba and the boy is also a knowledgeable fan of the big leagues, he speaks familiarly of the Sisler family history (entry 22:11–13).

22:11–13 **he, the father, was playing in the Big Leagues when he was my age:** A key sentence. This remark by the boy is one of several artistic uses of calculatedly ambiguous pronoun reference in Hemingway's narratives. It allows most readers to assume that the second "he" refers to Sisler, the son, and that he was the boy's age when his father was a player (and, therefore, affluent). But readers who are baseball historians or have researched the Sisler family history know that Dick's father, George (entries 21:19–20 and 22:11), began his professional career at twenty-two and retired when his son was ten. Such readers (and only they) know that, if the second "he" refers to the son, "the boy" in the novella is ten or younger, but, if the second "he" is the father, "the boy" must be twenty-two. Learning this, Hurley (96–97) has reasoned that the second "he" is the son (since a child could not play in the major leagues) and that the boy in the story must, therefore, be no more than ten.

But that would be considerably younger than most readers have felt the boy to be, and there are reasons for the widespread impression that the youth is older than ten. Philip Young, who computed the three-quarter-mile length of the lines the boy carries, saw it as a matter of common sense that no "young boy" could carry those lines "unless . . . the lad was actually a giant" (Young 274–75; cited in Sylvester, "Cuban Context" 256). And once readers have, in addition, researched the weight and size of these lines (entry 15:5), they are faced with a child of ten supposedly carrying a box weighing 130 pounds, while balancing a gaff and harpoon. The only logical conclusion is that the second "he" in lines 22:11–13 must refer to Sisler's father and that "the boy" can only be twenty-two (or older). Many readers must have suspected that the pointedly repeated, elaborate descriptions of the fishing lines, as well as the two beers of 20:15, provide more than a sense of local color or "the way it was." And many must have been equally uncomfortable with the syntax of the sentence on "the great Sisler's father." For Hemingway—a meticulous stylist—has not only composed an egregiously ambiguous pronoun reference but has called attention to that ambiguity with a conspicuously clumsy insertion that sustains the ambiguity while pretending to resolve it (see also Losada 79–83). Importantly, the insertion of "the father, was playing" was added by Hemingway in pencil to the typescript he submitted to Scribner's ("Old Man and the Sea," manuscript, box 90, item 12) in order to add to the ambiguity. Careful readers have found that these attention-getting anomalies converge to reveal a fact of the plot. "The boy" is a young man of at least twenty-two, rather than a youth from twelve to fifteen as readers and critics have generally assumed—though Baker does place him "on the edge of young manhood" (*Writer as Artist*, 305).

Of course, the boy's young adulthood seems at odds with the narrative's ostensible indications that this character is a child: that he is "a boy" who "must obey his father" (10:21–22). But for that apparent inconsistency we can find an explanation in the social history of Cuban villages like Cojimar. For example, many findings of Lowry Nelson's sociological study of Cuban working-class culture of the 1940s are directly relevant to this book. From the customs and terminology Nelson discusses (174–200), we can see that the appellation "the boy" for a young man is true to the time and place portrayed here. We see, too, why this young man would accept his parents' authority (as does Santiago) with a deference that has understandably misled American and European readers (10:21–23). The boy's unquestioning subservience to his parents (until the concluding scenes of the narrative [125:7])—and Santiago's endorsement of that subservience (10:23)—reflect a Cuban family patriarchy still modeled on that of feudal Spain and strict to a degree that would not occur to most North Americans or Europeans. Authority was slowly shifting, in the mid-twentieth century, from the family to the individual and the community. Yet, at this character's social level, a son's life, regardless of his age, remained dictated by his father until he married and actually set up housekeeping under a separate roof. A single man's deference was so great, for example, that he did not, in his father's presence, practice the male ritual (in that culture) of smoking.

Knowledge of Nelson's topical information, thus, makes the "boy" as a young adult credible to us and allows us to recognize the important thematic implications of his chronological maturity, as it is actually portrayed in all of his activities away from his parents. Adding credence is the fact that the Spanish nouns *chico* and *muchacho* can both be translated as "boy," but both terms are used among young men addressing each other, with the meaning of "guy" or "man." In Cuba, "chico" is frequently used to address friends. It roughly has the same meaning as "hey, man" or "buddy" in English.

As a young adult, "the boy" functions realistically, rather than fancifully, as a Parzival to Santiago's Fisher King (entries 124:11, 125:2). As an adult, he is literally comparable to the grown sons in the biblical "fishers-of-men" allusions (entries 10:9, 17:6 [first entry]). He is also credible, literally, in his advertent championship of old values in the social struggle against the growing materialism in Cuba at the time and as a dominant member of the cadre of adult males loyal to Santiago in that social and spiritual division (entry 29:23–24). It is important to realize that, at twenty-two, Manolin has fished with Santiago for seventeen years, since he was five (12:15), a long and very close apprenticeship, very much cementing the surrogate father/son relationship. (See Sylvester, "Cuban Context" 256–62, for more evidence of the boy's adulthood and for further comment on the thematic implications of his adulthood, as well as on Hemingway's purpose in presenting apparently inconsistent narrative details. See entry 14:24 for discussion of such apparent inconsistencies in Hemingway's works as, in effect, subtle research assignments—invitations to curious readers to account, themselves, for apparently unresolved issues.)

22:14 **before the mast:** Working as a "common seaman" on a sailing ship. Men of this rank slept in the forecastle (or forward quarters) in the bow (front) of the ship, and therefore ahead of the mast or masts; hence, the term, made common by Richard Henry Dana's 1840 memoir *Two Years before the Mast*. It is unlikely that Santiago would have been entrusted with a seaman's heavy, dangerous labor when he was the age the boy is now, if the boy is only ten or less—one of only two possibilities specified by lines 22:11–13. Santiago's occupation aboard the ships thus nudges us further to wonder if the boy might be considerably older than many readers have assumed.

22:15–16 **to Africa . . . lions:** The old man mentions important voyages to the northwest coast of Africa that are prefigured in 12:6 and 19:10 and are discussed in entry 24:19 as well as in several subsequent entries. We will learn that watching the lions "on the beaches" was one of several experiences deeply affecting the rest of Santiago's life (entry 25:14, second entry).

22:17 **I know. You told me:** A gentle chide, couched in the subtle understatement often used by both characters. Long-term memories typically preoccupy the aged; and, although Santiago's are very special, he does tend to repeat himself in relating them (entry 12:8). But the boy is also saying that he remembers his mentor's every word.

22:18 **Africa or . . . baseball:** Santiago archly acknowledges the boy's polite nudge (22:17) and considerately offers baseball (entry 17:1) as an alternative subject more likely to interest the young man, who hears often enough about Africa (see, for example, 19:10 and 22:15–16). Santiago's question here completes an exchange (22:15–18) in which appealing mortal flaws are balanced by the good humor and daunting selflessness of these protagonists (entry 12:8).

22:20 **McGraw:** John J. McGraw (1873–1934), nicknamed "Little Napoleon" for his dictatorial style, was manager of the National League New York Giants, 1902–32. (See entries 22:23–24, 23:6, and 23:9.)

22:20 ***Jota:*** Pronounced "HOE-ta," the Spanish word for the letter *j*.

22:23–24 **His mind was on horses . . . baseball:** McGraw owned part of the Oriental Park race track in Havana, so that he was commercially as well as emotionally divided in his commitments. Even though many baseball experts consider McGraw the greatest of all managers, even getting great praise from fellow manager and rival Connie Mack when McGraw was inducted into the Baseball Hall of Fame, the dedicated craftsman Santiago disapproves of McGraw's lack of focus on one totally absorbing vocation.

23:5 **here the most:** Santiago suggests the narrow perspective of the boy's father who, he believes, values only the familiar and picks the American coach who has come more often than any other to Havana. Also, McGraw had a business interest in Havana, after all (entry 22:23–24). And Santiago also apparently thinks of him as one of the rowdy Americans attracted to the gambling, prostitution, and drinking in Havana, a center of illicit activity at that time.

23:6 **Durocher:** Leo Durocher (1905–91), a controversial but successful manager who harassed umpires, fought with team owners and fans, and played hunches. In 1947, he was suspended from baseball for a year for his association with gamblers, and Santiago apparently categorizes him as he does McGraw (22:23). Santiago implies that the boy's father, lacking vocational dedication himself, is no better judge of baseball men than he is of the fisherman to whom he has apprenticed his son (14:11).

23:9 **greatest manager:** Cubans Adolfo Luque (1890–1957), known as Dolf, and Miguel González (1890–1977), called Mike, were successful Major League players for twenty and seventeen years, respectively. Both, notably, were very light-skinned. Hemingway's selection of these two particular men reminds baseball-oriented readers of the color line that kept nearly all other Cubans out of the Major Leagues until well after this novella was published. And because of a related unwritten law, González (assumed to be entirely white) was the only Cuban who had ever managed a Major League team: the Saint Louis Cardinals in 1938 and 1940. (See Barbour and Sattelmeyer 285; Burns and Ward 112; and Sylvester, "Cuban Context" 251–52, for more details on this racial exclusion.) Partly for this reason, Luque and González (both highly gifted) managed regularly in the Winter League in Havana. Yet we can assume that Santiago and the boy's high regard for these two managers is not a limited, provincial assumption like the boy's father's choice of Durocher (23:6–8), but is based instead on Luque's and González's considerable stature in the majors as well as in the Winter League. Santiago and the boy, who know a great deal about big-league players (entries 17:1–2, 22:11–13), are selecting two Cubans as the best of all managers. The entire exchange thus reveals the national identification with the sport that was a source of pride for informed as well as provincial Cubans, despite the color barrier in the Major Leagues. And this identification explains the association of baseball with heroism in the minds of the protagonists, even though Santiago's ultimate exemplar is the American Joe DiMaggio (entry 17:1–2). Luque is also mentioned in Hemingway's *Islands in the Stream*, 292.

23:13 **better:** Santiago believes that a few other fishermen are more effective in some aspect of the craft than he is. However, the boy's rejoinder, "But there is only you" (see entry 23:15), points up a different kind of measurement, making us think further about defining "best" and "great" in the context of the action to come.

23:14 ***Qué va:*** Pronounced "kay-va," an idiomatic expression of disbelief or (as here) dismissal; here it is translated as "Oh, come on now" or "That's nonsense."

23:15 **only you:** Partially a reflection of the boy's love and the faith the two share. But considered in the context of Santiago's characterization in the novella, the boy's words are a measured, qualified assessment, acknowledging the particular distinction of a special man (21:17).

24:3–4 **Why . . . so early:** Like most rhetorical questions in Hemingway's narratives, this query nudges us to look beyond literal answers and implications. Here we are prompted to explore, instead, the psychological and philosophical motives and issues suggested by Santiago's next question (24:4).

24:9–10 **as though I were inferior:** See entry 27:6–7 and, for contrast, lines 11:3–5.

24:16 **newspaper inside:** The papers add to the makeshift pillow's bulk and height. This detail calls attention to Santiago's poverty. We note that he is not only without a pillow but without a mattress. There is nothing between him and the bedsprings but a layer of newspapers (24:17–18) and the blanket that he rolls "himself in" (24:17) to get it beneath him (122:2). Yet his poverty enforces the material simplicity that is paradoxically turned to his ethical and spiritual advantage in the novella as a whole. He must make do with what is at hand, rather than rely on manufactured products or machines (entry 11:18–19). And such direct contact with his environment, viewed positively, will become thematically important (see entries 30:3 and 30:20–21).

24:19–20 **dreamed of Africa:** When he visited the northwest coast of that continent during his stint as a young seaman (22:1–16 and entry 22:14). The lines immediately following (24:21–25:3) reveal that Santiago's habitual memories and daydreams of his youth, hinted at earlier (entries 12:6 and 19:10), figure in recurrent, nocturnal dreams, as well as in his daydreams. We learn that watching the lions "on the beaches" was one of several experiences during those voyages that deeply affected the rest of Santiago's life (entry 25:14, second entry). Lines 24:21–25:3 give us some of the specific contents of those thematically crucial dreams. Together with lines 25:8–10, these lines reveal that Santiago was originally from the Spanish province made up of the seven Canary Islands off of the northwestern coast of Africa (see entry 25:8, also Figure 5). The passage also gives information leading to our realization that the vessel he sailed on to Africa (entry 22:1) was a trading vessel that stopped at "different harbours" of the various Canary Islands (25:9–10). (For the particular significance of this latter information, see entry 25:8.)

24:20–21 **the long golden beaches and the white beaches:** These phrases and those in the rest of this sentence are notable for their poetic rhythm and repetition. They convey the incantatory insistence of Santiago's associations with beaches and whiteness. The latter are two of the main features of the African shore (see entry 24:19–20) that were stamped in the young Santiago's memory with the force of a vision and have remained dominant in his imagination. (On whiteness and high mountains in Hemingway's works, see entry 25:8.)

25:1 **oakum:** A fiber obtained by untwisting and fluffing out the yarns of old, tarred hemp rope. It is commonly used to caulk (jam into) the seams of wooden vessels to make them watertight.

25:2–3 **smell of Africa:** Santiago actually smells the Cuban land breeze blowing outside his shack (entry 14:6) and works it into his dream as the odor of the African shore years ago. Past and present merge in his dream, for, despite his chronological age, in his unconscious mind, Santiago retains the identity he recognized during his youthful, African experiences of initiation as a champion of nature (entries 24:19–20, 25:8, 25:13–14, 25:1, 25:15 [both entries], and 25:16). Baker (*Writer as Artist* 309) sees a similarity between Santiago and Joseph Conrad's Captain Beard in *Youth*, a character Conrad's narrator describes as "sixty, if a day . . . [with] blue eyes in that face of his, which were amazingly like a boy's" (2). For Santiago's youthful, blue eyes, see entry 10:7. See entries 25:8, 25:13–14, 25:14 (first entry), 25:15, and 25:16 for the fixed, youthful focus of Santiago's imagination.

25:8 **white peaks:** The mountains of the several Canary Islands (25:10) as their rocky, sun-bleached peaks appeared to rise "from the sea" as the sailing vessel the young Santiago worked on (entry 22:14) approached the land. The Canary Island peaks are among the dominant visual memories, like those cited in entry 24:19, of Santiago's early voyages to Africa. Bright white natural forms (especially in high places) and land rising from its opposite, the sea, are both associated with mystical experience here, as elsewhere in Hemingway's fiction; compare *SS* 52 and 76, and *ARIT* 26–29, 34, 44–45ff.). These topographical memories dominate Santiago's dreams (25:13–14). Hemingway uses them as T. S. Eliot uses "the rose garden" in his poem "Burnt Norton" (I, l. 14), as both the memory of a real place, imbued with emotion, and as a source of symbolic meanings. Such memories mark the "places" (25:14) where Santiago experienced the initiation into life's mysteries that has changed his perception of life ever since. In using this associative device, both Eliot and Hemingway were influenced by the philosopher Henri Bergson (see immediately below), Eliot having heard Bergson lecture at the Sorbonne in Paris.

25:13–14 **only dreamed of places now:** The places mentioned in 24:20 and 25:8 and discussed in the entries on those places as dominant visual memories are associated with Santiago's first full sense of life's wondrous possibilities. The sites of those youthful discoveries merge past and present perpetually in the symbolic imagination that defines his identity and creates his dreams. According to Henri Bergson (entry 25:8), whose theories of psychology influenced T. S. Eliot, William Faulkner, Hemingway, and other modernists, the most intense experiences are more forceful and enduring in the imagination than are subsequent experiences of much greater actual duration. In Santiago's dreams, only the distant places where he first felt the power of his affinity with all of nature remain vivid in his subconscious. The places where he later in life experienced "great occurrences," "great fish," "contests" (25:12–13), or relationships—places where he subsequently applied that power—have lost their immediacy as the great events there have receded into the past. Only the initiation sites dominate his subconscious mind (his dreams). For the initiation experiences were more fundamental to his character than were his later exploits and, therefore, remain more powerful in his memory (entry 25:16). We notice, moreover, that even those powerful first impressions of his affinity to nature are themselves no longer re-enacted in his dreams. Except for the lions associated with one of those impressions (25:14), these dominant initiatory moments of self-recognition are represented only by the places where they occurred.

The dominance of place in Santiago's memory is psychologically plausible. The tendency of location to become fixed in the mind more readily than other aspects of experience was long ago demonstrated by classical rhetoricians in the Simonides-Quintillian tradition, who regularly used mnemonic systems based on spatial location to perform otherwise impossible feats of memory.

25:14 **lions on the beach:** Lions do frequently play on the African beaches (Wooster email). The text of *The Old Man and the Sea* poses this direct question: "Why are the lions the main thing that is left?" (66:18–19). Their importance and the importance of Africa, remembering, and dreaming are underscored by the last sentence of the book: "The old man was dreaming about the lions" (127:8–9). For a lengthy analysis of the role of lions and Africa in *The Old Man and the Sea*, see Grimes, "Lions on the Beach."

Santiago's personal identification with the lions he observed there was one of several moments of self-discovery he experienced during voyages to the African coast when he was young. These moments remain impressed upon his imagination and in his dreams (entries 24:19, 24:19–20, 25:2–3, 25:8, 25:14). Yet the lions are the only animate details of those momentous events that still appear in his dreams. For his dreams are now dominated almost entirely by topographical details of the places where he discovered that his way of looking at things gives him a sense of responsibility to nature (25:14). Only the lions and the topography remain because, apparently, Santiago's extreme excitement in the presence of impressive natural forms (24:20, 25:8) made him aware that he had some unusual role to play in nature. And the lions, as fellow creatures rather than inanimate natural features, defined for him the position he was destined to fill in that scheme. Moreover, the lions are an efficient narrative device because readers already associate lions with natural aristocracy: with the qualities of courage, confidence, and *joie de vivre* (entry 25:15), qualities that emerge in the narrative to set Santiago (and the boy) apart from many in their human community.

"Community" is a significant word here. Lions are social animals: they hunt in packs, and they form communities of integrated support. Thus, in addition to the qualities listed above, they remind us that Santiago, even when apparently alone on the ocean, is a member of such a human community, as well as a member of a larger, biological one. Similarly, Hemingway's sports hero has changed over time. Sports figures appeared in early Hemingway fiction—the boxers Ole Andreson ("The Killers") and Jack Brennan ("Fifty Grand"); the bullfighters Manuel Garcia ("The Undefeated") and Pedro Romero (*SAR*)—but these men practiced their sports alone, as individuals. In this work, the sports hero is Joe DiMaggio, who not only plays a team sport but who is the ultimate team player, the one who sparks other players to do their best.

25:15 **like young cats:** Santiago does not dream of young lions. He dreams of lions that behave *as if* they were young, as mature lions frequently do, romping and chasing each other like kittens (Wooster email). This distinction identifies them with Santiago himself, not simply as he was when he saw the lions but as he has been ever since and will be until he dies. Santiago feels an "intimacy" with the lions as they represent "the proud and often fierce heart of nature that for him is the repository of values" (Wells 101). And this intimacy accounts doubly for the language expressing his love for the lions ("he loved them as he loved the boy"). His love is compounded of fellow feeling and love or admiration for great forces of nature, both within his species (for the "boy," for example) and across species (for the lions, as well as for the marlin and mako shark) later in the novella. As Santiago's memory preserves them—playing—the animals demonstrate the perspective of nobility immemorially associated with the lion: an easy assurance of power, allowing for pleasure in being alive. Because he shares this perspective, Santiago is able to see these formidable creatures as many of us see domestic cats, as familiar and nonthreatening, attracting affection as well as respect.

Santiago's own freedom to be playful is an important part of his portrayal. Rather than solemnity, he shows spontaneous pleasure in his response to his young protégé, as well as to the lions (and to various admirable sea creatures later in the narrative). Despite the great seriousness, sacrifice, and responsibility of his accepted role as the human representative of nature's aristocracy (entry 25:8), his unassuming confidence ("faith," entry 11:1–2) leaves him emotionally capable of the light touch. We have seen him gently teasing the boy, for example (entries 12:8, 17:17, 22:18), and abandoning himself to the happy enthusiasm the two share for baseball.

Elsewhere, particularly at the time when he composed *The Old Man and the Sea*, Hemingway considered gaiety in the face of adversity one of the most attractive signs of heroism. In letters of the period, he remarked on such cheerfulness in General C. T. Lanham (*SL* 651), one of his models for Santiago. In this regard, Santiago reminds us of the allseeing elders of antiquity celebrated in W. B. Yeats's poem "Lapis Lazuli": "Their ancient, glittering eyes, are gay" (1.56).

25:15–16 loved them as . . . the boy: The sense of identification that attracted Santiago to the lions' easily borne power accounts for the feeling he has for "the boy" as well as for these beasts. We have seen that the lions, "the boy," and Santiago himself equally display the vitality and confidence marked by Santiago's blue eyes (10:7). Such confidence is singled out in portrayals of the "natural aristocrats," the champions among the natural creatures Santiago will contend with at sea. This unusual boy mirrors Santiago's memory of himself at emerging manhood, while at the same time mirroring the natural creatures whose appearance triggered his own first, intuitive conviction that such confidence was part of something larger than humanity. Thus, he loves the lions "as" (in the same way that) he loves the boy—and vice versa.

25:16 about the boy: Santiago dreams now only in symbols of timeless principles rather than in scenes where those principles are acted out—thus, his dream of the lions rather than of actions (25:13–14). The lions are already stamped in his unconscious as the primary animate symbols of the very qualities the boy might otherwise serve to represent. So Santiago has no more need to dream of the boy than to dream of "great occurrences" (entry 25:13–14) or any other individual *reflections* of the natural principles he lives by.

There is another implication of the boy's absence from the dreams, one essential to Santiago's characterization. Like the solitary marlin and the mako shark, who approach alone (entry 100:21–23), nature's other two champions he will encounter at sea, Santiago is ultimately autonomous within his species. It is true that Santiago depends on the boy for practical sustenance (106:7), wishes for the boy's help during his coming struggle (45:7, 83:6), feels gratified that many in his "good town" will worry about him (115:7), and is spiritually revived by the boy near the story's end (125:4–5). It is also true that Santiago's identification with lions, the most socially oriented of all the cats (Wooster email), also symbolically reinforces the social dimension in the book (entry 29:23–24). For some readers, then, this novella proves Hemingway's espousal of human solidarity and interdependence (see Burhans).

Yet Santiago's identity is ultimately marked by his capacity for self-containment throughout a champion's destined, solitary extremity (entry 61:3 and lines 66:9–14).

His dreams reflect that capacity for self-containment and autonomy. Dreams are the brain's way of processing dissatisfactions too disturbing to cope with in waking life. But Santiago's dreams are free of all need to dramatize his values or concerns by placing them in plots so as to deal with them. That is why there is no animate personification of any kind in his dreams, except for the lions associated with his all-encompassing discovery—in one of his numinous "places"—of his personal identity in nature's order. His dreams thus reveal the psychic integration of a mentality completely "together," as the slang term aptly puts it. As the narrator of Conrad's "Youth" says of Captain Beard, Santiago is "immense in the singleness of his idea" (quoted in Baker, *Writer as Artist* 310). In fact, a central reason for Santiago's effectiveness as an exemplar of human potential is exactly this concord between his conscious and unconscious motives. From "Out of Season" at the beginning of Hemingway's career to this novella of the sea near the end, his works stress a unification of conscious and unconscious goals as the key to "grace under pressure"—that outward sign of emotional and philosophical maturity throughout Hemingway's fiction (Sylvester, "Italian Waste Land" 82–83). Santiago displays this sought-after psychic unity in its purest form, despite a single loss of confidence (entries 121:4 and 125:3), when he does indeed have to rely on the boy (125:4–5). (See entry 121:4 for traditional religious implications of Santiago's temporary lapse; see entries 125:3 and 125:4–5 for his revival.)

Santiago's constant psychic identification of past and present, youth and age, reinforces various patterns of cyclicity and circularity that emerge in the narrative as a whole (compare with entry 88:21–89:7). See also Baker, *Writer as Artist* 310; T. S. Eliot, "East Coker," 123.l 1; and entries 9:2, 16:2, and 126:23). For a Jungian reading of circularity in the work, taking into account "the mystery of the mandala," see Strauch (194–207, 225–26 esp.) And see, for example, entries 24:19–20, 25:8, and 25:13–14.

26:11 Qué va: Rather than expressing disbelief, as in 23:14, the boy's "*Qué va*" here means "that's life"; that's "what a man must do" (26:11–12). The expression marks Santiago's mature recognition that humanity must endure the rigors of labor. This is an allusion to what all humankind "must do," according to Jehovah's pronouncement after the Fall: "In the sweat of thy face shalt thou eat thy bread" (Gen. 3:19–21). On the boy's maturity, see especially entries 12:23, 15:5, and 22:11–13.

27:3 Manolin: The boy's name, withheld until this late in the narrative (as Frederic Henry's name is withheld until Chapter 8 of *A Farewell to Arms*). The subtly dramatic effect of such a delay is particularly appropriate in Manolin's case, for Manolin is the diminutive of "Manuel," the Spanish form of the Hebrew name "Emanuel" or "Immanuel"—literally, "God with us." Partly for this reason, it is the name given by Isaiah to the Hebrew Messiah of his prophecy (Isa. 7:14; Matt. 1:23). This allusion is consistent with Manolin's role as Santiago's eventual successor, the Parzival to his

Fisher King, the next champion of the community's traditional values (entry 12:23 and Sylvester, "Cuban Context" 258).

Bullfighters named "Manuel" have commonly used "Manolin" as a professional name, a practice suggesting its appropriateness for a physically and morally prepossessing young man playing a central, exemplary role in his culture. Baker (*Life* 46, 50) thinks Hemingway partly had in mind Manolito, son of the cafe owner in Cojimar, a boy Hemingway had taken for a cruise on his boat, the *Pilar*, in 1948.

27:6–7 **he . . . himself:** "He" is the man with whom Manolin sails, and he brings the gear himself because "He never wants anyone to carry anything" (27:7–8), and "anyone" means Manolin. The unnamed and thereby disrespected new employer (14:11) does not trust Manolin and does not give him responsibility as Santiago does. Manolin brings up the subject at this point to explain why he has time to help Santiago, even though his employer's boat also must be loaded for departure.

27:12 **credit here:** But not everywhere. Literally, Manolin is reminding Santiago that they have an arrangement at this "early morning place that served fishermen" (26:23). Perhaps this is also a play on words, suggesting that they are "credited" (approved of) for their values, as they are at the Terrace (entries 20:6 and 20:14). But his remark also reminds readers that others in the community, Manolin's father included (entry 10:24), do not respect Santiago's values (line 11:7 and entry 29:23–24).

Readers considering autobiographical connections should know that, in his personal dealings, Hemingway apparently regarded the giving and accepting of credit as an exchange of respect and made a point of charging his drinks at spots he favored. These included the Terrace (La Terraza) in Cojimar.

PAGES 28 THROUGH 43

28:1 **Good luck:** More than a conventional parting remark. Luck is a complex concept in this novella (9:6–7, 116:15–117:5, 125:3–5, and esp. 32:23; see also second entry 17.1).

28:3 **thole pins:** A pair of wooden, cigar-sized stakes (or sometimes, as probably here, a single stake), inserted vertically into the gunwale (the top edge) of each side of the boat. Thongs attached to the pins are tied around each oar to keep it in place as it is stroked. The thematic significance here of the wooden pins and the thongs is that they are homemade and of natural materials. The old man does not use oarlocks, which are a manufactured, metal item (see entries 11:20, 29:23–24, 30:3).

28:3 **leaning . . . against the thrust:** Santiago apparently faces the bow of the boat as he rows—pushing, instead of pulling, against the water as he strokes. That he faces ahead even while rowing (although rowers usually face the stern and pull the oars) explains his constant view of ocean activity ahead of his boat, as befits his disciplined vigilance (32:22–23).

Artistically, his position is part of a pervasive iconographic pattern conveying Santiago's "faith" (entry 11:1–2) and resolution by his physical stance throughout the novella. See Luke 9:62: "No man, having put his hand to the plough, and looking back, is fit for the kingdom of God." Readers will notice that, except when performing an immediate task toward the stern, Santiago faces forward throughout the action at sea and on his return to land. The single exception to this pattern marks a significant, but temporary, lapse in Santiago's confidence (see entries 121:4 and 125:3).

28:18 **Gulf weed:** The current surging east through the Florida Strait carries large amounts of a greenish-brown seaweed (described by the narrator as yellow) of the genus *sargassum* from the Gulf of Mexico. The glow of "phosphorescence" in the dark comes not from the weed but from microscopic life forms floating near it. Here, the presence of the weed tells Santiago that he is entering the edge of the suddenly deep (28:19) main flow of the Gulf Stream. Yellow is the color of the Santeria *orisha* Oshún (see entries 35:11–13, 35:16, and 56:2).

28:19 **great well:** Created by the sudden depth at the edge of the island's coastal shelf. The sea floor surrounding a landmass slopes very gradually at first and then "drops off" dramatically, creating a haven for fish from the shoreline currents (entry 14:3–4). For this reason, most shoreline fishing precisely follows the lines formed by continental shelves. At a point only a few miles out from Havana, the bottom suddenly drops nearly half a mile, from approximately 280 to 704 fathoms (4,224 feet, or nearly three-quarters of a mile). A little farther out beyond this drop-off, Santiago will find his marlin in "water that was a mile deep" (40:18–19). For the importance of depth in this, see entry 30:20–21.

The description of the ocean's depths here is part of a pattern that becomes thematic in this novella. In Hemingway's works, generally, visual descriptions are painterly: they stress what is literally visible from a character or narrator's physical position (see the celebrated opening paragraph of *A Farewell to Arms*). Yet here the point of view moves immediately from the *visible* phenomenon (the predawn, phosphorescent glow of "Gulf [Stream] weed") at the surface of the sea (28:18) to details in the depths that Santiago can only *visualize* but that he knows account for the presence of the *visible* weed. Although in this instance we learn of the weed and the drop-off from the third-person narrative point of view, we know that Santiago, like all experienced commercial fishermen in the area, thoroughly understands the underwater dynamics of this central fishing spot. Thus, we imagine him to be thinking of the underwater shelf and currents. And repeatedly elsewhere, via Santiago's thoughts or comments to himself, Hemingway uses Santiago's "mind's eye" (or the third-person narrative's implication of his mind's eye) to show what goes on where the old man cannot literally see.

In this way, physically sensed natural phenomena are repeatedly connected with their interlocking natural causes and effects located beyond the immediate scenes. This is a device, a narrative strategy, in *The Old Man and the Sea*. Readers are thereby allowed to share the old man's seemingly omniscient overview of natural processes. Readers sense with Santiago his integration into nature's organic unity. (See entry 29:3. For a related observation, see Beegel, "Eye and Heart" 78–79; and Ott 69–70, 92–95.) The old man's mind's eye is one of many reasons that nature's order seems, for many readers, more fully and satisfactorily perceptible to the human mind in this novella than in any other Hemingway work.

29:3 **feel the morning:** Santiago registers, largely unconsciously, the combination of sounds, odors, and other sensations (including his own reflections) that he has repeatedly experienced at sea in the period just before first light. Thus, he feels stimulated by the feelings he has habitually experienced at that point in the day. The flying fish greeting him in the dark are an example of these stimuli, as is the familiar associative flow of his warmth toward the birds and toward the sea that represents the natural order that he loves (see lines 29:7–18 and entry 28:19).

29:5–6 hissing . . . stiff set wings: *Exocoetidae,* or "flying fish," do not actually fly, and their "wings"—the extended pectoral fins—never really move. An illusion of flight is created just as the fish breaks the surface, when it rocks slightly as it sculls the water with its tail. Seldom more than thirty centimeters in length, flying fish have been clocked at speeds up to thirty-five miles an hour and observed rising twenty to thirty feet out of the water.

29:8 friends on the ocean: Flying fish leap into flight to escape attacking dolphin-fish (their most common predator) and other large fish, thereby sending useful signals to fishermen seeking big fish for the market. Santiago, a sea creature himself, characteristically anthropomorphizes this usefulness as friendliness, although the fish leap here simply because they are startled by Santiago's approaching boat.

29:9 terns: Also known as sea swallows, they resemble gulls but are smaller, with slenderer bills, weaker feet, and a more graceful, dashing flight. They must try, while on the wing, to plunge their bills into the water and grab small fish. Santiago thinks they are in danger of being carried under by a wave when the sea suddenly becomes rough (29:15–16). See entry 54:17, on an exhausted little warbler at sea for another instance of Santiago's tender regard for nature's fragile creatures (55:15–18). It is a solicitude he does not exhibit for creatures like the tough "robber birds" (entry 29:12) and the inexhaustible "man-of-war bird" (entry 33:9), both probably the same species and better matched against the forces they must contend with in nature's competitive, demanding scheme (entry 30:3).

29:12 robber birds: Most likely frigate birds, also known as man-of-war birds.

29:14 the ocean . . . She: The ocean, representing all of nature in this novella, is a feminine entity, the "mother nature" of folklore. She is *la mar,* the feminine form in Spanish, "which is what people call her . . . when they love her" (29:19–20). And even when people who love the sea make negative comments about "her," they speak "as though she were a woman" (29:21–22). Their common expression, even of affectionate anger is in the feminine form, "*la puta mar,*" "that whore the sea." But those who do not love and respect the sea routinely use a masculine term, *el mar* (entry 30:3).

29:23–24 buoys . . . motorboats: Artificial devices the "younger" (modern) fishermen put between themselves and the sea, as Santiago does not (entry 30:20). They are almost certainly using the "Cuban three-hook rig" (Farrington 28–30), a fishing device employed for generations. Although used specifically by shark fishermen in this novella (entry 11:18–19 and line 30:1), the practice is all too effective for many kinds of large fish. It is actually an early form of today's notorious "long-line fishery," which proliferated in the Atlantic shortly after this work appeared. Typically, each "motorboat" (29:24) of the kind the younger fishermen would use at that time put out eight or ten "sets," each set consisting of a line across the water connecting three "buoys" (floats) forty to fifty feet apart. Hanging from each float in a "rig" was a line with a baited hook at the end, one line usually reaching 120 feet of depth, the next 300 feet, and the third 480 feet (Farrington 30). Such fishermen often left their sets overnight before returning to collect any large fish that had exhausted itself pulling against the floats and had drowned when no longer able to move enough for their gills to "breathe" the oxygen in the water.

As Hemingway portrays such fishermen, they are ignoring the purest traditions of craftsmanship in the Cojimar fishery. They are letting an artificial apparatus fish for them, instead of matching themselves against the fish—and against the sea's forces—by discovering, chasing, and killing their quarry. They represent an accelerating, exploitative attitude competing with the old fishing culture championed by Santiago and his disciples and affirmed by the novella as a whole.

These three-hook sets had not been extended at the time of the book (1952) into today's "long lines," with hundreds of floats and hooks, now sometimes stretching seventy miles across the Pacific, set out by factory ships and power-winched aboard many hours later. Yet despite Farrington's assumption that Hemingway never imagined such a future practice (35), Hemingway's selection of this particular practice as the epitome of destructive commercialism in this work suggests that he did foresee something of what has now come to pass. (For reports on a worldwide crisis in large fish stocks, see Myers and Worm 283, as well as Vergano's summary for the general reader.) And Hemingway clearly portrays the early long-line procedure as a threat to the sense of kinship with nature that has made the ancient craft of fishing historically a source of spiritual as well as physical food (cf. Beegel, "Eternal Feminine" 143–45).

There is a division in the novella's Cuban community, then, that gives the narrative a social dimension it has been criticized for neglecting (Friedman 284–85). Manolin's biological father feels antagonistic toward Santiago, the spiritual father who has "blooded" (initiated) the boy into nature's order (12:23). The father's opposition reflects a conflict between the merchants and the mystics that is, of course, common to all cultures and economies and becomes part of a subplot in this novella. Santiago, supported by a cadre of young men led by his chief disciple, Manolin, has a local reputation for traditional craft passion that, in fact, reflects his sense of oneness with nature. But Manolin's father represents a "progressive," materialistic, new Cuba, anxious for change and frustrated by this charismatic old man's appeal to a faction of the young men. Manolin's family is apparently too poor for him to hope for a career as a floatfisherman with a motor boat. So his father requires him to work with one who is at least materialistically practical—a cautious businessman making a tidy profit from the consistent supply of relatively small fish in the waters near shore (14:11).

This subtly conveyed social conflict does not lead to such disastrous results as does the similar conflict explicitly proclaimed in Faulkner's "The Bear" (1942), that great precursor of this novella. "The Bear" suggests that the efforts of spiritually dedicated individuals—like Sam Fathers and Ike (whose roles parallel Santiago's and Manolin's)—cannot prevent humanity's alienation from nature by the demands of civilization. "The Bear" suggests, further, that dedication to nature's patterns eventually destroys one's capacity to function within the flawed yet necessary patterns of human society. But *The Old Man and the Sea* focuses, rather, on a natural scheme that will abide forever, regardless of human imperfection, and will always produce rare individuals like Santiago and Manolin, who will sacrifice themselves to maintain the vital connection between nature and humanity. This positive focus in Hemingway's narrative somewhat glosses over the ostracism such heroes would typically face in the human community. Still, the materialists' disdain for nature's champions is an important dimension of *The Old Man and the Sea* (see entry 50:17–19 for a discussion of this phenomenon and Hemingway's references to it), and puts the novella in contention with "The Bear" as social commentary. (See Hays, throughout, for the many other parallels between these two works. See also Bulkington in "The Lee Shore" chapter of Melville's *Moby-Dick*.)

29:24–30:1 **had motorboats, bought . . . had brought much money:** The Second World War cut off cod fishing in the North Atlantic, due to the presence of German submarines. To supply vitamin A, then largely supplied from cod liver oil, drug companies, processed-food producers, and animal-feed producers switched to shark liver, and Cojimar had three shark-liver processing plants during the war and bought as many sharks as local fishermen could catch. Hence, the reference to "when shark livers brought much money" is also a reference to the war, both a subtle historical reminder and a foreshadowing of Santiago's battles with the marlin and the sharks. It also reminds us later readers that, when Hemingway wrote this work, America was engaged in the Korean War. As Susan Beegel writes,

> In 1952 [the date of the publication of *The Old Man and the Sea*], Allies staged the largest air strike of the Korean War, pummeling the ancient city of Suan from dawn to dusk with bombs, machine gun bullets, and napalm, while six thousand American troops with flamethrowers and tanks smashed a Communist prison on Korea's Koje Island. General Dwight D. Eisenhower and running mate Richard Nixon won the presidency in a landslide, vowing to end the Korean War with honor. Meanwhile, the war in Vietnam widened, as French soldiers pressed north to Hanoi. The British sent troops to Kenya to suppress the Mau Mau rebellion [near where Hemingway's son Patrick had a farm in what was then Tanganyika and later became a safari guide, and where Hemingway would visit in two years]. ("Thor Heyerdahl's Kon-Tiki" 544)

Compare Beegel's "Monster of Cojimar" 14–15.

30:3 **contestant . . . enemy:** In contrast to Santiago's sense of identification with the sea and its creatures (see 29:8–18, for example), these fishermen are separated from nature psychologically as well as physically. Because they regard the sea as an entity apart from and opposed to themselves (a "contestant" or "enemy"), they can think of the sea as a competing male ("*el mar*"). They are barred, then, from Santiago's symbiotic and loving feeling toward the sea (29:19–20), an attitude evoked by his gender terminology (entry 30:7). Emotionally detached from the sea and her creatures, in fact from nature itself, these new fishermen can comfortably use machines that give them an unnatural advantage over their quarry and minimize their personal struggle against the sea's forces, while Santiago's is the reciprocative, respectful approach of the sportsman. It is paradoxical that those who see the sea as an "enemy" do not contest her but passively receive her bounty. It is equally paradoxical that Santiago's reciprocative approach will be shown to require aggressive, hands-on violence and an opposition to nature's forces that is essential to his craft as a fisherman. That courageous approach to life is dictated by his sense of his role as a champion (an advocate and human exemplar) of total, self-sacrificing dedication that reflects a principle of dynamic tension in all of nature. The paradox that nature favors those who serve that demanding principle by risking their material comfort and safety in respectful opposition to her forces is introduced early in the book by the boy's bloody, perilous initiation into the craft of fishing (lines 12:15–23; entry 12:23). And that paradox will emerge in the action to come as a central theme of the novella.

For a differing view of what it means to oppose the sea, see Beegel's ecofeminist reading, "Santiago and the Eternal Feminine" (146–47). See Strauch (208–18) for a Jungian reading of the sea's gender, using Christian mysticism to reconcile nature's seemingly contradictory roles as mother-cherisher and witch-betrayer. Finally, see Tyler (133–35) for further gender-oriented commentary, which, like Beegel and Brenner, sees Santiago's behavior negatively.

30:7–8 **as it does a woman:** The moon's gravitational pull on the earth's surface generates the movement of the ocean waters known as tides, which wax and wane in monthly cycles as does the moon. Tradition and folklore make a causal connection between a woman's physiological cycle (and its psychological effects) and the moon's monthly cycle. Santiago's anthropomorphic personalization of the sea, "her," suggests something about the atavistic primitivism that is part of the old man's belief system (entries 12:23 and 25:8). Like his companionable view of the lions as resembling young cats (25:16), his affection for the sea implies the familiarity as well as the respect of one force of nature for another (entries 63:15–16 and 75:4–5). For comment on gender issues, see entry 29:14. For a feminist comment on the female sea's "wild or wicked things" (30:6), see Beegel's "Santiago and the Eternal Feminine" throughout but especially 147 and Tyler 133–35.

There is a probable source in Hemingway's experience for this observation by Santiago. In the "EH Fishing Log, 12 Apr.–15 July 1933" (5), Hemingway had mentioned the "theory on the moon" of Carlos Gutíerrez, his knowledgeable, Cuban tutor in ocean fishing. Gutíerrez's by-no-means original "theory" was that the phases of the moon affect all creatures, from men and women to fish that lose their appetite with the new moon. Hemingway frequently relied on his fishing-log entries for observations and events in this novella, sometimes after incorporating them into a journalistic piece. This was a frequent pattern in his creative process throughout his career. For examples outside of his sea experiences, see Mandel's *Reading Hemingway* throughout. For a thorough analysis of the sea log, see Mark Ott's *A Sea of Change*; of particular relevance to *The Old Man and the Sea* are pages 31, 88, 100–105.

30:16 **deep wells:** Santiago has recently been fishing where the swirling current gathers and churns up feed against the edge of the island's coastal shelf (28:18–24). As Beegel notes ("The Eternal Feminine" 136), this well is described as symbolically womblike; for more on this spot, see entry 28:19. However, Santiago has not been successful at this location. And brisk as the stream's flow is on this day, marlin should be feeding in every part of the current, not just at this drop-off near the current's inner edge. So he has decided to go out where the marlins' prey, the bonito and albacore, will also be feeding actively in schools. Their feeding activity may attract the attention of passing marlin.

30:20–21 **baits out . . . drifting with the current:** This method of fishing is called "handlining." The boat drifts or maneuvers very minimally while keeping deep lines as straight down as possible. The heavy lines (entry 15:5) are baited with dead fish and lowered most often to between 40 and 150 fathoms. Once hooked, fish are "played" without the aid of rod and reel, by letting line slip though the hands when the fish runs away from the boat and taking up slack hand over hand when the fish moves toward the boat.

Hemingway himself occasionally tried this method of fishing (but using rods and reels rather than bare hands on heavy lines) and took several marlin (recorded first in "EH Fishing Log, 4 Feb.–17 July 1936," entry for July 9, and then in "On the Blue Water" (*BL* 240–43). He tried drift fishing deep when no fish appeared on the surface or struck his trolled lures and baits, usually because the water was too calm for productive trolling. (When "trolled"—towed through the water to simulate moving prey—bait fish or artificial lures will not skip provocatively in flat water.)

It is difficult, however, to adjust the drift of a large boat minutely enough to keep lines straight down to the considerable depths most opportune for "still" or drift fishing (entry 30:22). With oars, however, such fine adjustments are easily made; and for poor fishermen, limited in any event to small boats without motors for trolling, handlining is the only feasible method to use. Deep fishing from rowboats has, therefore, long been a commercial method of taking fish, including bottom fish on the Grand Banks and (especially during the Depression) salmon off the West Coast of the United States and Canada. Furthermore, hand-held lines must be used for billfishing from a small boat because nobody could maneuver a skiff while playing fish of that size and speed on a rod and reel, even if poor fishermen could afford such gear.

Handlining is ideally suited to the thematic and symbolic purposes of this novella. The hands-on-the-line method necessarily requires more skill, resolution, and kinesthetic rapport with a fish than does any other method—while none of these capacities is demanded of commercial fishermen passively using mechanical devices. (See esp. entries, 29:23–24, and 30:3.) Once again, therefore, Hemingway's metaphoric plot detail is based on what he believed to be topical reality: that the largest marlin are likely to be deep, particularly during the September run. (See entry 41:22.) Stan Ulanksi, in *The Billfish Story*, writes of Hemingway's experiences in marlin fishing that "[t]he prevalent theory of the day was that the biggest marlin could only be caught on a deep-set line. Cuban commercial fishermen routinely brought back big marlin weighing five hundred pounds and more, caught by handlines that were deployed deep down" (52).

30:22 **forty fathoms:** Since a fathom equals six feet, the bait is lowered 240 feet. The second bait is at 456 feet, and the third and fourth at 600 and 750 feet, respectively. These lengths should be taken into account by those accepting Hemingway's challenge to readers to compute for themselves the total amount of line Santiago has on board. (See next entry and entry 15:5. For the literal and symbolic importance of depth in the book, see entry 30:20–21.)

31:16 **big pencil:** This comparison, associated with written rather than fishing "lines," has drawn the attention of many readers to the element of "self-reflexivity" in this narrative; it is, at one level, a book about the writing of a novella. The fisherman Santiago and the writer Ernest Hemingway are both precise and dedicated craftsmen who pride themselves on using their different kinds of "lines" with "precision" (32:19). The writer is exact in his observation and expression of reality, the fisherman "exact" (32:22) in the location of his baits and in every other detail of his craft (30:20–31:9). As Mark Schorer was one of the first to point out, Santiago's struggle to take and keep a fish of great size is—in addition to its even larger dimensions—a "parable" about "a great artist in the act of mastering his subject, and more than that, [in the act] of actually writing about that struggle" for mastery (19–20). Schorer might have added that both craftsmen, Hemingway and Santiago, sacrificed much in their dedication to their vocations.

Both Hemingway and Santiago also depended greatly on luck, despite their craftsmanship and hard work. In his Nobel Prize acceptance speech, Hemingway said that a writer (or fisherman) should try for what "others have tried and failed. Then, sometimes, with great luck, he will succeed." Hemingway said also in that same speech that a writer, in order to succeed, is—as was Santiago—"driven far out past where he can go, out to where no one can help him" (quoted in Baker, *Writer as Artist* 339).

31:21 **three hundred fathoms:** That means a fish on any one of the four lines he has out. A fish on even the shortest of the lines now in the water could take out "over" three hundred fathoms of line, including, of course, whatever length was already down with bait on that line. But this three hundred fathoms does not count the varying lengths of the three other baited lines. The sum of all the latter lengths is one of two sets of measurements, each adding up to the total length of Santiago's lines that remain in the water after their spare coils (two apiece) are detached and tied to the line with the running fish. (See entries 15:5, 30:20–21, 30:22, and 41:14. Note also lines 51:7–18.) These summations are, of course, another of Hemingway's challenges to readers (see entry 14:24). He deliberately challenges readers to calculate the various combinations of lengths, in this case so as to make us actively participate in the action by thinking along with Santiago as he plans ahead, preparing to be instantly ready for various sudden contingencies. Since the descriptions of the lines are placed well apart in the text, we must work an additionally complex puzzle to arrive at the total length of the lines. But our reward is a personal appreciation of an important part of the old man's craft and a clear picture of the lines' arrangement in the boat and in the water.

Hemingway, however, seems to have made an error when he wrote "three sticks" (31:22), for there are four baits, hence four sticks holding them over the side of Santiago's small boat.

32:15–16 **Others let them drift:** See entries 32:23 and 33:17. And, following the line of interpretation opened by "pencil" (entry 31:16), Hemingway could be accusing other writers of drifting from their topics, rather than staying tightly focused.

32:23 **ready:** If he is "exact" (32:22), his baits will always be near the depths where experience tells him very large fish are most likely to be. Thus, his baits will have their best chance of intercepting such a fish at any time, no matter how unexpectedly (entry 33:17). Santiago's precision will shortly be rewarded (41:6).

33:7–8 **morning . . . painful:** Figuratively, this distinction between the effects of early and late sunlight, traditionally associated with youth and age, makes us think of Santiago's consistent orientation late, "all [his] life" (33:4), toward accepting the challenges of adversity—the harsh realities exposed by the light of each new day—face forward, exactly as he sits in his boat. He has always been able to adjust after some exposure and "look straight into" each reality "without getting the blackness"

(33:6)—the blindness—of either depression ("black ass," as Hemingway called it) or of denial. Or to put it another way, all his life—despite his early initiation into a transcendental view of the fact of evil—Santiago has found initial experiences of objective, flawed reality (the first light of each new day) "painful." Yet his champion's perspective has always allowed him to adjust and "look straight into" reality's most forceful effects "without getting the blackness" of either the "black ass" or denial.

But whatever metaphorical application we decide best fits the narrative, the figurative is based on fact once again (as in entry 30:20–21, for example). Sunlight hits the water at the same flat angle in both the evening and the morning. But, in the evening, the light is partially blocked by molecular particles of moisture and other materials raised off the water by the heat of the day, while, at dawn, the light rays are unobstructed, and more of them reach the eyes. The setting sun appears more red and forceful than the rising sun because the refraction of the scattered evening rays causes a more marked color; but rays of the thinner morning light move straight ahead, striking directly into the eyes.

33:9 **man-of-war bird:** A sea hawk, also known as a frigate bird, of the genus *fregata*. Noted for its powerful flight, the man-of-war bird has webbed, clawed feet for grabbing prey from the water or other birds (see entry 29:12).

33:17 **But he crowded the current:** "Crowd" is a rare nautical term for "driving or hastening on." Instead of drifting passively with the current, the old man has already been rowing very slowly with the current to make his boat move a little faster than if carried by the current alone. Only in this way could he have been keeping directly over his lines (32:11). For the lines present a much larger surface to the current than does the boat, as they extend for hundreds of vertical feet in the water, while the shallow boat sits lightly on top. The lines, thus, constantly threaten to be dragged out at an angle ahead of the boat by the current. This would move the baits up and away from their designated depths (entry 32:23), as it does the baits of "others" less "exact" (because less dedicated) than Santiago (32:15–18).

However, Santiago now needs to gain on the circling bird and feeding fish, which are also being carried by the current, "ahead" or downstream of him, as he rows facing forward in the boat in the direction of the flow. Thus, he has to go a little faster in the direction of the current than he has needed to go when he only wanted to keep even with his lines. The "but" in the cited phrase refers, then, to his having to accelerate enough to drag his lines a little behind and higher, yet not enough to pull his baits markedly higher than their proper depth because his big fish may not be in the feeding activity directly under the bird. It may be somewhere in Santiago's course on the way there—so that he must keep his lines down every moment during his approach to the bird (32:22). This is the second explicit reference to Santiago's rigorous craftsmanship in the activities leading to the marlin's strike (41:6–7).

34:1 **Dolphin:** These are not porpoises; they are dolphinfish, also known as mahi-mahi or dorado. The old man knows that these dolphinfish are the predators most likely to frighten flying fish (entry 29:8) and that only large dolphin could make them leap so "desperately" into the air. Also, he can see the "bulge" in the water made by large fish moving just under the surface (34:13). The text scrupulously distinguishes between dolphin(fish) and porpoises (bottlenose dolphins).

34:3 **leader:** A "leader" is a yard or more (usually) of abrasion-resistant monofilament, gut, or wire placed between the hook and the main fishing line to prevent a fish from cutting the line with its sharp teeth, gill covers, bill, or tail. Wire, which Santiago uses and which is the strongest of all leaders, is used for fish with abrasive mouths or for very large fish. Santiago here plans to hook one of the large dolphin he knows are feeding on the flying fish (34:1).

34:20 **too fast:** Up to thirty-five miles per hour (entry 29:5–6).

35:1–2 **my big fish:** In using the possessive "my," Santiago thinks not of ownership but of a meeting he views as if luck or destiny had foreordained it (see entry 16:20). He believes that, by acting always on that principle, he will be supporting (championing) a fundamental law of nature, one that requires total dedication and focus (entries 30:3, 32:15–16). But being human, he and the boy need to use their "as if" trick of the mind to help them maintain their resolution in the face of the adversities all mortals face and the added deprivations of poverty in their particular lives. (For references to this device and sample demonstrations of it in action, see the passages discussed in entry 11:1–2 and in the other entries listed there.)

35:3 **rose like mountains:** It is now mid-morning, and cool, dry air from the north has calmed this part of the sea (for an explanation, see entry 14:6). The dry air has increased the visibility at sea, so that Santiago can see the clouds over the land. According to Dean Churchill, "In good weather, clouds develop sooner in the day on the land than on the sea, as land heats up faster in the sunlight than does the ocean surface. And updrafts of warm air ashore push up mountainous plumes of cumulus clouds," marking fair weather (email).

35:5 **dark blue:** Ocean water far from land usually appears a somewhat deeper, clearer blue than the cloudy, often greenish-brown coastal sea that takes its color from the land. But the Florida Current, as part of the Gulf Stream, is a much deeper blue than is the surrounding water. In *Islands in the Stream,* Thomas Hudson explains that the Stream is "a different density of water" and theorizes that "the plankton [see entry 35:7] make it look almost purple because they add red to the blue I think" (107).

In *The Old Man and the Sea,* there are thematic implications of the darkening water as noon approaches at this point in the narrative. (See entries 35:7 and 35:8). In Christian iconography, blue in sea and river sustains Santiago through Mary's color, calling into the text the presence all around Santiago of the Virgin of Cobre. Among adherents of Afro-Cuban religion, blue and white are the colors of Yemaya, the *orisha* of the sea and sister of Oshún, *orisha* of the river (that is, the Great Blue River, the Gulf Stream) whose color is yellow and who is the Afro-Cuban manifestation of the Virgin of Cobre. For a discussion of the *orishas* and their colors, complete with color plates of costumes and altars, see Flores-Pena and Evanchuk. This is the sacred surround of Santiago's struggle.

35:7 red sifting of the plankton: A drifting mass of tiny organisms, often microscopic, that are the bottom of the food chain in the sea. Plankton are fed on by the smallest sea creatures and tiny fish, which, in turn, are consumed by progressively larger fish, like the marlin, that are consumed by people. (See also Beegel, "Guide to Marine Life" 282, 284.)

Hemingway's description fits several kinds of plankton found in this region; perhaps the most common are the comb jellies and the bacterial algae, trichodesmium. The trichodesmium is a bacterium. The comb jellies are ctenophores, a family including the much larger *agua mala* that Santiago will comment significantly on, a few lines later in the narrative (35:18; see Wrobel et al. for a useful guide to various plankton, including those in tropical Atlantic waters). Both of these organisms have tiny, moving parts that are "iridescent" (35:17). That is, they refract light so as to create a "rainbow" of colors. But when viewed through the water, these colors appear in the aggregate as red, the color Santiago sees. Santiago begins to see that light when the sunlight strikes the plankton in this scene during the late morning, when the "higher" sun (35:12) of later morning, moving toward noon, strikes down on them at various angles approaching ninety degrees from the water's surface. For at those higher angles, the light from the many, tiny organisms is refracted back toward the surface, rather than horizontally through the water. It is important to know, however, that when "high" noon arrives (40:16), with the sunlight straight down on the water, Santiago will no longer be able to see the light from the plankton (40:10–19). The redness in the water is also allusive, pointing toward the blood of the fish and the blood of Christ. Beegel writes that "this coloring aligns the plankton with all the blood of life spilled in the sea" ("Eternal Feminine" 137).

In early Christian iconography, the sign of the fish was used by Christians as an acrostic consisting of the initial letters of five Greek words forming the word for fish (*Ichthys*), which words briefly but clearly described the character of Christ and his claim to the worship of believers: *Iesous Christos Theou Yios Soter,* that is, "Jesus Christ, Son of God,

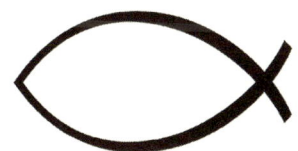

Fig. 8. Christian sign of the fish.

Saviour." See Figure 8. The moment of Christ's crucifixion is said to be at noon, hence a reason for Hemingway's attention to the color red and noontime in this paragraph.

35:8 **strange light:** As stated in entry 14:21, "strange" for Hemingway connotes the numinous, and this noon moment, and the light that presents it, anticipates Santiago's catching the largest fish of his lifetime, the culmination of his career as *el Campeón*. That it is significant is underscored when Hemingway repeats "strange light" at 35:12 (see also entry 98:21–23).

35:11–13 **light . . . meant good weather:** The insistence that this "strange light" means good weather is affirmed by the lines going straight down, the color and shape of the clouds, and the presence of Oshún's color, yellow. It is contradicted by the absence of the bird and the presence of the Portuguese man-of-war (*agua mala*). This contrast continues Hemingway's exploration of the paradox of nature.

35:16 **Sargasso weed:** Another name for gulf weed (entry 28:18, and entries 16:9 and 35:5 for Hemingway's insistence on yellow as the color of this seaweed usually described as brown in color: http://oceanexplorer.noaa.gov/facts/sargassum.html). See also Beegel, "A Guide to Marine Life" 293.

35:17 **formalized:** Having a discernible outline or shape, despite being as close to transparent as a "bubble." Also remarkably applicable, in context, is an obsolete usage listed in the *Oxford English Dictionary*: specious in appearance, beguiling (see 35:22, 36:15).

35:17 **iridescent:** see entry 35:7.

35:18 **Portuguese man-of-war:** The violent marine invertebrate *physalia physalis*, a type of jellyfish. Generally found in open waters, it resembles a balloon floating on the surface and varies in color from nearly transparent to dark blue or purple. It trails wispy, pale blue tentacles up to forty feet in length, seductively harmless in appearance but equipped with numerous stinging cells containing coiled tubes tipped with poisonous barbs. If a fish or even a tiny particle of plankton touches a tentacle, the tubes stab into the flesh and the tentacles retract, drawing in the poisoned victim. The poison is highly toxic, and sometimes fatal, to humans (36:4–10).

The *aguamala*'s rainbow-like colors become a deceitful beauty. Like its nearly invisible tentacles, the menacing *aguamala*'s colorful floating body is totally misleading. The *aguamala* kills and feeds passively, not by direct attack but by beguilement—attractive deceit—a way of life Santiago detests: "You whore" (35:22).

Yet the *aguamala* is, paradoxically, a cnidarian, and, therefore, genetically related to the ctenophores that make up part of the reddish cloud of plankton supplying life for the entire food chain (35:7). Moreover, as the old man later acknowledges (50:14–18), in order to fulfill his positive purpose in nature, he must kill fish partly by a "trickery" that has something (but not everything) in common with the *aguamala*'s. This is part of the paradox of necessary sin, another of the several paradoxes of nature that are affirmed in the novella as a whole (see entries 36:15; see also Sylvester, "Hemingway's Extended Vision" 134, 136).

35:20 cheerfully: see entry 36:11.

35:22 Agua mala: The correct Spanish for "jellyfish" is a single word, *aguamala*. When the two words are separated, as here, they do not refer to the Portuguese man-of-war. They mean "bad water" and are particularly used as a Cuban colloquialism for seawater infested with tiny, almost invisible jellyfish that leave unwitting swimmers covered with welts resembling insect bites. Of course, jumping to the conclusion that Hemingway is in error about a topical detail is never wise. Many earlier and later entries in this book prove the value of searching carefully, first, for some purpose in his apparent anomalies. Here, therefore, it is tempting to notice that, in using the split form of the word "*agua mala*" Santiago makes a clever pun on the name of this large, highly visible relative of the merely annoying, tiny jelly fish. For anywhere near the *aguamala*'s long tentacles, the water is, indeed, "bad water" and more; it is potentially lethal, even to humans (entry 35:18).

However, Hemingway uses the incorrect term again (36:9) when writing as the third person, or "omniscient," narrator. It appears, then, that Hemingway was, in fact, either confused by the two sound-alike usages or intentionally put the two-word term in Santiago's line for the reason suggested above, then carelessly repeated that spelling in his own sentence.

35:22 whore: Santiago utters a standard Spanish exclamation about anything distasteful. But his remark aptly refers to the deceitful trickery of this predatory creature (entries 35:17 and 35:18; lines 36:11–12). But presently Santiago will acknowledge the "trickery" in his own craft of fishing (entry 36:11).

36:3 immune: The small (ten centimeters) man-of-war fish (*nomeus gronovii*) swims unharmed among the stinging tentacles.

36:10 whiplash: The poison of the Portuguese man-of-war is neurotoxic, causing an instant paralysis of muscles, organs, and lungs. It can be fatal to a human whose skin is widely exposed.

36:11 **beautiful:** The iridescence (35:17) of the globe-like "bladder" (35:17–18) of these "jellyfish" is technically a prismatic dispersal of light into a spectrum of colors. It creates an effect much like the "rainbow" on the surface of a compact disc, as was noted of the less elaborate, reddish reflection of the sunlight off the tiny, individual plankton Santiago saw underwater, a short time earlier, in the drifting cloud of those organisms that meant the likelihood of fish in the area (see entry 35:7).

36:15 **carapaced:** The turtles' heads and appendages are entirely shielded by the extremely tough, horny skin of their heads and feet, while the rest of their bodies are covered by their shells, technically their true "carapaces." When their eyes are closed, therefore, the turtles are completely protected from the man-of-war's poison. Unfortunately, sea turtles cannot draw their heads and limbs into their shells for protection as land turtles can, so that sharks sometimes bite off their legs (108:3–4). With their eyes closed, however, the loggerheads are safe from the man-of-war's poisonous barbs, and Santiago loves to see these creatures using the armor that makes them (ironically) nature's blind instrument (36:14–15, 37:2) for destroying creatures that kill by visual deceit: the "*agua mala*" (35:22; and see 36:11–12). Thus, even his "contempt" for the clumsy, stupid, barnacle-encrusted, commercially worthless loggerheads is "friendly" (36:22).

Santiago's hostility toward the *aguamala* is significant. It is central to Santiago's portrayal that his Whitmanesque sense of nature's paradoxical order allows him to accept as part of nature yet detest and (elsewhere) destroy the sea's dishonest creatures with relish (102:3–4 and 107:24–108:3). He detests such creatures because he has faith that his natural role is to advocate and exemplify total, direct commitment, without concern for his material survival, and to oppose people and other creatures that survive by passivity and deceit (107:24–108:7). Yet he does not question the purpose of such creatures or the ethic they represent (both natural and supernatural), even though their presence is an example of what philosophers worry over as the fact of evil in a just universe. Especially since his early mystical experiences in the Canary Islands and Africa (entry 25:2–3 and entries cited there), he accepts on faith and intuition a governing wisdom in the universe, a wisdom he must champion at all costs (entries 25:2–3, 37:3, and entries cited in these entries). Therefore, he does not seek to understand what is beyond his personal knowledge (104:24–105:3) or defies human logic (necessary sin, for example; Santiago discusses necessary sin with himself on 105:4–106:8). Nor does he try to accomplish what is beyond human means (see 75:6). All of the capacities and attitudes just listed contribute to his saintliness, a quality that will emerge as the characterization develops (Stoneback, "The Name Is No Accident" 175–77. See Brenner, esp. 38, 56, and 67, for an opposing view of Santiago's portrayal).

36:20 **green turtles:** Vegetarians with the most valuable meat and the greatest speed of all the sea turtles, moving as fast as a human can run.

36:20 **hawk-bills:** Usually called "hawksbill." Their valuable shells provide "tortoiseshell" for jewelry and artwork.

36:23 **strange:** Several features of the loggerheads' copulation are unusual enough to seem beyond natural norms to Santiago, as well as to lay readers, and therefore qualify as "strange," as Hemingway customarily uses the word (entries 14:21, 35:8, and 98:21–23). Hemingway recorded at least one personal observation of "two loggerheads hooked up" ("EH Fishing Log—Cuba Trip, 12 Apr.—15 July 1933," p. 5). When copulating, captive male sea turtles have been observed remaining mounted for five hours (sometimes longer). And before sensing themselves ready to "nest" (lay fertilized eggs), females have been observed accepting a continuous succession of males for an average total of 25.5 hours, with a nearly incredible ("strange"), observed maximum of 195.3 hours (Wood and Wood 500). And whether Hemingway was aware of this scientific observation, he refers in *To Have and Have Not* to turtles copulating for "three days" (113).

Throughout these marathon couplings, the pairs constantly thrash about on the surface, each male fending off his competitors. And when a couple sinks beneath the surface, the female must paddle both of them back to the surface to breathe, unaided by the preoccupied male on her back. Both would otherwise drown. The male's reptilian penis is at the end of its tail and the female's cloaca is at the end of hers. During copulation, the male's tail must curve down beyond the edge of the female's carapace for the penis to reach into the cloaca in her upturned tail. Accordingly, a large male's tail is on average eighteen inches in length (Zug 9–11, and remarks to author; Eckert email). Possibly it is this sort of observable, reptilian phenomena in turtles that has appeared anomalous—mysterious—to Santiago.

37:3 **mysticism:** Venerated by many Native American cultures, the sea turtle was seen in their mythologies as a sort of Atlas carrying the world on its back. Therefore, many North and Central American tribes avoided eating this turtle or its eggs, even though they harvested it for export after Europeans arrived. But not entirely sharing the natives' mysticism in this case, Santiago will eat the eggs, which ties in with other cultural traditions, that of absorbing qualities of a prey by consuming it, as Santiago will do later with the marlin.

However, Santiago's own mysticism is central to his character and his function in nature (entries 16:2, 17:1, 24:19–20, 25:2–3, 25:8, 25:13–14, and 25:16). And readers aware of the turtle's Atlas-like role in Native belief can reflect that in the "mysticism" of this novella, Santiago's responsibility is comparable to the turtle's responsibility in the legend. In the myth, the world rests on the turtle's back. In the natural scheme developing in the book (entry 17:1–2), all of humanity depends for psychological and spiritual survival on its champions (70:2), figures like Santiago who go out "beyond all people" (see entry 50:17–19), each becoming a crucial "towing bitt" (45:8) between the human community and the rest of nature. For this aspect of the champions' role in the novella's ontology, see entries 94:22–23 and 98:21–23.

37:7–8 **will beat for hours:** The cardiac muscle of all vertebrates is myogenic (able to stimulate itself without signals from a central nervous system); even an excised human heart will beat until the oxygen in its tissues is exhausted. But turtles (with low temperatures and a slow heart rate) have hearts that will beat up to two days after death. (See next entry and esp. entry 125:20–21.)

37:9–10 **heart . . . feet . . . hands:** The skin on Santiago's hands and feet, so weathered and scarred by age that it looks like the skin of turtles, has by the same process become as thickened and tough as theirs. As for Santiago's heart, he will later be seen to share, metaphorically, a turtle's ability to endure, despite the extreme emotional and physical laceration he has experienced in the past and will experience on this voyage. Moreover, at the end of the narrative (entry 125:20–21) there will be a physical as well as metaphorical parallel between Santiago's heart and a turtle's.

37:10 **white eggs:** Female turtles come to shore to lay as many as 150 eggs in the sand at one time. Only a few of these hatchling future turtles are destined to survive predators such as humans and animals on their way back to the water, at which time they face further risk from large fish, such as sharks. Caribbean folk myth describes the eggs as aphrodisiacs capable of increasing male virility. They are eaten raw or pickled and are usually purchased by men from containers that sit on bar countertops. The old man would have eaten them "all through May," (37:11) when turtles begin to lay their eggs.

37:13 **shark liver oil:** Taken from the shark's disproportionately large liver—up to 25 percent of a shark's weight—the oil is rich in vitamins and has often been marketed as cod liver oil, especially during World War II when the war prevented cod fishing in the North Atlantic (see entry 11:18–19).

37:23–38:1 **scattering of bait fish:** "Bait fish" are schools of small fish that feed on plankton and move along the ocean's surface as ready prey for larger fish. They often smash the water white in an attempt to escape large fish, such as marlin.

38:8 **I will get into them:** The old man will move his boat into the midst of the school of bait fish, hoping that his own bait below them will be taken by the large fish he believes has caused the disturbance. Marlin have mechanoreceptors along the lateral line of their bodies, neuromasts, essentially tiny hairs that register changes in the "movement and change in their surroundings by sensing magnetic field and electrical impulses" (Ulanski 95). They help these predator fish find prey. The scene described here is bait fish being attacked by larger fish, here tuna, what Cuban fishermen call a *faje*. Marlin, although down deep, will respond to this aquatic turmoil through their mechanoreceptors, hoping to catch some of the tuna pursuing the bait fish. Federico Gomez de la Maza in a 1936 article describes fishing "with a float or buoy placed a few fathoms above the hook so it remains near the surface" (56). For years, this was interpreted literally, until, in 1957, Gomez de la Maza and Sánchez Roig explained that the hook was actually twenty-five to thirty fathoms down, just above where Santiago places his highest hook (24; Almeida email). The Cuban fishermen know that the turmoil in the water will draw large fish to it. Although marlin hunt primarily by sight, "If light conditions are far from optimal . . . [marlin] may rely on mechanical perception, sensitivity to vibrations in the water, for finding prey" (Ulanksi 106).

38:13 **The bird is a great help:** The presence of the bird alerts the old man to the movement of the fish, giving him an aerial view.

39:4–5 **Albacore. . . . He'll make a beautiful bait:** The old man's decision to use commercially viable fish as bait demonstrates his lack of interest in fishing simply for profit (see entry 9:2). According to Jeffrey Herlihy-Mera, this type of tuna is called *albacore* in Cojimar, Cuba, although later (58:4), Santiago will call it *bonito*, its more common name in the Canary Islands ("Eyes the Same Color" 36).

40:2–3 **That which I was born for:** The old man's self-professed destiny is to capture a large fish, as well as his self-identification as a fisherman.

40:6–7 **Everything . . . travels very fast and to the northeast:** The current is running especially strong, either in this particular spot or on this particular day, as a river runs at varying speeds at different points along its length. When the current runs strong, more marlin are seen on the surface, and more are caught at greater depths; the state of the current at present portends success for the old man, although his question indicates that he is unaware of it.

40:18–19 **A mile deep:** One mile equals 880 fathoms. By now, the old man has rowed and drifted with the current to a point at least ten miles east-northeast of Cojimar, where ocean maps mark the average depth as varying between 850 and 900 fathoms.

40:23 **were down again:** The tuna have left the surface of the water to swim at a deeper level.

41:4 **bight of line:** A loop in a length of line.

41:8 **shipped his oars:** Santiago took the oars from their row locks (here thole pins; see entry 28:3 first entry) and lay them inside the boat.

41:22 **This far out, he must be huge in this month:** Santiago knows that older, larger marlin swim the Florida Straits in late summer and early fall. See entry 18:13. It also reflects the belief, the desire, that extra effort should bring greater reward.

42:1 **How fresh they are:** Marlin prefer fresh bait. Often they will not even consider taking stale bait.

42:2 **in that cold water in the dark:** Heat and light waves from the sun are rapidly absorbed by the upper inches of water, leaving greater depths colder and darker.

42:2 **make another turn:** The marlin's tentative behavior hints at his being more curious than hungry, a response noted by game fisherman. The amount of time a marlin takes to seize bait indicates either hunger or curiosity.

42:21–22 **Maybe he has been hooked before:** This speculation on Santiago's part echoes one Hemingway recorded in his fishing log for May 1932: "saw big marlin/ behind bait on surface he/ *rushed it but refused it*/ . . . or/ else took it by the tail only/ acted sly as though he had been hooked [before]" (quoted by Ott 15; emphasis in original).

43:12–13 **He has it sideways in his mouth now:** Hemingway is again granting Santiago exceptional ability to sense how the marlin, 600 feet deep (100 fathoms) is holding the bait in its jaws. But Hemingway had seen marlin on the surface doing so. In his essay "Marlin off Cuba" for *American Big-Game Fishing,* he records, "[S]ometimes they come in from the side and take the bait off sideways in their mouth" (61). Beegel, "Guide to Marine Life" (271), quotes marine biologist Charles O. Mather from his book *Billfish: Marlin, Broadbill, Sailfish* (48), agreeing with this observation.

43:15–16 **he knew that . . . it might not happen** Superstition that, if you "put your mouth" on a bad thing, it will happen and on a good thing it won't happen. It was a common belief among practitioners of Obeah, a Bahamian form of Santeria.

PAGES 44 THROUGH 53

44:12 Are you ready: The standard fishing technique used for marlin involves waiting several seconds after a fish has taken the bait and then striking, or setting the hook, with a sudden pull on the line. Here, the old man asks if the fish is ready for the strike.

44:19 Nothing happened: Normally a marlin will rise to the surface immediately after a strike and engage in jumping and fighting with the line. Its pugnacity has earned a reputation as the elite of big-game fish. This marlin's seemingly indifferent response to being hooked would thus be mystifying and disappointing to the old man.

45:2 the pull: That is, from the fish.

45:2–3 The boat began to move . . . toward the northwest: The marlin is towing the boat against the easterly current.

45:7 I wish I had the boy: One of the few times Santiago speaks aloud on this voyage. Of the eight instances of wishing for Manolin's presence, Santiago speaks aloud the first five, thereby emphasizing the importance of this wish. The old man's request can be seen, of course, first as the practical desire for help in boating an extremely large fish. Second, despite Santiago's seeming isolation, it speaks to his feeling that he is part of a larger community. And, third, since the young man's name stands for the Hebrew Emanuel, God is with us, it can be seen as a prayer. This is the first of a series of spoken and unspoken wishes for the young man's help. See also 48:6, 50:9, 51:24, 56:19, 62:5, 83:6, and 83:7. Since the novella is less than half over, Hemingway devotes more space—and time (two days, as opposed to less than one)—to Santiago's adversity in killing the marlin and trying to bring it to shore than in catching the big fish.

45:8 bitt: A small post on the deck of a ship used to fasten lines or cables to the boat. Santiago likens himself fastened by the fishing line to the marlin to a bitt.

45:14 if he sounds: Dives to the bottom.

45:15–16 **things I can do:** If the fish "sounds and dies" deep down in the water, at least one of the "many tricks" (14:24) that Santiago can employ to raise it is to use his sail to get enough speed to plane the body upward. Then he can "come about" and sail (or row, depending on the wind) back toward the fish and quickly pull in what slack he can gain in the line. By repeating this maneuver many times, he can get the inert fish to the surface and tie it to the boat—unless sharks appear and strip the fish on its way up.

46:1 **It was noon when I hooked him:** Normally, a marlin jumps immediately following a strike, and although a fisherman may occupy several hours reeling it in, these hours would be full of jumps, antics, and constant struggle between fisherman and fish. Given the many allusions to the Christian Passion story in *The Old Man and the Sea*, Hemingway's decision to have Santiago hook the great fish at noon connects the event with the moment during the crucifixion of Jesus when the whole world goes dark (Mark 15:33, Matt. 27:45). Santiago too is approaching many difficult, and therefore dark, hours now that the fish is hooked.

46:10 **un-stepped mast and sail:** The mast is not placed vertically in the socket or "step" that holds it upright, but here is lying flat in the bottom of the skiff.

46:10–11 **tried not to think but only to endure:** "Endurance" can be physical, mental, or spiritual. The old man's mental and physical trials echo the spiritual trials of endurance for attaining salvation as depicted in the New Testament: "And thus Abraham, having patiently endured, obtained the promise" (Heb. 6:15); "But he who endures to the end will be saved" (Matt. 10:22, 24:13; Mark 13:13). Hemingway explored turn-of-the century "muscular" Christianity in the short story/play, "Today Is Friday." See Joseph M. Flora 145–54, for commentary on the story, including a relation to *The Old Man and the Sea*, 150, entry 272:29–36. A motto of Hemingway's "*il faut (d'abord) durer*," with which Carlos Baker concludes his biography of the author (*Life* 564), translates as "one must, above all, endure, or last."

46:12–13 **no land was visible:** Under good conditions on the ocean, the visibility of a person in a small skiff will not exceed ten to fifteen miles, indicating that the old man must be at least that far out to sea.

47:14 **I can do nothing with him:** The old man recognizes that his strength is no match for the marlin's size, making impossible any effort to bring the marlin up by himself. He knows that he must wait for the marlin to surface.

47:20 **the glow of Havana:** Havana is ten miles west of Cojimar, from which Santiago sailed (see 11:3–4).

48:6 I wish I had the boy: The second in the series of wishes for Manolin, again voiced, a rarity, since Santiago does not usually speak aloud. See entry 45:7 for the other times Santiago either speaks this sentiment aloud or thinks it. Eight repetitions testify to their closeness, to the extent the old man now depends on Manolin, and to the eventuality of Manolin's succeeding him.

That Santiago has developed the habit of talking aloud when he is alone is first mentioned on 39:6–7. There he admits that this habit is not common among fisherman and others would consider him "crazy" (39:21). On 42:16–17, Santiago says, "'He'll take it.' . . . 'God help him to take it'"—talking aloud to God—that is, praying. Thereafter, many of Santiago's remarks made aloud can be seen as prayers, though not always of the intentional sort. They escape from him in phrases secularized across time—phrases like "Christ knows he can't have gone (42:20–21); "Thank God he is travelling and not going down" (45:11–12); "God let him jump" (53:18); "God help me to have the cramp go" (60:4); "thank God, they are not as intelligent as we" (63:14–15); Christ, I did not know he was so big" (66:5–6); "God pity him and me" (68:16); "God knows he has had enough chances to learn" (85:8–9); and "God help me endure" (87:17).

48:14–15 He could tell the difference: Another testimony by Hemingway to Santiago's exceptional prowess, his champion abilities. In this case, as in the day-long arm wrestling mentioned later, it is a fictional invention of Hemingway, poetic license (see Ott 104–5; Sylvester, "Hemingway's Extended Vision" (Jobes 95). Marine biologists say there are no noticeable differences between the sounds that male and female bottlenose dolphin emit from their blowholes. Porpoises have no vocal cords. They exhale through their blowholes, and there is no more difference in the sounds they make than between men and women exhaling (emails from Acevedo, Dudzinski, Steinessen, and Tyack).

48:17 They play and make jokes: The old man's porpoises are bottlenose dolphins (*tursiops truncatus*), whose mouths are drawn in a permanent grin, hence their reputation for being happy creatures. In addition, they engage in many forms of play with each other. The dolphin has long been considered a friend to humans, having developed a reputation for leading ships safely into harbor and protecting shipwrecked sailors from sharks (see, for example, the myth surrounding the Greek poet Arion). There is no biological evidence that precisely supports this sympathetic behavior.

49:6 He took the bait like a male: The size of this marlin (see 97:3) means that it must be female, since the male blue marlin rarely exceeds three hundred pounds, while the females can weigh as much as two thousand pounds. These facts were known when Hemingway wrote the novella. In 1935, in an article he wrote for

American Big Game Fishing (see entry immediately below), he states that "the male always hangs back until the female fish has taken a bait, but since the male is often only a fraction of the size of the female, this may not be true altruism" (77, quoted in Ott 102–3). Hemingway probably chose male as the marlin's gender (as he did for the trout Nick catches in "Big Two-Hearted River") in order to make the contest male-to-male, more macho, and not a male attacking a female. See Claire Rosenfield on Hemingway's "emphatically male bias" (51). However, he also wrote that male marlin fight harder ("Marlin off Cuba" 56).

49:10–50:1–2 **The male fish always let the female fish feed first . . . to see where the female was:** This phenomenon that Santiago reports is one that Hemingway was told and also witnessed himself. In July 1932, recording what experienced Cuban fisherman Carlos Gutiérrez told him, Hemingway wrote, "*male rush boat and refuse to leave when female hooked*" (quoted by Ott 13; emphasis in original). In May 1933, writing in his log for the boat *Anita*, Hemingway indicated, "*mate followed him to boat*" (Ott 30; emphasis in original). Hemingway repeated this account of marlin behavior in his "Marlin off Cuba" for *American Big Game Fishing* (77), quoted in Ott 102–3. That Hemingway writes of Santiago's remembering the seeming gallantry of the male fish and the bond between the male and his mate may be a reference to Santiago's nostalgic memory of his dead wife.

49:19 **rapier bill with its sandpaper edge:** The bill of a marlin is smooth on top and has rasp-like sides and ventral (underside) surfaces.

49:21 **almost like the backing of mirrors:** When alive in the water, a blue marlin has a cobalt-blue back, golden-copper sides, and fairly distinct vertical stripes, either a different shade of blue or purple (see Color Plate 4). When the fish dies, the stripes disappear quickly, the blue back deepens to dark gray or black, and the sides turn a silvery color—hence the comparison to the backing of mirrors. Compare Ulanksi 90. This is the first of three times that Hemingway used the image of mirrors in the novella; the other two are at 96:23 and 110:6–7. At all three, Hemingway requires readers to understand at the technical level what is being compared to what. Each image speaks to the complex optics that allows us to see ourselves in/through the mirrors of dying creatures. As to the mirror backing, the reader is asked to see a particular silver color. The comparison goes beyond color. The silver coating allows one to see a reflection in the mirror, so the simile not only establishes the color of the fish but also allows Santiago/readers to see our reflection in the clubbed and dying fish (49:18–21); the same reflection of our own inevitable death is implied in the optics on 110:6–7.

50:8 **begged her pardon:** Hunting rituals of many peoples include an apology to the spirit of the prey that has been killed, a hope that the method of killing has not

Left: Color Plate 1. La Terraza in 1997.

Below: Color Plate 2. La Terraza in 2015, with a new sign, fully neon, marlin pictured on each. (Photos by Peter L. Hays)

Color Plate 3. Painting of the Virgin of Cobre by Raúl Villarreal, in the manner of posters commonly found in Cuban homes in the 1930s. (Courtesy Raúl Villarreal)

Color Plate 4. Blue marlin by Duane Raver, who made this painting for Ulanksi's book. (Courtesy Duane Raver)

Color Plate 5. Mako shark. (Photo by Mark Conlin. Courtesy Southwest Fisheries Science Center NOAA)

Color Plate 6. Oceanic whitetip shark. (NOAA)

been disrespectful, and an invitation to return in another body so that the hunt may continue.

50:9 I wish the boy was here: Another repeat of Santiago's wish/prayer to have the boy help him. Again, it is spoken aloud. See entry 45:7.

50:14–15 through my treachery, it had been necessary to him to make a choice: "Him" refers to the marlin. For the paradox of Santiago's using treachery, deceit like the jelly fish, see entry 75:4–5. Santiago is a carnivore: he catches fish for himself and others to eat. He would no more consider being a vegan than would the native inhabitants of most seacoast cultures. Fishing is not just a job but a vocation of dedication to craft, which includes respect for his prey, in contrast to the growing commercial fishery around him, which often discards any fish it catches that lacks commercial value. But to catch larger, more powerful creatures, involves deceit, trickery, a hook hidden within a fish. Santiago acknowledges this, and laments it, but it is part of his life cycle, whereby he must kill to live, one of many paradoxes in the book, including loving the fish that he kills or how "the fish came alive, with his death in him" (94:6). It is the paradox of necessary sin, of killing to live, which we justify in war and self-defense. For Santiago, named for a saint (St. James), killing is a sin, but a necessary one, both self-defense and fulfillment of self-identity. As he thinks, "[E]verything kills everything else" (106:5), Santiago apologizes to the fish afterward for his act, but, until the sharks take his prey, he does not regret it. Like his author, who presents this universal paradox, Santiago sees killing as a necessary way to live. (See Sylvester, "Extended Vision" 134, 136–37).

50:17–19 far out. . . . Beyond all the people in the world: As noted at entry 14:6, Hemingway repeatedly tells us that Santiago sails out beyond sight of land, out beyond other fishermen. In doing so, Hemingway may well be referencing Friedrich Nietzsche, the German philosopher who denounced small-minded pieties and the conventional morality of late nineteenth-century Europe. Nietzsche advocated for the autonomous individual, championing the person who took charge of his own destiny. In ways applicable to *The Old Man and the Sea,* Nietzsche recognized both the possible achievement and the pain of going out too far. In *The Birth of Tragedy,* discussing the Prometheus myth, he saw "the imperative necessity of [transgression] for the titanic individual," even while recognizing that "[m]an's highest good must be bought . . . and paid for by the flood of grief and suffering" (Golffing trans. 63–65; editor's substitution of "transgression" for Golffing's more mythic-minded translation of the German noun *Frevel*). Prometheus disobeys Zeus and brings the gift of fire to humanity but pays with eternal torture; humankind benefits from his suffering. In other words, to achieve much, one must risk much, or, in simpler sports lingo, no pain, no gain. Santiago catches the huge fish because he abandons safe territorial waters and ventures far out to sea, leaving behind the timid, conventional, and more commercially minded fishermen; he loses the fish because his distance from shore allows ample time for the sharks to strip him of his catch. He has no material gain, but he has the satisfaction of knowing that he caught and killed an enormous fish, that his skills are intact. He has re-established his credentials as *el Campeón* (the champion) among the other fishermen. And he has renewed Manolin's faith in him. Charles Taylor also read *The Old Man and the Sea* in Nietzschean terms, concluding that "the value of the heroic individual taking the greatest risks [is] to achieve the greatest fulfillment" (642).

"Too far" is repeated five times in *The Old Man and the Sea,* "far out" nine times, although several of these overlap the first count ("far" is repeated twenty-four times in the novella). In the sense that Nietzsche considered it—that is, the individual going beyond customary boundaries—Hemingway repeats it eight times, and the lines on this page make explicit Santiago's exceptionalism: the fish's "choice had been to stay in the deep dark water far out beyond all snares and traps and treacheries. My choice was to go there to find him *beyond all people. Beyond all the people in the world*" (50:18–19; emphasis added). The first introduction of "far out" is on 14:6, where Hemingway repeats the phrase three times (14:6, 8, and 11), insisting that we notice it and consider its implications. Interesting also is that Hemingway repeated this situation in *Islands in the Stream* when David, almost attacked by a hammerhead shark while spearfishing, says, "I just went too far out and I lost that good yellowtail . . . and he bloodied the water and that called the shark" (86).

Hemingway withdrew from Sylvia Beach's library a 1926 edition of Nietzsche's *Thus Spoke Zarathustra* and kept it from May through September 1926 (Reynolds, *Hemingway's Reading* 163). He also had a French biography of Nietzsche, Guy de Pourtalès' *Nietzsche en Italie* at the Finca Vigía, where *The Old Man and the Sea* was written (Brasch and Sigman, *Hemingway's Library* 298). See also entries 110:8, 115:12, 116:15–16, 120:15.

50:23 **the thing that I was born for:** Santiago's self-identification as champion fisherman, as a vocation, not just a way of earning his livelihood. Both he and the boy are "born for" fishing in all the old ways. Theirs is an exceptional "borning" that makes them different and strange in modern times. It also gives them the necessary skills and strength to do great things, to be champions. Henry David Thoreau wrote of a fisherman that he met: "His fishing was not a sport, nor merely a means of subsistence, but a sort of solemn sacrament" (*Week on the Concord* 31).

51:3 **gunwale:** The upper edge of a ship's side; a piece of timber extending around the topside of the hull.

51:4–5 **sheath knife:** Any fixed-blade knife carried in a sheath, usually leather in Santiago's time, for the protection of both the carrier and the blade of the knife.

51:18 **Catalan *cardel*:** Rope or line from, or in the fashion of, Catalonia, a province in northeast Spain. "*Cardel*" should read "*cordel*," the Spanish term for line or rope.

51:20 **cuts him off:** That is, the presence of another fish near the line holding Santiago's marlin increases the risk of that fish inadvertently severing the marlin's line.

51:22 **broadbill:** A swordfish so named for its bill, which is broader and flatter than that of a marlin.

51:24 **I wish I had the boy:** Again, spoken aloud. See this most repeated refrain in the novella at 45:7, 48:6; 50:9, 51:24, 56:19, 62:5, and 83:6–7.

52:7 **made a cut below his eye:** This is the second blood sequence, following Manolin's being marked with blood at 12:23. The fish surges, and Santiago is pulled down on his face in the boat, receiving a cut over his cheekbone, below his eye. The imagery used to describe the wound comes from boxing and underscores the violence and competition inherent in the blood bond between humans and nature. The stuff of life becomes visible in the struggle, through the wounds. The blood quickly coagulates. Santiago rests a moment, readjusts the line, and the contest continues. However, in Hemingway's biblical imagery in the book, Santiago's bleeding face recalls the blood dripping down Jesus's face, caused by the crown of thorns; this symbolism is repeated at 87:9–11, along with black spots Santiago sees before his eyes: "and the sweat salted his eyes and salted the cut over his eye and on his forehead." These wounds, together with the cuts to his hand, eventually build to a direct evocation of Jesus's crucifixion wounds and elevate Santiago's hand wounds toward the level of stigmata.

52:10 **rested against the wood:** Given the previous entry, and its suggestion of Jesus's crucifixion, this line also carries the same suggestion: Santiago's resting against the wood reminds us of Christ's suffering on the Cross. Melvin Backman recognized the allusion in 1955 (9).

53:22–23 **he'll fill the sacks along his backbone:** Fish have air bladders along their spines that they can control for buoyancy among the varying water pressures of different depths. If a deep-dwelling fish surfaces, reduced water pressure allows the bladders to expand, increasing buoyancy, making dives more difficult. Surfacing too quickly from great depths can cause injury, even death. And for fish like the marlin (physoclistous species), reabsorption of air in these bladders takes time (Fangue email). Santiago wants the fish on the surface where he can see it and harpoon it, not at great depths. Hemingway wrote in "Marlin off Cuba," "[J]umping . . . tires the fish greatly and also fills the air sacks along his backbone, . . . with air that prevents him from sounding deeply. If he jumps enough he cannot sound at all. If you fight him fast enough there is no time for his pressure apparatus to adjust itself" (69).

PAGES 54 THROUGH 77

54:7 **throw it:** That is, work the hook loose.

54:10 **There was the yellow weed:** See entries 28:18, 35:11–13, 35:16, and 56:2.

54:12–13 **that had made so much phosphorescence in the night:** See entry 28:18.

54:14–15 **Fish . . . I love you. . . . But I will kill you dead:** Santiago's vision of life in nature is consistently paradoxical. There is always great passion in his response to all creatures great and small and to the sea itself. He does love the natural world and its gifts of life. He knows, however, that, to receive gifts of sustenance from nature, humans must kill, hence the pardon begged in 50:8. Santiago's paradoxical understanding of the relation of humans to nature is much like that expressed by Romero in *The Sun Also Rises* (189–90). Compare entries 59:18–19, 75:4–5, 94:22–23, 105:18, 105:20, and 106:5.

54: 17 **A small bird came . . . from the north:** Warblers—and there are over fifty species in the United States alone—are small birds, five inches or less, smaller than sparrows, that migrate from North America to Mexico, Central, or South America in winter and back north in the spring. Hemingway based this incident on personal experience. He wrote in the *Esquire* essay "There She Breaches! *Or* Moby Dick off the Morro" (May 1936): "[T]he small birds that are going south are deadly tired sometimes as they near the coast of Cuba where the hawks come out to meet them, and the birds light on the boat to rest and sometimes we would have as many as twenty on board at one time in the cabin, on the deck perched on the fishing chairs or resting on the floor of the cockpit. Their great fatigue makes them so tame that you can pick them up and they show no fear at all. There were three warblers and one thrush in the cockpit" (*BL* 247). Similarly, Hemingway recorded in his Fishing Log (April–July 1933), "A pretty little parakeet just flew on board exhausted. Charles [Thompson] caught it and put it in a box to take home," saving it from the hawks.

55:4 **It's too steady:** A steady line means that the great fish remains persistent in his movement against the current and out to sea.

55:6 What are birds coming to: The old man could intend this question in two senses, that is, the literal—what are they approaching?—or the figurative—what will happen to them?

55:7 the hawks: The old man responds to his own question above with an answer to both the literal and figurative meanings: the migrating birds approach the land-based hawks and will most likely be attacked by ruthless predators, a prefiguring of what will happen when Santiago tries to tow his prize to shore.

55:17 small breeze . . . rising: On 55:5, we are told that the previous night had been windless; now the breeze is freshening. The trade wind that the old man expected the night of his first day at sea (14:6) begins instead in the morning of his second day out. Santiago now has been at sea for over twenty-four hours, with the fish towing him since noon of the previous day.

56:2 bleeding: This third mention of blood occurs during Santiago's long struggle (*agon*, contest) to land the marlin, 55:23–56:2. Santiago and the fish have reached a stalemate in the contest. This stalemate is presented by allusion to things sacred, both African and Catholic. Attention is drawn to the color yellow, Oshún's color (54:10–13 and entries 16:19 and 35:5), and to Santiago's conversation with the warbler (perhaps also yellow), which recalls conversations with birds by Saint Francis of Assisi. The holy calm of the stalemate is broken when the line jerks suddenly, cutting Santiago's hand. Santiago literally feels the marlin's hurt. He bleeds because of that hurt, and he mingles his blood with that hurt as he washes his hand in the ocean and watches "the blood trail away and the steady movement of water against his hand as the boat moved" (57:1–3). Something of the holy quiet of the stalemate is returned as a result of the wound, of the blood, and this creates a new kind of bonding between the old man and the fish. No longer is the binding merely fishing line; it is now mutual pain, a blood bond. They are ritualized blood brothers.

56:4 turn the fish: Force the fish toward the boat, to be within harpoon range.

56:10 liked him for company: Insisting on the social network that sustains Santiago and that he is part of.

56:19 and that I had some salt: Seasoning the raw fish with salt would make it more palatable. The line also contains another wish for Manolin's company: 48:6, 50:9, 51:24.

57:1 blood trail: While Santiago's blood trail from his cut hand is miniscule, it foreshadows the trail left by the harpooned marlin, a trail that will attract the mako shark.

58:4, 58:18 bonito: Jeffrey Herlihy[-Mera] suggests that Santiago named the tuna he caught on 39:4 as "albacore" because that was the Cuban name for this variety of tuna; but now, more tired, he reverts to the dialect of his birth and youth and calls it by the Canarian name for this fish, "bonito," as he will also do, still more tired, on 74:8 ("Eyes the Same Color as the Sea" 36).

58:8–9 his left hand was cramped: Santiago's left hand suffers a muscular cramp, of which the Mayo Clinic says, "Long periods of exercise or physical labor, particularly in hot weather, may lead to muscle cramps" (http://www.mayoclinic.org/diseases-conditions/muscle-cramp/basics/definition/con-20014594); another recognized cause is an imbalance in electrolytes, the effect of dehydration, an early indicator that Santiago is not drinking enough water. As with other details in the novella, this, too, has a basis in Hemingway's experience. A friend of Hemingway's and frequently his boat captain was Edward "Bra" Saunders, whose "hands were often afflicted with fisherman's cramp" (Baker, *Life* 655).

With the cramp, Hemingway suggests multiple readings. First, that Santiago, *el Campeón* though he is, is human, subject to human's physical limitations. It is now the second day at sea: Santiago is tired, strained, and somewhat dehydrated. With its acknowledgment of human limitations, the passage also suggests Captain Ahab in Melville's *Moby-Dick*, a novel to which *Old Man and the Sea* has often been compared (and Hemingway wrote of Melville and *Moby-Dick* in *The Green Hills of Africa* [20]). Ahab, too, seeks to define his place in the universe. But unlike Santiago, who seeks merely to live in the world, Ahab seeks to dominate it and curses when his physical limitations curtail his ability to impose his hubristic will. When his artificial leg is snapped off in pursuit of Moby Dick, the white whale, Ahab cries, "Accursed fate! That the unconquerable captain in the soul should have such a craven mate!" (Melville 422). All we humans have our aspirations limited by our corporeal mates, our minds and bodies. But Ahab's "unconquerable captain in the soul" also suggests Santiago's "pain does not matter to a man" (84:21–22) and "man is not made for defeat" (103:14). Finally, it is Santiago's left hand (*sinister* in Latin) that cramps. Later, Santiago speaks of the hand's "treachery" (61:24) and calls it "a traitor" (71:3). In the Christian Passion imagery of this book, such treachery recalls that of Judas.

58:20 It was not unpleasant: Since Hemingway wrote the novella in 1951, the Japanese custom of serving raw tuna in sashimi and sushi is now widespread in the United States; it was not then. Although the old man would not have been accustomed to the taste, it would not have been too strong or offensive.

59:18–19 He is my brother. But I must kill him: Compare Romero's similar statement in *The Sun Also Rises*, when he describes the bulls as his best friends. Brett asks him if he kills his friends: "'Always,' he said in English. . . . 'So they don't kill me'" (189–90). Both statements, Santiago's and Romero's, insist on the acknowledgment of death as part of life, as well as the professional obligations of both men in the careers they have chosen and in which they identify themselves. See 54:14–15.

60:4 **God help me:** Santiago engages in a simple direct prayer for divine intervention. Such direct calls for intervention are common in the Psalms, among them Psalms 12, 28, 69, and 102. Santiago does not hold fast to Catholic orthodoxy (64:24—"I am not religious"), even though he says Hail Marys as promised (65:1–15, 87:16–19, 116:9). As the pictures in his shack suggest, his spirituality is a mix of Catholic and Afro-Cuban beliefs and practices. His prayer life in *Old Man and the Sea* tends toward the Afro-Cuban and Catholic folk traditions of bargaining prayer, manipulating divine favor and intervention rather than praying "thy will be done."

60:22–23 **strange undulation . . . building up:** If, during the absence of wind, the sea gets agitated by a long, rolling swell, a gale may be expected, a phenomenon well known to sea men. When trade winds blow, cumulus clouds form in lines, called "cloud streets," that are parallel to the wind direction (Churchill email). Now being pulled straight north (53:9), Santiago is probably looking east (from which the trade winds come) and seeing "streets" forming upwind of him, before the full wind reaches him.

Fig. 9. There are few clouds at sea in this picture taken by Hemingway himself of a boat with two occupants, but the photo reveals the emptiness of the ocean for one in a small boat out in the enormously wide sea. (Courtesy Ernest Hemingway Collection. John F. Kennedy Library and Museum, Boston)

61:3 he knew no man was ever alone on the sea: See 29:8, 38:13, and 48:18 for examples of the old man's ability to commune with sea life. He has the sea beneath and around him, with its numerous prisms (40:14) and its equally numinous ("strange") motion-in-stillness, a rhythmic "undulation" elsewhere anthropomorphizing the sea as "making love with something under a . . . blanket (72:11–12). Thus personified, his beloved *la mar* (29:19) is a companion, albeit much more than human (compare Beegel, "Eternal Feminine" 136–38). He has his "brother," the marlin, reassuringly on the line "stretching ahead," connecting him to the creature of the depths. His eyes sweep the sky from the friendly clouds above to the ducks far away. "Etched" as individual creatures no less alone than he in this vastness, they become blurred as they merge with the sky above and the sea below (as does Santiago himself), yet maintain their individual identities (as does Santiago). Thus, Santiago situates himself, as well as the ducks, in nature's circumambience, integrated into nature, even when ostensibly "alone."

61:10 If there is a hurricane: Santiago's knowledge of natural forces, like his way of fishing, reflect his experience. If a hurricane were coming in the next few days, the cumulus clouds accompanying the trade winds would disappear and the higher atmosphere would be fully clouded over with cirrus clouds. Instead, Santiago sees "friendly piles" of cumulus (61:16–17). These are cumulus humulus, puffy, vertically shaped, fair-weather clouds. And in the higher atmosphere, the cirrus are in "thin feathers" against a clear sky (61:18–19), rather than in a solid film over the sky. All these features, good and bad, are clearly visible at sea for great distances, so that they can be recognized long before a hurricane arrives.

61:13 The land must make a difference too: Cloud patterns are most visible without the disruption of air currents that exist over land. For this reason, weather forecasters have found that the most accurate forecasting takes place by satellite or at sea, and sailors have been surprisingly accurate in their predictions of approaching storms.

61:20 light *brisa*: A "light breeze" on the Beaufort Scale measures four to six knots or six to eleven kilometers per hour. This wind would be accompanied by slightly increased wave and current activity, both of which would tire the marlin more quickly than a dead calm would. There is also a bilingual pun. The previous lines mention ice cream; *brisa* in Cuban Spanish also means "hunger" (Herlihy-Mera, "Hemingway's Cuban Spanish").

62:2 ptomaine poisoning: A form of food poisoning caused by deconstructing proteins in meat or fish.

62:3 *calambre*: Muscle spasm or cramp.

62:5 **if the boy were here:** Another wish for Manolin's presence and help. See entry 45:7 for a list of such wishes.

62:21 **as long as a baseball bat:** Hemingway's simile ties the marlin's bill to the baseball-related references in the novella (see entries for page 17), furthering the interconnectedness of the various elements.

63:10 **convince:** That is, persuade or conquer.

63:15–16 **more noble and more able:** Although at first glance this statement seems exaggerated, perhaps even untrue, one needs to remember that Santiago's focus is on this "great fish," not just any fish. He has called attention to its beauty to match the brightest rainbow and strength, far beyond that of any human. Moreover, unlike Santiago, the fish conducts its life with no trickery, unlike fishermen who hide hooks in bait and, unlike Santiago, who has gone out of his conventional fishing places to seek the fish where it may have considered itself safe. Thus, this fish is nobler and abler than Santiago or any human. See 50:14 and 75:4.

63:18 **many that weighed more than a thousand pounds:** Although fish weighing over one thousand pounds have been harpooned by commercial fishermen off the coast of Havana, landing a fish of that size was a rare occurrence when the novella was written.

64:2–3 **There are three things that are brothers:** The language used here, like that used in 55:11–18, calls to mind St. Francis of Assisi, specifically his much loved "Canticle of the Sun," a song Francis wrote praising God for the creation of, among others, Brothers Sun, Wind, and Air. For Santiago, named for a saint, Brother Hand, Brother Hand and Brother Fish are literally bound to each other by blood, and by pain, and by the awe and anguish that is the relationship of fisherman to fish.

64:14–15 **and took his suffering:** "But rejoice, inasmuch as you are partakers of Christ's sufferings" (I Peter 4:13). Compare also Hemingway's short story/play "Today Is Friday," in which three Roman soldiers discuss Christ's endurance during his crucifixion.

64:17 **small sea rising:** That is, waves of only a few feet.

64:24–65:1 **I will say ten Our Fathers and ten Hail Marys:** According to Catholic theology, one prays *not* to bring about the eventual accomplishment of a specific goal, but rather to dispose oneself to receive what God wills. For a brief introduction to types of prayer, see Scott P. Richert. Santiago's offer of prayer in exchange for the capture of the fish suggests that, as he says, "I am not religious" (64:24), at least not in an orthodox Catholic way. His understanding of prayer as a tool for manipulating fortune suggests an Afro-Cuban understanding of religion where one engages in various activities to get the gods to cast the future one wishes. His expedient attitude toward religion would not have been uncommon in prerevolutionary Cuba; the Catholic Church never had significant influence in the country so never gained political and social control over the population, particularly over those who came from nations with historically important non-Christian and syncretic religious cultures, as Santiago does, coming from the Canary Islands. For a discussion of magico-religious behavior of the sort Santiago manifests here, see Grimes, "'Bad Luck or No Luck at All.'"

65:2–3 **pilgrimage to the Virgin of Cobre:** See entry 16:2.

65:22 **If the fish decides to stay:** Note the old man's passive acceptance of the fish's power and strength, as in 47:14 and 53:11.

66:3 **But I have no light to attract them:** Flying fish are attracted to light at night and can be brought to a boat if a light is suspended just below or on the surface of the water.

66:5 **Christ:** Part exclamation, part prayer. (See entry 48.6 for elaboration.)

66:7–8 **In all his greatness and his glory:** Deut. 5:24: "Behold, the lord our God has shown his glory and greatness." Compare the Lord's Prayer's "power and glory."

66:9 **Although it is unjust:** Santiago considers it unjust to kill such a magnificent fish but does it anyway. Such opinion versus action is one of the contraries or paradoxes within the novella. See discussions at entries 12:23, 54:14–15, 58:8–9, 75:4–5, 105:18, 105:20, and 106:5.

66:11 **strange old man:** A repetition of 14:21. Note that the old man also describes the fish as "strange" at 48:23 and 67:21, strengthening their identification.

66:18 **Why are the lions the main thing that is left:** The old man asks himself why he now dreams only of lions. Traditionally, the lion is a symbol of power, pride, strength of soul, vigilance, and superior courage. According to legend, a lion's presence in a dream indicates a powerful adversary. In heraldry, a lion is a symbol of deathless courage. It is also considered a symbol of Christ's resurrection, stemming from the belief that the lion's whelp was born dead and remained so for three days and then is brought to life. The Aberdeen Bestiary asserts that, when a lioness gives birth to her cubs, she produces them dead and watches over them for three days, until their father comes on the third day and breathes into their faces and restores them to life. Thus the Almighty Father awakened our Lord Jesus Christ from the dead on the third day; as Jacob says: "He will fall asleep as a lion, and as a lion's whelp he will be revived" (Gen., 49:9). (https://www.abdn.ac.uk/bestiary/translat/7v.hti)

For an alternative reading, see Grimes, "Lions on the Beach," referred to in entry 25:14.

67:1 **small sea:** See entry for 64:17.

67:7 **east of north:** The tiring fish is now swimming more with the easterly current. Again, this is based on Hemingway's own experience. In "Marlin off Cuba," he wrote of a caught marlin, "When he begins to tire he will usually go with the current" (69).

67:13 **horse . . . can see in the dark:** A horse's eye is larger than any other animal's, except the whale's. Due to its eyes being widely set apart and placed far back on the horse's head, it can detect movement or objects in the front, at the side, or even behind; and horses have high visual acuity. Sylvester linked horses with large eyes, the marlin's large eyes, and Santiago, with his ability to see in the dark, as all "strange." Of Santiago, Sylvester says, his vision suggests "his perception of the paradoxical logic of nature" ("Extended Vision" 132). Marlin, with their large eyes, hunt primarily through their vision. Ulanski writes, "At approximately six hundred feet in the open ocean [one hundred fathoms] the light intensity is 1 percent of that at the surface. . . . The marlin' s eye is specifically adapted to cope with low light levels encountered during a dive" (103).

67:15 **almost as a cat sees:** The retina of a cat's eye is extra sensitive to light, but the cat relies more on its hearing than on its sight in a night hunt, just as a fish relies on senses other than sight in deep, dark water. In the marlin's case, these include neuromasts along its lateral line. See entry 38.8.

68:4 *juegos:* Games.

68:8 *un espuela de hueso:* Santiago translates "bone spur" literally from English to Spanish; he is not certain if a Spanish idiom exists for the condition.

68:9 **Can it be as painful as the spur of a fighting cock:** A cock's spur is a sharp, hard projection on the bird's ankle, also known as a back claw. If a spur is not naturally prominent, a metal gaff is attached to the leg of a game cock for a fight; sometimes these gaffs are sharpened. Either the natural or metal spur would be painful if a person were injured by it in the course of a cockfight.

68:12 **Man is not much beside the great birds and beasts:** That is, a person often has less courage and persistence against fighting the odds than do these beasts. Humans may not be much beside the great birds and beasts; nevertheless, Psalm 8:5 claims that they were made little less than God and crowned with glory and honor. Hemingway's text reflects this ironic and paradoxical view of humans and nature.

68:16 **God pity him and me:** One of many "accidental prayers" uttered by Santiago (see entry 48:6), this one calls up the irony and paradox of human struggle in and with nature, a struggle dictated by the order of creation, by the Creator. In its anguish, it calls to mind the lament that begins Psalm 22—"My God, my God, why have you forsaken me?"—repeated by Jesus on the Cross, Mark 15:34. The awe and terror that accompany the paradoxical relation of humans to the natural order evoke pity, even divine pathos.

68:17 **Do you believe:** "You" refers to the old man. Alone at sea, Santiago has begun to carry on a dialogue with himself.

69:1 **Casablanca:** Casa Blanca, a small community on the east shore of Havana harbor, connected at that time to Havana by ferry. It was a coaling station.

69:2 **hand game:** Arm wrestling. Although most arm wrestling matches end in seconds, a few in minutes, there have been long matches marked by incredible strength and endurance, some perhaps lasting up to twenty minutes—see http://northeastboard.com/thread/23554/longest-match. Here Hemingway has exaggerated even the greatest of real matches to establish Santiago as a true champion among champions. Hemingway distorts the contest, fictionalizes it, to demonstrate Santiago's strength and endurance.

69:2 **negro:** "Negro" was treated as an adjective in American English when this novella was written and was not capitalized at the time as a proper name.

69:3 **Cienfuegos:** A city and major sugar port on the southern central coast of Cuba.

69:13 **blood came out:** Blood as sports reference becomes factual rather than figurative when Santiago tries to give himself "more confidence" by remembering an arm-wrestling contest between him and "the great negro from Cienfuegos" from which Santiago emerged as *El Campeón* (69:2–3) One might not expect an arm-wrestling contest to be bloody, but, as Santiago recalls it, in a moment of great tension "blood came out from under the fingernails of both his and the negro's hands and they looked each other in the eye and at their hands and forearms" (69:13–15). Much like blood bonding through knife slashes on the palm, the great Negro and Santiago become blood brothers rather than enemies during their contest. As with the marlin and the old man, a blood bond is forged by the contest.

There is some change in the nature of the blood trope as the struggle with the marlin reaches its climax in the death of the fish. In the ebb and flow of life, blood not only flows out from wounds leading to death, it is also contained by flesh and sustains life. *The Old Man and the Sea* recognizes this yin and yang in blood. Santiago knows that blood contained in the flesh nourishes. He decides not to gut a dolphinfish he has caught for nourishment, but rather to "save the blood in the meat" (73:19) that he will later eat.

The life/death pulse of blood reaches its apotheosis when Santiago harpoons the fish. We are told that, when the harpoon is pushed into the marlin with all of Santiago's weight, "the fish came alive, with his death in him" (94:6). This figure is a perfect image for the mysterious tango of life and death carried in the trope of blood. That mystery is celebrated as the old man apprehends, for a moment, that the marlin rises and seems "to hang in the air above the old man in the skiff" (94:8–9). The mystery infused in that moment cannot be sustained, and the fish crashes into the water; soon "the sea was discoloring with the red of the blood from his heart" (94:17–18). Blood is the focus of Santiago's consciousness in the moment of the crash. It is seen first as "dark as a shoal" in the mile-deep water. "Then it spread like a cloud" (94: 20). References to blood in the final pages of the story emphasize the dispersion of blood in the water, its capacity to be present beyond sight and appear, rather, as "scent." Once spilled, blood (life) seems to be infused into everything and, again, serves as a metaphor for the bond that unites all creatures great and small. Beegel, referring to the red color of the drifting plankton, calls plankton "the blood of life" ("Eternal Feminine" 137). Santiago concludes his reflection on the apotheosis of the marlin by acknowledging this *bond*, saying, "I have killed this fish which is my brother and now I must do the slave work (95:4–6). (See also reflections on the red color in entry 35:5).

Those reading the story, on some level, as Christian allegory may recall in this scene the picture of the Sacred Heart of Jesus that Santiago's wife hung on their shack wall, for Santiago thinks, concerning the harpooning, "I think I felt his heart" (95:18). This perception extends from the early Christian representation of the word "Christ" with a stylized drawing of a fish (Figure 8). A caution, however, is needed: the blood of the fish seems to have no soteriological (saving) function and serves no ritual function of any sort.

The blood trope across the novella functions primarily as that which bonds life to death, death to life, and all creatures to each other in a great paradoxical mystery of ecstasy and pain, conflict and calm, horror and beauty. That this is blood's primary function is affirmed in the reference to it as the sharks attack the marlin. The image that emerges from Santiago's battle with the sharks is not a simplistic picture of nature bloody in tooth and claw. It is bloody, for sure, but it is neither chaos nor accident. The text is specific: "The shark was not an accident. He had come up from deep down in the water as the dark cloud of blood had settled and dispersed in the mile deep sea" (100:3–5). The phrasing here is nearly a literal recapitulation of 94:18–20. Santiago, marlin, blood, mystery, and shark are connected, are one thing in the deep oceanic version of nature presented in *The Old Man and the Sea*. The binding together of Santiago, marlin, and shark continues as the old man's harpoon attack on the first shark condenses and recapitulates his harpooning of the fish (93:15–94:5): "He hit it with his blood mushed hands driving a good harpoon with all his strength. He hit it without hope but with resolution and complete malignancy" (102:10–12). The binding of images from the catch of the marlin with the attack of the sharks serves to unite the contraries of life (blood) in nature—pain, agony, loss, malignancy, death, life, pride, triumph, and brotherhood.

As the fish bleeds again (103:3), attracting more sharks to come, Santiago reflects on the mystery that spreads like the blood over the natural struggle in which he is involved. He says, "[M]an is not made for defeat. . . . A man can be destroyed but not defeated" (103:14–15).

The presentation of blood shifts almost completely from sight to smell during the mass shark attack (108:10–11:5). This shift in senses reinforces the image of blood infusion and the oceanic unity of all things and actions in the natural world. Imagery in this section also returns the blood trope to its initial presentation (12:18–23) where the boy remembers "the sweet blood smell all over me." As he fights the sharks, Santiago thinks the sharks would strike a man even if he "had no smell of fish blood nor of fish slime on him" (108:6–7). The old man, of course, has that smell all over him, as did the boy in the moment that bound them in ontological vocation one with the other. The bond includes the sharks that kill as well as the marlin that would sustain.

Triumph turns to lamentation as Santiago looks at the great fish "drained of blood" (110:5). Full of sorrow and regret, he says, "I shouldn't have gone out so far, fish. . . . Neither for you nor for me. I'm sorry, fish" (110:8–9). Here, perhaps, Nietzschean readings of *The Old Man and the Sea* fold paradoxically into a humbling saint's tale as the sharks reduce the marlin to head and bones. Loss and gain, like life and death, are one cloth. Saint Francis and the *Übermensch* are one flesh.

The blood trope ends with another shift in the senses, this time from smell to taste and touch. Completely exhausted from his great struggle too far out, the old man "felt a strange taste in his mouth. It was coppery and sweet and he was afraid of it for a moment. But there was not much of it" (119:3–6). It is his own blood (life/death) he tastes. The significance of the blood in his mouth is cryptic and opaque. It can be read as an indication that he is bleeding internally from his exertion; perhaps it signals impending death. Santiago neither seems overly concerned about the blood in his mouth nor does he explore the matter. Rather, the taste of his own blood calls forth indignation and a defiant attitude toward the sharks: "He spat into the ocean and said, 'Eat that, *galanos*. And make a dream you've killed a man" (119:7–8). Whatever the state of his body, the old man's blood is on the rise, and the drive within him that once made him *El Campeón,* and that sent him "too far out" still pulses in his blood. It will not extinguish. As he reflected earlier, "A man can be destroyed but not defeated." That's the taste of blood.

69:22 **The odds:** The odds in betting: the ratio between Santiago's chance at winning and that of the Negro fluctuated as each man gained or lost apparent control, that is, as their hands moved straight up from the table.

70:2 *El Campeón:* The champion, Santiago's title as arm-wrestling winner, but also his role as champion of craft fishing against younger, profit-oriented fishermen and also champion of the natural universe, with its inherent contradictions. Jeffrey Herlihy[-Mera] also points out that Saint James was believed to have fought on behalf of the Spaniards against the Moors in eleventh-century Spain and that Spanish hero El Cid's battle cry was "Santiago! Santiago!" El Cid won the sobriquet *El Cid Campeador (campeón* in modern Spanish), and *campeón* became a popular Iberian nickname. Thus, for Herlihy[-Mera], that Santiago receives *campeón* for his wrist-wrestling win points to his Spanish background ("Eyes the Same Color as the Sea" 27).

71:3 **traitor:** The treacherous left hand, a traitor, like Judas. See entry 58:8–9.

71:8 **An airplane passed overhead on its course to Miami:** Most likely, but we learn later (124:16) that planes searched for Santiago when he did not return to Cojimar at the end of his first day at sea.

71:13 **to gain any:** That is, to gain any line. Santiago would like to pull the fish closer to the boat.

71:22 **cross-trees:** A pair of timbers or metal bars placed crosswise on a masthead to spread the vertical lines supporting the mast and leading to the mast above. Crosstrees often act as platforms for sailors searching the horizon.

71:23–24 **The dolphin looked greener from there:** Since a dolphinfish's true color is gold—hence, the Spanish name *dorado*—the blue water makes it appear green. See 74:9.

72:14 **true gold:** The sun's light enhanced the golden tint of the fish, lending it an even more pronounced auric hue when it leapt into the air.

72:20 **When the fish was at the stern:** Notice Hemingway's pattern of repetition in this description in 72:20–23, especially with the words "fish," "over the stern," "at the stern," and the possessive pronoun "its."

73:14 **it was perceptibly slower:** The fish is tiring, pulling the boat and swimming more slowly.

73:18 **It would be better to gut the dolphin:** See entry 69:13. Beegel writes that dolphinfish, mahi-mahi, taste better if not filleted until just before eating ("A Guide 243).

73:22–23 **The setting of the sun is a difficult time:** Probably not true, especially for a deep-swimming fish like this marlin, which only sees the sun when it surfaces, but included by Hemingway as further demonstration of Santiago's years of experience and knowledge. In general, fish are more active at sunrise and sunset, technically called crepuscular. Ismael Léon Almeida writes, "Anglers know that game fishes' activity comes more intensely at daybreak and sunset" because they are reacting to the feeding patterns of bait fish (email). See also Beegel, "A Guide" 283–84.

74:9 **He called it *dorado*:** The Spanish word *dorado* means gilded or golden. In Cuban Spanish, it also applies to *coryphaena hippurus*, a fish celebrated for its splendid coloring and the velocity of its movements. Santiago also calls it "dolphin," but it is a fish, not the mammal we call porpoises. It is also called mahi-mahi. See 34:1, 48:17, 71:23.

75:1 **Rigel:** Pronounced RY jel in English, ree-GEL in Spanish, the second star in the constellation Orion or the Hunter. This constellation is not visible in the sky of the northern hemisphere until midnight of 1 October, at the earliest. Santiago could not have seen any of the stars of this constellation just after sunset in September; Hemingway admitted that he had made an error after people wrote him to say that Santiago could not have seen Rigel at that time of year. Baker wrote of Hemingway's response: "'They were so good to write,' said Ernest, magnanimously" (*Life* 514).

The mythology surrounding Orion, however, makes it an appropriate choice. According to legend, Orion the hunter boasted that there was not an animal on earth that he could not conquer. To punish his vanity and pride, a scorpion sprang from the earth and bit his foot, causing his death. Rigel is Arabic for foot, and Kenneth Johnson linked it to DiMaggio's bone spur (391).

75:3 **all his distant friends:** Since the beginning of civilization, stars have been regarded as important to the welfare of earthly inhabitants. Even in earliest societies, no course of action was taken without consultation of the heavenly bodies. The old man's communion with the stars partially reflects this mystical tradition, that somehow the stars play a part in the fate of his quest. In a more recent Christian context, the star is a symbol of a spirit struggling against forces of darkness and, more specifically, of the birth of Jesus Christ: "and lo, the star which they had seen in the East went before them, till it came to rest over the place where the child was. When they saw the star, they rejoiced exceedingly, with great joy" (Matt. 2:9–10).

75:4–5 **The fish is my friend. . . . But I must kill him:** Compare 59:18–19. The paradox of being in a world where all living things end in death, where we kill to live (if we eat meat) and exist in space vacated by the dead. Moreover, Santiago's self-identity is as a fisherman: he kills to feed himself and others, even though he feels guilt about killing the magnificent marlin. Beegel writes that Santiago believes that his fishing "is ethical so long as the killing is followed by eating, the act of communion, of sharing the blood of life" ("Santiago and the Eternal Feminine" 140); she continues, "He understands that the lives [of the fish he catches] are part of the 'celebratory gift,' part of the fisherman's communion with life" (141). It is also what Hemingway's hunter/doctor father taught him (Baker, *Life* 10 and esp. 16). This paradox is one of a series in the novella, beginning on the first page with Santiago's "benevolent skin cancer" (9:17) and continuing with "Then the fish came alive with his death in him" (94:6). It includes Santiago's hatred of those, like the *agua mala,* which succeed through trickery and deceit, although, as he acknowledges, it is something he practices himself (50:14). Related entries are at 36:15, 54:14–15, 59:18–19, 66:9, 75:11–13, 94:6, 105:18, 105:20, and 106:5 Hemingway in this book portrays life's inevitable, yet insoluble, paradoxes, mysteries, contraries.

Hemingway has Santiago say, "[E]verything kills everything else in some way" (106:5–6). Recognition of death and its place in the life cycle was a prominent theme of Hemingway's, evident in "The Natural History of the Dead"; in *Death in the Afternoon,* where he writes that "all stories, if continued far enough, end in death. . . . Especially do all stories of monogamy end in death" (122); and in his eulogy for Gene Van Guilder in November 1939, where Hemingway said, "Now Gene has gotten through with that thing we all have to do" (Baker, *Life* 343). Death is an inescapable fact. It is a paradox that we are born to die, and Hemingway insisted on our recognizing death's constant, inevitable presence without a romanticized view of it.

Through consistent allusions to Christ's passion in *The Old Man and the Sea,* Hemingway connects Santiago's paradoxical relation to nature with the awe-filled relation of Creator to creation, a relation fraught with the anguish felt by Santiago as he must kill the fish that is his brother. Both Jesus and Santiago undergo a passion required by any who love and live under the paradox of creation itself. From the perspective of these Christian allusions, Santiago's passion elevates him to the status of "Saint Iago" inside *The Old Man and the Sea,* making it a saint's tale.

75:6 **I am glad we do not have to try to kill the stars:** Santiago recognizes with humility that he is an actor, not a director, on life's stage, unlike Ahab in his wishes, and that he has no choice but to respond to his predestined role as the most intelligent and cunning predator.

75:8 **The moon runs away:** A figurative description of the moon's monthly cycle of waxing and waning. During this process, the moon rises and sets on the horizon each night, but it disappears entirely from view in the night sky for approximately three days, hence the old man's observation that the heavenly body "runs away."

75:11–13 **Then he was sorry for the great fish . . . and his determination to kill him never relaxed in his sorrow for him:** See 75:4–5 above.

76:11 **oars are a good trick:** Santiago speaks early about his craft as a fisherman schooled in the old ways, saying "there are many tricks" (14:24). Using the oars as a drag is one of them. He knows these tricks because he has been called to be a fisherman; he was born for and into this vocation (40:2–3, 50:23).

77:8 **you have not slept yet, old man:** Hemingway reminds us through Santiago's caution to himself that he has been two days at sea without sleep and that he is, indeed, an old man; he is nearing exhaustion and is dehydrated and needs to sleep if he is to continue effectively.

77:12 **might become unclear in his head:** Grimes wrote, "The language used to describe the catch suggests that Santiago succeeds in landing the fish because of his supreme skill as a fisherman (masculine) and because he is able to keep his head clear, something he has accomplished through the power (*ache*) of Ochun"—or as spelled in this book, Oshún. For a fuller discussion, see Grimes, *Hemingway's Religious Odyssey* 158. Clear headedness is mentioned often in this work: 77:13–14, 85:13, 92:20–21, 99:20, and 101:14. Its opposite is mentioned in 87:14.

The topic is one that would resonate with Hemingway, who, as recent books and articles have pointed out, most likely inherited a depressive illness from his father, suffered multiple concussions, and was a heavy drinker, all obscuring clear-headedness.

PAGES 78 THROUGH 96

78:14 **maw:** Stomach.

78:18–19 **Leaving a trail of phosphorescence:** See 28:18.

78:20 **leprous:** Resembling leprosy, a contagious disease that forms shining white scales on the skin of afflicted humans, hence the comparison to a fish. Lepers are cured by Jesus several times in the New Testament (for example, Matt. 8:2), and he instructs his disciples to cleanse the lepers in Matt. 10:8.

79:6–7 **His back was bent with the weight of line across it:** This description suggests Jesus's long walk toward Calvary carrying the Cross, as described in John 19:17. The weight Santiago bears as he pulls against the fish is the weight of the paradoxical relation of humans to the natural world—we must love it, and we must kill in it.

79:19 **particles of phosphorus:** These are the dinoflagelates, too small to see individually, but seeming to be visible because they illuminate particles of plant life floating in the water.

80:4–5 **I will never go . . . without salt or limes:** Salt or limes would make the raw fish more palatable and may have masked any unpleasant taste. Ceviche, a dish popular in South and Central America, composed of raw fish "cooked" in the acid citrus juice of limes or lemons, along with spices, onions, sometimes tomatoes, was not well known in 1950.

80:15 **There will be bad weather in three or four days:** Santiago observes the first specific signs of an easterly wave, a trough of low pressure embedded in the easterly trade winds, which oscillate in a wave-like manner, hence the term "easterly wave." This wave is a transition in which weather changes gradually but definitely from fair to unsettled, until it develops into a storm. A keen and practiced observer would know the pattern and would easily recognize the first signs. Most easterly waves are stable and predictable, usually ending in a moderate rain and wind storm, except in September and October, when hurricanes are likely to develop.

81:8–9 **a vast school of porpoises:** Santiago dreams of a large school of bottlenose dolphins (see entry 48:17). Dolphins are heraldic symbols of love and kind affection, and Christian symbols of resurrection and salvation, based on stories of dolphins rescuing drowning people. Porpoises, like lions, are social creatures, so Hemingway is again insisting on Santiago's connection to a network of living creatures, human and not. Hemingway's use of dream throughout *The Old Man and the Sea* is significant. It is linked closer to ancient understandings of the natural world, rather than to more modern understandings of the unconscious. No qualitative distinction seems to be drawn between dreamtime reality and cognitive consciousness in the world. Both serve to connect humans to Being itself, though in very different ways. Dreams and dreamtime connect people to totemic animals like lions and porpoises. Through dreamtime, individuals receive strength, healing, deliverance, and even the affirmation of resurrection and salvation. The power of totemic dreamtime culminates in the last sentence of *The Old Man and the Sea*: "The old man was dreaming about the lions" (127:8–9). Reading *The Old Man and the Sea* through dreams and dreamtime one can proclaim a victory of *el Campeón* and expect him to rise from ruin and raise the tattered flag again.

81:14 **there was a norther:** A sudden, violent winter gale originating in the north, the mythological realm of darkness, where evil powers lurk, along with the mysterious and unknown.

82:8 **burned his back:** Another reference to Christ's scourging.

82:15–16 **breaking point:** Because this phrase is repeated again, both times without the definite article, the omission seems deliberate. Special emphasis on the phrase "breaking point" suggests more than an issue with the tensile strength of this particular line, in contrast to what Hemingway writes in *The Garden of Eden,* where David's "pole was bent to the breaking point of the line and trace by the fish" (8). Here, rather, it conjures existential breaks that mark divides between one realm of being and another. Such breaking points may be Nietzschean in nature and associated with going out "too far" (see entry 50:17–19 or entry 77:8). Or it may conjure up broken places like those that, in *A Farewell to Arms,* Hemingway says grow stronger at the point of breakage (249).

82:22 **make him pay for the line:** To compensate for the line run-out while he slept, Santiago now increases pressure on the fish to make him suffer a price for the line taken out. For readers attracted to the Passion narrative embedded in *The Old Man* *and the Sea*, this may also suggest classic blood-atonement theory as posited by St. Anselm of Canterbury—Christ (*ichthys*—fish) paid the unpayable debt owed by fallen humans through his Passion, thus canceling that debt with his blood. The payment that begins here reaches its culmination as the fish is torn apart and consumed by the sharks; it pays and pays with flesh and blood, pointing toward the power of the Eucharist.

83:6 **If the boy . . . would wet the coils of line:** Wetting the coils would cool the friction caused by the line passing quickly through Santiago's hands. These lines are the last of Santiago's on-sea wishes to be accompanied by Manolin. Other entries are at 45:7, 48:6, 50:9, 51:24, 56:19, and implied at 62:5. From 45:7 through 56:19, Santiago says "I wish" the boy were here. At 62:5, he shifts to the conditional "if." In this passage, the conditional is stressed. "If" is repeated three times in this four-sentence paragraph. The shift speaks to Santiago's current condition and a change in that condition—"if the boy were here." The movement is from wishing, hoping, to a conviction or faith that, "if" the boy were present, then all would change. Given the power of dream and memory in *The Old Man and the Sea*, perhaps Santiago's conviction in the truth of this conditional beyond his present state provides renewed strength, and even youth, in his on-going struggle with the fish. Echoes of Kipling's poem "If-," which begins "If you can keep your head when all about you/ Are losing theirs" can be heard in the repetition of the conditional "if." Hemingway read Kipling as a child (Reynolds, *Young Hemingway* 24, 39) and owned numerous volumes of Kipling throughout his life: Reynolds lists fourteen titles, including a nine-volume set of *Works (Hemingway's Reading* 144–45); Brasch and Sigman list seventeen titles, including the ten-volume *Works,* as well as *Collected Verse* (201).

83:21 **he cannot go deep to die:** The marlin cannot go deep because, by rising to the surface and expanding the swim bladders along his spine, he has made it impossible to dive deeply; the buoyancy of the air-filled bladders prevents the fish from diving to the depths, and marlin can only absorb the air gradually through their blood stream. See 53:22–23.

83:23–84:2 **I wonder what started him . . . suddenly felt fear:** For all his experience, the old man cannot get into the mind of the fish and cannot explain its every action. Nor can we. The fish's actions—why it swam without jumping at first, the direction it took in swimming—are among the many unresolved mysteries in the novella, like the place of violence in nature, or the blood that sustains life but also calls the sharks to take life, or that the fish can seem to come alive with his death in him.

84:21–22 **and pain does not matter to a man:** On one level, Santiago is saying that, if the fish started jumping because of inability to endure the pain it felt, then he, as a human with a human's will, has the ability to control his pain and make rational choices, that he is the superior creature, *el Campeón*. (Compare 88:10–12 and also 50:17–18, the Nietzschean self-determining individual). Santiago and Hemingway would probably say "man" instead of "human," making this not only a species contest but also a gendered one (see entry 49:6). On another level, Hemingway is anticipating what he will say later in the book, that "a man can be destroyed but not defeated" (103:14–15). That is, Hemingway is stating that the measure of an individual is not success or failure at an endeavor, but rather one's goals and one's dedication to those goals. Hemingway was a realist. Death is the inevitable failure of our bodies; thus, obviously, we all fail. But achievements in life mitigate such failure, and most Hemingway protagonists, in novels and short stories, do fail at achieving some desired goal: Jake seeking happiness with Brett in *The Sun Also Rises,* Frederic Henry with Catherine in *A Farewell to Arms,* Robert Jordan in conquering the Fascists or continuing to be with Maria in *For Whom the Bell Tolls.* Hemingway seems to say that failure in pursuit of an admirable goal is better than success at something less praiseworthy, for example, coming in with a boat load of small, commercial fish. Hence, Santiago's quest—and we use that term from the Fisher King and Grail tales consciously—is admirable, and the more pain he endures in pursuit, the more admirable he becomes.

85:6 Why was I not born with two good hands: Reference to hands occurs often in *The Old Man and the Sea.* Certainly, Hemingway makes reference to those appendages with opposable thumbs that make homo sapiens special in nature. But hands are also personified and become "beings" with whom Santiago holds conversation. Clearly projected beyond flesh and bone, they are signs of human agency and figure into both the Christian and Nietzschean dimensions of the novella. Attention is given to both the right (Latin: *dexter* [dexterous]) and the left (Latin: *sinister*) hand, suggesting that hands/human agency is paradoxical. Our reaching and grasping take us out "too far" and allow us to catch and bind (if not keep) the transient fish that "seemed to hang in the air" (94:8–9). Hemingway's focus on hands is lengthened to blood, wound, and the "sudden lurch" of the great marlin into the story (55:19). For the five pages following this action by the marlin (55:19–60–19), resulting in a cut to the old man, Santiago expresses concern about his wounded right hand and his cramped left hand, culminating in a question posed to the "sinister" hand: "What kind of hand is that?" (58:11). The reader is left to decide as concern over the nature of hands continues along with the struggle to land the marlin. A deep human question is raised on this page: "Why was I not born with two good hands?" Why is human agency problematic, limited? Why can we, must we, reach and grasp but only bring in the bones? We are reminded of Ahab's "That the unconquerable captain in the soul should have such a craven mate [the body]!" (*Moby-Dick* 422) and also of Robert Browning's "A man's reach should exceed his grasp" ("Andrea del Sarto," l.98). No clear answer to our human dilemma is offered. Is the wounded and bleeding right hand to be seen as a sign of redeemed human agency, as stigmata? Or is the cramped sinister hand a sign of human limitation and the pain of overreaching? Both and—paradox? Hemingway seems to tip the scale in the direction of Nietzsche as he offers up his last significant reflection on hands:

> The hands cure quickly, he thought. I bled them clean and the salt water will heal them. The dark water of the true gulf is the greatest healer that there is. All I must do is keep the head clear. The hands have done their work and we sail well. (99:4–9)

85:11 **let the line cut him off:** See Matt. 5:30: "If your right hand causes you to sin, cut it off and throw it away." Also Matt. 18:8 and Mark 9:43. This allusion to the Bible passages is reinforced by the phrase "God knows" in the same paragraph and reinforces the Christian religious themes in the text.

86:4 **The sun was rising for the third time:** Hemingway is again reinforcing the Christian symbolism, here with the three days that Jesus was in the tomb prior to his resurrection.

87:2 **Now I must convince him:** See entry 63:10.

87:9–10 **black spots before his eye:** These are technically called scotomata, blind spots, and are usually associated with migraines, even without usual migraine symptoms such as headaches, and then called migraine equivalents. They can occur under stress, such as Santiago is experiencing, from sunlight reflecting off the water from the just-risen sun, causing temporary retinal burns, or from hypotension due to dehydration (emails from Keltner, Park, O'Hara, and Schwab). Whatever the possible medical reasons, and whether such spots would actually endure for an hour, Hemingway most likely introduced this added symptom to Santiago's suffering to suggest a crown of thorns surrounding his head, increasing the symbolism linking Santiago's torments to those of Jesus's agony.

87:11 **the cut over his eye and on his forehead:** This cut, plus the black spots of the previous line, have been likened to Jesus's crown of thorns. See 52:7, where the narrator describes the cut as occurring below the eye. It would seem that Hemingway forgot where he had placed the cut earlier in the manuscript. The "sweat salted his eyes" suggests that tears may ensue to clear the eyes; thus, we have blood from the cut, sweat, and tears, alluding to Christ's agony and crucifixion together. Blood flowing from a cut by the eye might also suggest tears of blood, a reference to Luke 22:44, Christ in the garden before the Crucifixion: "And being in agony, he prayed more earnestly; and his sweat was, as it were, great drops of blood falling to the ground." Certainly, Santiago, like Jesus in his agony, is undergoing a mortification of the flesh.

87:17 I'll say a hundred Our Fathers: See entry 64:24–65:1.

87:24 the wire leader: See entry 34:3.

88:10–12 I must hold his pain. . . . Mine does not matter: See entry 84:21–22.

88:21–89:7 He kneeled against the bow. . . . gained. Hemingway's emphasis on the marlin's turns and circling calls attention to the cycle of nature against which the action of the story takes place. Bickford Sylvester explains that Santiago sails north from Cojimar until he catches the marlin. The marlin initially also swims north until tiring, and then swim east with the current. After Santiago kills the fish and sets sail, he seeks to sail southwest (97:21), but, despite the trade winds, the current pushes him somewhat to the east before he can reach Cojimar. Thus, in order to return home, his journey is a large circle, like the circles the marlin swims around Santiago's boat, like the cycles of nature, like life into death and then new life, including Manolin as Santiago's successor, as Parzival replaced Amfortas as the next Fisher King.

Larry Grimes provides an alternative analysis of the circles and circling based on Afro-Caribbean understandings of that cycle, particularly as manifested in the rituals of Palo Monte and art associated with those rituals. Citing the work of Robert Farris Thompson, Grimes sees the camino followed by Santiago, and the great turns of the fish, in African cosmogram shown in Figure 10, Kongo Cosmogram (adapted from a drawing in *Flash of the Spirit* by Robert Farris Thompson).

The diagram pictures a cross whose intersection represents a sacred point on the ground of the dead and under an all-seeing God. The horizontal line separates the dead from the living, with God at the top, the living at the bottom, and water in between. The four circles at the poles of the cross represent the movements of the sun. The diagram also represents Santiago's skiff and the circular movement of the marlin around it. See Thompson 108–9 and Grimes, "Hemingway's Religious Odyssey" 158–59, for the complete argument.

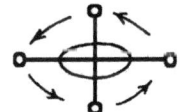

Fig. 10.

89:9 trade wind: See entry 14:6.

89:22 it is a long island: Cuba is indeed a long island, measuring 696 miles (1140 km.) from tip to tip.

90:7–10 pale lavender . . . purple stripes: The fish Santiago has hooked is a blue marlin. Ulanski, who titled his chapter on this fish "The Ultimate Billfish," describes the blue marlin as having a dark blue back, silvery white flanks and belly, and light blue or lavender stripes along its sides (90).

Hemingway caught many blue marlin. His description of them differs slightly from Ulanski's generalized description and Duane Raver's painting (see Color Plate 4), but a marlin can rapidly change aspects of its color, due to iridophores or chromatophores, cells containing pigments that can change color, and light-reflecting skin cells. These changes occur when the fish is excited over prey and also when it is caught and dies. Hemingway described a swimming marlin's tail as "a light, steely lavender" ("Marlin off Cuba," *BL* 57) and wrote that they appear "plum colored" in the water (ibid., 65), much like the purple color Santiago sees. Another fish he describes as "purple-black" (ibid., 63). In his "Out in the Stream: A Cuban Letter" for *Esquire*, he wrote of a marlin's "great blue pectorals . . . and the stripes around him like purple stripes around a brown barrel" (*BL* 173). For the ocean-based viewer, the blue of the water has added to the color of the fish.

90:10–11 **His dorsal fin was down:** Hemingway wrote that, when surface-feeding marlin approach a bait, their dorsal fins are always up: "The minute a marlin sees the bait . . . he raises his dorsal fin" ("Marlin off the Morro," *BL* 141). That may be to increase maneuverability in pursuit of its prey. But raising the dorsal fin implies that, while swimming, the fin is down, so as to reduce drag and increase speed, and Hemingway says as much in the same essay, where he describes a fast-moving fish with both pectoral and dorsal fins tucked close in to the body (139). Here the fish is resisting Santiago's effort to pull it close to his skiff, and having the dorsal fin down does reduce its drag in the water, allowing it more energy—and the fish, too, is tired after pulling the boat for two days—to resist the old man's efforts. Symbolically, the lowered fin, a sail, may also be a lowered flag, signaling the fish's ultimate defeat. Compare 9:12–14: "The sail . . . , furled, it looked like the flag of permanent defeat" (emails from Almeida, Fangue, and Schratwieser).

90:14 **the two gray sucking fish:** Remoras. See entry 14:24 for a description of these fish. In "Marlin off Cuba," Hemingway wrote, "All marlin seem to suffer much from remoras" (78).

91: 6 **too far:** These repetitions of "too far" very subtly echo Hemingway's earlier discussion of Santiago's going "too far" out. See 14:11, and especially 50:17–18, 110:8, 115:12, 116:16, 120:15.

92:14–18 **You are killing me. . . . I do not care who kills who.** The second part of that is not literally true. Santiago does care, and he has invested time, blood, and energy in capturing the marlin. But he recognizes the marlin as a fellow creature, a fellow champion, whom he caught through "trickery": going where the marlin thought it would be safe and hiding a steel hook within fish (see entry 50:14–15). In his exhaustion, he declares that he doesn't care who wins the contest, prefiguring his more serious lapses of confidence, 116:15–16 and 124:4–5.

93:15–17 He took all his pain . . . and put it against the fish's agony: In this searing sentence, Hemingway describes Santiago's ultimate dedication of purpose, neglecting pain, age, and exhaustion, as the human overcomes the equally afflicted fish. It is a triumph, but a temporary one.

94:1 into the fish's side: The Greek acronym for Christ among early followers was *Ichthys, the Greek word for fish*, ΙΧΘΥΣ, standing for Jesus Christ, son of God, the Savior, as noted at entry 35:7 (see Figure 8). Not only does Santiago suffer scourging and stigmata, but the fish also suffers; and here Santiago assumes the role of the Roman centurion, spearing Christ in the side. Hemingway is again insisting on the linkage and holiness of all living things.

94:6 then the fish came alive with his death in him: This phenomenon can be scientifically explained as a last burst of energy, a moment of clarity and peace before death, but science is not what is wanted here. Given its context in 94:3–11, there are apparent references to the crucifixion of Jesus, beginning with "he felt the iron go in," an allusion to the spear thrust into Christ's side. The paradoxical phrase "he came alive, with death in him" has a correspondence with the death of Jesus as the necessary condition of resurrection. Resurrection imagery is reinforced by the phrase "rose high out of the water showing all his great length and width and all his power and beauty" (94:7–8). This image of resurrection is extended in the Santiago's perception that he "seemed to hang in the air above the old man" (94:8–9), as Jesus hung on the cross above those viewing him. Not only do these passages amplify the Christian allegory in *The Old Man and the Sea*, but they also underscore the paradoxical cycle of life/death in the natural order of all things.

94:8 all his power and his beauty: A paraphrase of the doxology of the Lord's Prayer's "his power and glory." Theologically, "glory," "shine," and "beauty" are all synonyms.

94:9 to hang in the air: This unusual occurrence marks the instance as numinous and parallels a similar timeless instance in Faulkner's "The Bear" as Boon kills the bear: "they almost resembled a piece of statuary" (241). Both incidents mark the death of totemic animals. (Compare Rosenfield throughout.)

94:12–13 he could not see well: A late addition to the text, penciled in on the typed manuscript ("The Old Man and the Sea," ms 90, 77), indicating the physical strain the old man is enduring and adding to the constricted vision created by the black spots before his eyes (87:9–10).

94:17 discolouring: This spelling, archaic in American English is used here, along with "colour" at 96:21, for its visual and tonal effect, to associate the fish and the entire event of its death with the ancient and therefore eternal, as is appropriate for a creature associated with Christ (*Ichthys*). The King James Version of the Bible would be one first readers of *The Old Man and the Sea* (1952) were brought up on, so Hemingway could count on their associating spellings like "colour" with the Bible in particular, as well as other icons of antiquity and authority. The "Revised Standard Version" that has largely replaced the King James Version in popular use did not come out until after this work was published. Hemingway uses the "*our*" spelling throughout *The Old Man and the Sea*, for example, "harbours," 25:9.

94:18 red blood from his heart: Blood, of the marlin and of Santiago, as well as the blood-red-appearing plankton, figure prominently throughout the novella. See entries 12:23, 35:7, 52:7, 56:2, and 57:1. The large flow of the marlin's blood provides the spoor that will attract the mako shark, making ironic Santiago's prayers on 65:1–3 to catch the fish—he does, but cannot keep him—and 68:15: "If the sharks come, God pity him and me." The Christology suggested in *The Old Man and the Sea* is paradoxical in nature and reflects the various passages in the Gospels suggesting that those who save their lives shall lose them and vice versa. The shed blood of Christ is the culmination of this paradox, a paradox echoed in Santiago's victory through loss in *The Old Man and the Sea*. See Matt. 10:39, 16:25; Mark 10:8:36; Luke 9:21, 17:33; and John 12:26.

The fish's death, the red blood in the water, echoes the red plankton Santiago sees just before hooking the giant marlin (see entry 35:7).

94:22–23 glimpse of vision: Literally, the statement refers to Santiago's clearing vision from the blind spots he has been seeing (87:9–10), as well as from the sweat salting his eyes and causing tears to cloud his sight and from the strain mentioned at 94:12–13. But "vision" also suggests something more than corporeal; it suggests a mystical view, one that Santiago has held throughout the novella, from seeing the white peaks in his home Canary Islands, to the lions on the beach, to his realization of the dynamic tension in nature's larger order, expressed in such paradoxes as comfortable pain (47:13), killing for kindness (39:1), compassionate killing (asking the female marlin for pardon, 50:8), and life in death (94:6), as well the Christian mystery of eternal life through Christ's death and resurrection. See also the previous entry.

95:9 swamped her: Sank the boat below the surface of the water by filling it with water—doing so would allow a large fish to be landed more easily into the boat, especially by one man. The wooden boat, however, retains its buoyancy and does not sink completely.

95:11 **step the mast:** Prepare for sailing by placing the mast vertically in its hold and then unfurling the sail.

95:18 **I think I felt his heart:** Notice Santiago's concentration on the heart of the fish, here and at 94:18, as well as an earlier passage on turtle hearts, 37:9, and critics' interpretation that his own heart might fail following his exertions at sea (see entry 125:12). Hemingway again insists on the linkage of all living beings.

96:8 **But the fish did not come:** Normally, the old man would be able to pull an average-sized fish toward him with relative ease. Due both to the size of the marlin and to Santiago's weakened physical state, the standard fisherman's approach will not work.

96:22–24 **the fish's eye looked . . . as a saint in a procession:** Both similes point to objects or people linking two levels: the periscope links two separate altitudes, and the saint in procession links the quotidian with the holy. Similarly, Santiago's daily activity of fishing has linked him to a numinous event. These two similes reinforce the physical and spiritual detachment from the marlin that the old man feels upon the death of the fish. They also suggest a residual holiness that lingers beyond, perhaps through, the dead eye. The first simile, the second mirror simile in the novella (the first is at 49:21), stresses a physical distance from the fish created by viewing it through its dead eye—the fish through its death is now in some fashion a refracted rather than an objective presence. Exactly how the fish's eye works as refracting mirrors is obscure, perhaps even numinous. (Beegel links the periscope simile to the submarines of World War II ["Monster of Cojimar" 26]). The second simile in the passage is both more obscure and more complex. The eye of the dead the fish is likened to a saint being processed from its holy shrine. The first level of detachment is the saint's removal from its holy shrine, perhaps related to the removal of all animated life from the fish. A second level of detachment comes in the contrast between the lively crowd forming the procession around the saint and the inanimate figure being processed. The holiness in the midst of the moving procession is still, quiet, inanimate—a mystery of holiness in stillness and death.

PAGES 97 THROUGH 106

97:5–6 If he dresses out . . . at thirty cents a pound: Once the fish is gutted and butchered, it should provide a thousand pounds of marketable meat, which, if sold at thirty cents a pound, would yield a profit of 300 dollars/pesos. (The Cuban peso and the American dollar were valued at par in 1950.) The Cuban national per capita monetary income in 1950 was 304 dollars/pesos annually, making the old man's catch worth a year's salary. Note that this catch confirms Santiago's wish at 16:22 for just such a large fish, and thus the early desire becomes a narrative prefigurement.

97:27 He only needed the feel of the trade wind: Since the trade winds originate in the northeast and blow southwest, the old man could allow them to carry him home with a minimum of navigation. As long as he sailed with the wind, he would continue a straight course southwest, which would bring him back to Cojimar, with some adjustment for the current pushing from the east.

98:1 a spoon: In this case, a bright piece of spoon-shaped metal attached by a swivel to a fishing line above the hook, which twirls to attract fish and is used as artificial bait to lure them.

98:2 and drink for the moisture: It is important in evaluating Santiago's health to realize that he has been working and sweating under the hot sun of the Florida Straits for three days with only a small water bottle and whatever moisture he can gain from the fish he eats. He is, most likely, severely dehydrated.

98:5 small shrimps: There are at least six species of shrimp, all mottled brown in color, found living on the floating Sargassum weed. "Shrimps," with a final "s" as the plural form, is an acceptable spelling, though an infrequent one, one that Hemingway favored in most of his works. For example *SAR* 210, 211; *DIA* 93.

98:21–23 hang motionless in the sky . . . great strangeness: Hemingway's repetition of these descriptors emphasizes the numinous quality of the event, echoing 94:6. Not only is there an emphasis on "strangeness," but this strangeness is experienced as a tactile event although framed between dream ("this had truly happened and was not a dream" [98:18] and "he had thought perhaps it was a dream" [98–19–20]) and vision ("Then he could not see well, although now he saw as well as ever" [99:1–2]). Here numinous experience is presented as something that "truly happened." The image of the fish hanging motionless in the sky is also significant. As a Christ symbol, it suggests the Ascension. And, in an Afro-Cuban religious context, it suggests the ritual passing of the body of a sacrificed animal over a person who seeks healing and harmony in life (Nordel and Ramos 167–86).

99:6–7 **The dark water of the true gulf is the greatest healer that there is:** Because of its high saline content, but the line also contains the essential paradox of the novella: what the sea gives it also takes, and, when it wounds, it also heals.

99:21 **high cumulus clouds:** Indicating clear weather through the night. Compare 61:10 and 61:17.

100:3 **The shark was not an accident:** Harpooning the marlin, piercing its heart as Santiago does, causes the fish to bleed profusely; and, since he cannot boat the fish, it continues to bleed into the water, as the next line indicates. The blood, of course, attracts the shark, and, since Santiago caught the marlin so far off shore, the sharks have ample space and time to devour the old man's catch. Going out far enables Santiago to catch the largest fish he has ever taken, but it also allows the sharks to take it from him. Again, we see the paradox at the heart of nature.

100:3–4 **He had come up from deep down:** Santiago knows that the mako has come up from depths because its rush has developed enough momentum to carry it all the way out of the water.

100:9 **picked up the scent:** Seventy percent of a shark's brain is devoted to the olfactory function, and, from distances of fifty feet or more, the sense of smell is more important than vision in pinpointing prey. The smell organs in the noses of some sharks are able to detect one droplet of blood in one million drops of sea water, according to an article of 11 June 2010 in *The Daily Mail* (dailymail.co.uk/sciencetech/article-1285652/Mystery-sharks-astonishing-sense-smell-solved.html#ixzz3GRFVzG3G; compare Tricas et al. 101).

100:12–13 **He swam fast and hard:** The average mako shark (see next entry) can swim thirty to forty miles per hour.

100:13 **a very big Mako shark:** The mako, or *isurus oxyrinchus*, is generally regarded as the most graceful, beautifully proportioned, and spectacular shark, reaching an

Fig. 11. Mako shark. (Photo by Mark Conlin. Courtesy Southwest Fisheries Science Center NOAA)

average length of twelve feet. (See Figure 11 and Color Plate 5.) It is a favorite of game fishermen because it causes greater than average excitement with its struggles and its tenacious, sometimes violent rejection of being landed and killed. Mako sharks have another distinction: they are warm-blooded sharks.

100:15 **except his jaws:** The teeth of the mako are the deadliest looking of all sharks and are visible without the fish having to open its jaws.

100:21–23 **Inside the closed double lip . . . teeth were slanted inwards:** Generally, only a single row is easily visible and functional at any one time, but sharks do possess six or more rows of replacement teeth that are arrayed behind the first row and move forward individually as teeth are lost. The teeth are slanted inward, barb-like, to prevent prey from escaping.

101:2 **nearly as long as the fingers of the old man:** The teeth of a mako resemble curved knives, being flat on the forward surface and sharply pointed at the tip.

101:4 **a fish built to feed on all fishes in the sea:** Due to the mako shark's great speed (see entry 100:12–13), it can pursue even the fastest billfishes; one of its favorite meals is marlin or swordfish. Its tenacity and vicious teeth make it a match for fish that are much larger.

101:12–13 **The rope was short . . . to lash the fish:** Harpoons are designed with long ropes, one end of which is fastened to the boat. Longer ropes allow a fish to fight and jump without straining the rope to the breaking point. Santiago's harpoon no longer has this flexibility.

101:15 full of resolution but he had little hope: In Hemingway's fiction, major characters persist to achieve a goal despite overwhelming obstacles against them, and we admire them for their courage and determination, characters such as Manuel Garcia in "The Undefeated," Jack Brennan in "Fifty Grand," Jake in his love of Brett in *The Sun Also Rises*, Harry Morgan in *To Have and Have Not*, and Robert Jordan and Pilar against Franco's forces in *For Whom the Bell Tolls*. We admire the determination of these individuals to do what they have set out to do, despite overwhelming odds and even likely defeat. Compare entry 84:21–22 and Baker, *Writer as Artist* 293–94. While pie-in-the-sky hope is certainly not an attribute of Hemingway's characters, it should be noted that Santiago is not without hope. "Little hope" may be part of the mix of courage and determination that pushes characters forward despite overwhelming obstacles. Compare entry 104:24. See also Sylvester, "They Went through This Fiction," throughout and Baker, *Writer as Artist* 273.

101:18–19 I cannot keep him from hitting me: Note the old man's use of the pronoun "me." Santiago does not fear the shark's attacking him, but rather the marlin, a fish with whom he has become closely identified.

101:19 Dentuso: A Cuban derivative of the Spanish adjective *dentudo*, which means possessing large, uneven teeth.

101:20 Bad luck to your mother: An insult, but not the most derogatory of Cuban insults. To quote Cuban journalist Ismael León Almeida, "to make a depreciatory mention of the mother of another person is one of more common offenses between low people here [in Cuba] (email).

102:4–5 the line between his eyes: Where the shark's brain would be. In "On Being Shot Again," an *Esquire* essay from 1935, Hemingway described where to shoot a shark to kill it: "[S]hoot him anywhere along a straight line down the center of his head, flat, running from the tip of his nose to a foot behind his eyes. If you can . . . intersect this line with a line running between his eyes and can hit that place it will kill him dead" (*BL* 198). The title of Hemingway's account refers to the fact that he wounded himself in the legs with a bullet with which he meant to kill a gaffed shark when the gaff broke and struck his hand holding the gun and moving it; the shot ricocheted off brass combing on his boat with bullet fragments going into both legs.

102:16–17 but the shark would not accept it: Once hooked, makos tenaciously resist death, often charging at boats and even jumping into them. They have been known to bite and seriously injure fishermen even after being gaffed and landed: hence, the game fisherman's warning that one can never be too sure of a mako shark's death.

103:6–7 **It was as though he himself were hit:** Santiago's sympathy with the marlin is obvious. See entry 101:18–19. David, in *Islands in the Stream,* similarly identifies with the broadbill he has hooked and fought for hours, saying, "I couldn't tell which was him and which was me" (134).

103:14 **But man is not made for defeat:** Hemingway's much-quoted line about the indomitableness of humanity, again voiced in gendered terms. For Hemingway, victory is not necessarily in success but in effort, in attempting something if not noble then at least worthwhile. Humans will be destroyed, inevitably by death, but that destruction need not signal defeat, as testimony of Santiago's achievement will endure in his fishing community for years and as Hemingway's fiction has endured long beyond his own self-destruction. Compare 84:21. This assertion is central to Nietzsche's philosophy and also attested to in the Christian story of Christ's Passion and in the magico-religious world rituals of Afro-Cuban religion.

103:17–18 **The *dentuso* is cruel and able and strong and intelligent:** This anthropomorphic description of the shark acknowledges its well-tuned survival skills as "cruel" and its high level of adaptability as "intelligent," thus giving the animal more capacity for intentional, premeditated evil than it really has. Analysis of a shark's brain shows that its cerebrum—the section used for memory and rational thinking—is very small, while its cerebellum—the section that controls coordination, reflexes, and instinct—is substantially larger. Since sharks are so well adapted, they are often mistaken for being "intelligent," a term that, when Hemingway wrote the novella, biologists applied only to human beings.

104:6 **sting ray** According to an on-line encyclopedia, "stingrays are a group of rays, which are cartilaginous fish related to sharks. They are classified in the suborder Myliobatoidei of the order *Myliobatiformes* and consist of eight families. . . . A stingray's diet includes small fish, snails, clams, and shrimp, and some other small sea creatures" (https://en.wikipedia.org/wiki/Stingray). See Figure 12 for a picture of a stingray.

104:12–13 **the pattern of what could happen . . . the inner part of the current:** As Santiago worried about what would happen as the warbler that rested on his boat came closer to shore and to land-based hawks awaiting it (55:7), so he knows that there are more sharks waiting to take his prey from him. Foreknowledge, however, does not deter his determination to fight the sharks as they come.

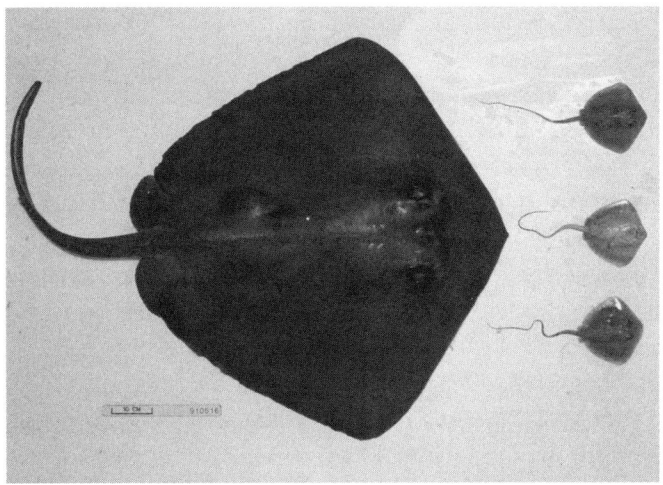

Fig. 12. Bluntnose stingray. (Courtesy Northeast Fisheries Science Center NOAA)

104:18 **sheet of the sail:** A "sheet" is a rope or line attached to the lower corner of the sail that helps maneuver the sail in or out, depending on the direction of the wind.

104:24–105:1 **Besides, I believe it is a sin:** Hope is considered to be a virtue, along with faith and charity (love), and it figures prominently in the Old and New Testaments. In Catholic theology, hope is believed to be necessary for justification and salvation and is an intermediary virtue between faith and charity. See entry at 101:15.

105:9 **there are people who are paid to do it:** That is, priests and lay servants of the church.

105:11 **San Pedro was a fisherman:** San Pedro is the Spanish form of Saint Peter, whom Jesus did encounter fishing, Matt. 4:18; of course, Santiago's namesake, Saint James (Sant Iago) was also a fisherman (Matt. 4:21). See entry 10:9.

105:17–18 **You killed him for pride and because you are a fisherman:** Santiago's use of the term "pride" is ambiguous: he may be referring to either the pride of a hunter such as Orion (see entry 75:1) or the pride of a human who acts outside God's will. In a theological context, pride is viewed as a sin of attitude rather than an act, an attitude that results in a person's assuming that his strengths are self-created, not given by God, and that, with these strengths, he may accomplish great tasks. Catholic theology defines pride as the inordinate desire to excel, when a human being isolates himself from God and the rest of humanity and makes the power of the self absolute or central. So defined, pride is not only a sin, but it is a deadly sin because, in this attitude, one willfully separates self from God. Santiago reflects on pride in the middle of a complex meditation on sin. As he concludes this meditation with this self-accusation, he also qualifies it by affirming that he is a fisherman. Since he considers being a fisherman a gift, a vocation, a calling, and not a job, his pride may be theologically justified. It is good to take pride in God's gifts. Pride, like sin, is a complicated thing. Hemingway lets Santiago end his mediation with a question rather than a conclusion: "If you love him, it is not a sin to kill him. Or is it more?" (105:20–21).

Santiago's self-identification as a fisherman confirms for him a way to earn a living shared with Saints Peter and James, as well as Joe DiMaggio's father. It is a vocation, something for which he feels himself to have been born; see 12:16, 40:2–3, and especially 50:22–23. Fishing defines his life, his attitude toward taking life and feeding not just himself but others with his catch. It is a craft in which he takes great pride, even as that craft diminishes in the face of commercial fishing. He shares this dedication to craft with the bullfighters Manuel Garcia in "The Undefeated" and Finito in *For Whom the Bell Tolls,* who also suffer for their commitment to their chosen careers.

Although Santiago's pride has provided him with much of the extra bursts of strength required to land the fish (see 93:15–16), it has also inspired his desire to venture out so far into the Gulf Stream. His superstitious version of Catholicism causes him to phrase the excesses of pride as a violation of his "luck" (116:15–16). Contrary to this Catholic view is Nietzsche's, which praises the individual confident in his own power, one who does go out far.

105:20 **If you love him, it is not a sin to kill him:** Santiago thinks that perhaps the greatest virtue, love, can outweigh the less charitable killing of the fish, but then wonders whether the act of killing the fish is not, in fact, in direct conflict with the fact that he has loved and respected it. This is, of course, one of the many paradoxes that the novella presents. Compare Beegel, "Thor Heyerdahl's *Kon-Tiki*" 535–36.

105:24–106:1 **He is not a scavenger nor just a moving appetite:** Generally, sharks are opportunistic feeders, eating when they find available prey, whether they are hungry at that time or not. There is no evidence that the mako is less of an opportunist than other types of sharks, but the fact that he is more selective in his choices to begin with (see entry 101:4) may make him seem to be less of a "moving appetite."

106:5 **everything kills everything else:** Hemingway's anti-Romantic, realist attitude: we exist on the planet through the death of others. Compare entries 54:14–15 and 75:4–5. It is also a way for Santiago to justify his profession, especially his killing of the fish he has come to respect and love. As William Cain describes Santiago, "If he is human, it is because he is a killer" (Wagner-Martin 562). The rest of the brief paragraph—"Fishing kills me exactly as it keeps me alive. The boy keeps me alive, he thought. I must not deceive myself too much"—was added in pencil to the typed manuscript (90), adding to Santiago's realistic awareness.

106:11 **He chewed it:** Santiago ingests part of his totemic beast and does so again at 107:2. Originally, this practice was assumed to impart to the eater aspects of the totemic animal. Not only does this connect Santiago with the old religions, since he eats flesh from the Christ fish, but this is also a Eucharistic moment.

106:17–18 **It had backed a little further into the north-east:** The old man observes the next sign of an approaching storm. (See entry 80:15, which describes the first sign.) In a typical easterly wave, just before towering cumuli storm clouds form, the east or northeast trade winds back to the northeast or north.

PAGES 107 THROUGH 119

107:5–6 "Ay," he said aloud. There is no translation for this word: A Spanish phrase dictionary does list the English translation as "oh" or "ouch," but the word carries much broader implications than this. What is concealed here, or only subtly revealed, is that the *galanos* hit at three o'clock on a Friday afternoon, as Jesus died at three o'clock on Good Friday. We know from the baseball lore (entry 17:1–2) that the novella begins on Tuesday, 12 September, and ends on Saturday, 16 September. Santiago killed the marlin at noon on Friday (96:5). The mako attacks one hour later (100:1). Then the *galanos* hit two hours later (107:1). As with the length of line that Manolin carries, and what such weight must mean about Manolin's age and size, Hemingway has carefully included the facts to let us know that this crucifixion reference (as the next entry makes clear) occurs at the reputed time of Jesus's death.

107:7–8 Feeling the nail go through his hand into the wood: A clear reference to a crucifixion, the act of putting a person to death slowly and painfully by nailing or binding him to a wooden cross. Use of such a method ensures that the person will endure long suffering through slow asphyxiation before death, as Jesus did when he was crucified on Mount Calvary (see entry 121:11). This metaphor caps the numerous references to Christ's Passion throughout the book, and Santiago's parallel suffering, making it a very important moment in *The Old Man and the Sea* as a saint's story.

107:9 Galanos: In Cuban Spanish, *galano* is an adjective meaning "elegant" or "fancy" and is applied to oceanic white-tipped sharks (*Carcharhinus longimanus*), a large brown shark with a broadly rounded white-tipped dorsal fin and very long, wide, white-tipped or mottled pectoral fins; the upper lobe of the tail fin is longer than the lower lobe, both white-tipped. They grow to eleven feet in length and weigh four hundred pounds. The oceanic whitetip prefers warm waters, over seventy degrees (F) and has a short and bluntly rounded nose and small circular eyes that have nictitating membranes that rise from the bottom of the eye to cover and protect the eye when feeding (see Castro, Klimley, and Tricas et al.).

Hemingway's description of the "white-tipped wide pectoral fins" (107:23–24) confirms this identification. José Castro, in his book on sharks, says of oceanic

Fig. 13. Oceanic whitetip shark showing its wide shovel mouth and small eyes. (lemga/iStock)

whitetips, "Authors writing in the 1950s called it the most abundant warm-water shark" (440); he continues, it "has been estimated that, since the 1950s, oceanic whitetip sharks have declined by more than 99%." It is now nearing or at endangered-species status, protected in some areas, because its fins are favored for shark-fin soup; its hide is also used for leather; and, because of its scavenging nature, it is also attracted—and caught—by long-line fishers. The shark that once ate more people than any other (see entry at 108:1) is now itself being eaten in large numbers, or rather, its fins are, and the shark, deprived of its fins, is then thrown, alive, back into the water. (Identification from Ismael León Almeida, email; Beegel, "Guide to the Marine Life," 246–47; and Mandel, *Reading Hemingway* 352.)

107:11 **shovel-nosed sharks:** A descriptor of a variety of blunt-nosed sharks and, thus, distinguished from the pointed-nose mako. What are now technically called shovel-nosed sharks, or *Rhinobatos productus,* are a completely different species, very unlike the aggressive oceanic white-tipped sharks that would have attacked Santiago's catch at sea off Cuba. (See Color Plate 6.) Shovel-nosed sharks are actually a species of rays, also called guitarfish, only five feet to five feet, six inches long, are bottom feeders, and are only found in the Pacific. Shovel-headed sharks are bonnet-headed sharks, *Sphyrna tiburo,* found in Cuban waters, but are only two to three feet long, with a maximum size of about five feet, and quite shy. There are over five hundred different species of sharks.

Figure 13 reveals the shovel-nosed aspect of the whitetip, as well as its small eyes. Note the white-tipped dorsal and pectoral fins in Color Plate 6.

107:13–14 **the stupidity of their great hunger:** Sharks are rarely motivated to attack solely to satisfy hunger; since they are opportunistic feeders, they will attack when prey is available. It is less likely that the old man observes physical hunger in these sharks as much as he observes an instinctual and strong desire to consume any prey available, a vicious but nonetheless effective survival skill.

107:16–17 **made the sheet fast and jammed the tiller:** Santiago fastens the line controlling the sail and secures the tiller so that it will not move left or right and thus take the boat off course. He makes these preparations in order to free both his hands for the fight with the sharks.

108:1 **bad smelling scavengers as well as killers:** Whitetips are likely responsible for most human deaths by sharks, the reputation of great whites notwithstanding. A torpedoing of a ship in whitetip-infested waters occurred with the sinking of the British RMS *Nova Scotia* off Natal Province, South Africa, in 1942. Out of 1,052 people on board, 858 people were lost, mostly Italian prisoners from Eritrea being transported to South African prison camps. Many drowned or died of exposure, but many were taken by oceanic whitetip sharks, including many of the dead. Susan Beegel, in her "The Monster of Cojimar," writes of the *Nova Scotia* tragedy: "Rescuers, when they finally arrived, had to club sharks away. Many were oceanic whitetips, the *galanos* of *The Old Man and the Sea,* known for their mobbing behavior" (21).

Closer in time to the composition of the book was the torpedoing and sinking of the cruiser USS *Indianapolis* in July 1945, whose resting place at the bottom of the Pacific has just been located. Again, the oceanic whitetip, the most abundant oceanic shark in the tropical Pacific, was one of the species responsible for many of the deaths attributed to sharks at that time. In one of the accounts of the sinking (Lech 72), the characteristic dorsal fin provided a clue to the identity of the attackers: "The dorsal fin was," José Castro adds, "'almost as white as a sheet of paper' while the body was of darker color. The shark could therefore always be seen because of the visibility of its white-tipped fin in the water" (443). The *Indianapolis* carried 1,197 men aboard; 317 survived four days in the water. Many died of the explosion, wounds, dehydration, and drowning; but many also died from whitetip shark predation. In the movie *Jaws,* Robert Shaw plays Quint, an *Indianapolis* survivor who describes the watery ordeal and thereby his hatred of sharks. (Compare Beegel, "Monster of Cojimar" 22–23.)

One month after Hemingway returned to Cuba in the spring of 1945 after participating in the battle for Hürtgen Forest during World War II, Cojimar fishermen hauled in a seven thousand pound white shark. That monster, plus the shark attacks on sea-adrift sailors from numerous torpedoings in the Gulf of Mexico and the Atlantic just five years before his writing of *The Old Man and the Sea*, are, in Beegel's view, behind the hatred Hemingway gave Santiago for the *galanos*; and the war is also subliminally there in her reading of the novella: "its sharks reminding us that *Old Man* too had its origins in war" ("Monster of Cojimar" 25). She also reminds us that Hemingway wrote this work during the Korean War (30). Beegel continues, "[T]he Sisyphean violence and loss represented by the sharks [are] simply the existential condition of man, something that could only be bravely endured" (31).

108:14 **slitted yellow eyes:** The whitetip has a nictitating membrane that can narrow its eyes, and perhaps that is the slit Hemingway is referring to; but, on a sunny afternoon at 3:00 P.M., which is when the *galanos* attack (see entry 107:5–6), oceanic whitetip sharks' pupils would retract to a vertical, narrow pupil, even without the nictitating membrane. "This pupil narrows to a vertical slit in high light intensities" (Klimley 191).

108:20 **yellow cat-like eyes:** In appearance, the narrow pupil in a yellow eyeball is like a goat's or cat's eye.

109:14–16 **drove the blade between the vertebrae and the brain. . . . he felt the cartilage sever:** Sharks have no bone. The spine and jaws are constructed of cartilage, reinforced with calcium crystals in the jaw, but still just cartilage; they have no ribs.

110:6 **awash:** Level with the surface of the water; washed by the waves, flooded.

110:6–7 **the silver backing of a mirror:** See entries 49:21 and 96:22.

110:8 **I shouldn't have gone out so far, fish:** Since 14:6, Hemingway has insisted that Santiago has ventured out far, that his achievement is due to his willingness to go beyond most of his fellow fishermen, as Nietzsche said was necessary for the autonomous individual, and that his loss is also a consequence of that adventuring spirit.

110:13 **I wish I had a stone for the knife:** That is, to sharpen the knife for the next attack.

111:6 **He was a fish to keep a man all winter:** That is, the marlin, if undamaged, would have been financially profitable and would have sustained Santiago for quite some time. See entry 97:5–6.

111:8–12 **The blood smell from my hands . . . from cramping:** The blood from Santiago's cut hand is negligible in terms of attracting more sharks compared to the copious amounts spilling from the shark-eaten marlin. As noted earlier (12:23), Hemingway has established a blood trope that runs through *The Old Man and the Sea*. The blood trope as deployed in the novella has roots in ancient cultural and religious rituals of the hunt, calls to mind the picture of the Sacred Heart of Jesus in Santiago's hut, and is linked to the Passion of Christ. In this particular passage, the blood trope also reflects sacrificial rituals practiced in Afro-Cuban religions, both Regla Ocha (which is called Santeria in the United States) and Palo Monte (Regla Kongo). Santiago's long bout of bad luck (*salao*—the worst kind [9:6–7]) has come to an end. He has caught the giant marlin and secured it to his skiff. While the old man's skill and tricks have helped him catch the fish, he has also been blessed by the action of two water *orishas* (deities) venerated in Afro-Cuban religion—the sisters Yemaya (ocean *orisha*) and Oshún (river *orisha*). Oshún's prominent role in the story is announced in the painting of the Virgin of Cobre (see Color Plate 3), a possession of Santiago's dead wife. Her color, yellow, appears often and at crucial moments (see entry 16:9 and other references there) in the novella. The great fish, blue-backed itself, stands out boldly from the blue of the sea, Yemaya's color, so the marlin not only bears Christian marks (*Ichthys*), but is also identified with the ocean *orisha*, Yemaya. Together, the water sisters have worked to return the power of the feminine, lost at his wife's death, to Santiago, providing a balance disturbed by that death. (For a similar interpretation, see Beegel, "Santiago and the Eternal Feminine.") Given his change of luck, Santiago, in blood references from page 99 to page 111, makes the requisite blood sacrifice to the *orisha*s for the blessing he has received. This particular blood offering may also "keep the left (hand) from cramping" (see entry 111:11–12, below).

Raúl Villarreal has provided an Afro-Cuban reading of this blood trope in *The Old Man and the Sea*. It should be noted that Villarreal's father, René, who served as Hemingway's majordomo at Finca, Hemingway's Cuban abode, was a high priest in Palo Monte and passed the *fundemento* (core teaching) to his son, Raúl. Villarreal writes, "My father often spoke of Oshún and Yemaya in that one may offer something to Oshún in order to obtain a favor, or especially a deep cleansing to get rid of bad luck or *malocchio*. The offering could be placed in a river that flows to the sea and the sea [would be] able to cleanse anything . . . even the worst of luck, *salao*" (email of 17 Oct. 2015). He also says that he asked his father who he thought were Hemingway's guardian deities; his father replied: "Yemaya, mother, and Oggun, father." For more on Oggun, see entry 111:11–12 below.

111:10–11 There is nothing cut that means anything: The injury to Santiago's hands will heal well and leave no permanent damage.

111:11–12 The bleeding may keep the left from cramping: There is no medical justification for such a statement; nor have we discovered anything in Cuban folk medicine to account for it. Rather, Santiago seems to be making a blood sacrifice for good fortune. (See entry 64:24–65:1.) According to Raúl Villarreal, identified above, Hemingway seems to be following the tradition of the Regla Ocha or Yoruba strain of this Afro-Cuban religion. Says Villarreal:

> Santiago is washing his bleeding hands in the ocean (Yemaya), and she (*la mar*) will heal the wounds and receive the offering of blood (*la ofrenda*). The colors of the marlin are the colors of Yemaya. One can also note that Santiago el Grande is syncretized in the Yoruba religion with Oggun, the male deity of iron, metal (knife, machete, keys), and firearms. (email, 17 Oct. 2015)

Santiago could, however, be offering the sacrifice, not to Yemaya, but to the river *orisha* Oshún (the Gulf Stream is a great blue river). See entry at 35:5.

111:13 Nothing: As the shark attack strips the marlin to bare bones, echoes of the "nada" (nothing) motif, set forth with great clarity in "A Clean Well-Lighted Place," occur in *The Old Man and the Sea*. The nada prayer has roots in the tradition of negative theology articulated by St. John of the Cross and advocates a stripping away of all things to obtain a direct, unmediated encounter with the divine. For a detailed study of Hemingway and negative theology, see Nickel throughout.

111:19 so wide that you could put your head in it: The wide spectrum of food consumed by the whitetip shark, unfortunately including humans, is aided by its massive jaws and broad, serrated teeth.

112:1–3 showing first life-size . . . But he did not even watch it now: Another late addition, penciled into the typescript of the novella ("Old Man and the Sea," manuscript, 90, 96), showing the old man's extreme exhaustion.

112:8–9 I will try it as long as I have . . . the tiller: A reiteration of Santiago's "a man can be destroyed but not defeated." He refuses to accept defeat, fighting against overwhelming odds and, in so doing, demonstrates an unquenchable human spirit. (See also 2 Corinthians: 4–9: "Cast down but not destroyed," KJV.)

112:21 quartering on the scent: "Quartering" means to zigzag back and forth, for the sharks, to track a scent. Here, the scent is so obvious that they need not do so.

114:9 bone: Not actual bone but hardened cartilage. Hemingway's repeated statements of bone (at 113:16 and here) are incorrect, but Santiago is unlikely to know the difference between actual bone and hardened cartilage. See Klimley 52–54.

115:2 **one of the new beaches:** The old man is most likely referring to Playas de Este, east of Havana, including Boca Ciega and Guanabo.

115:3–7 **I hope no one has been worried. . . . I live in a good town.:** Santiago knows that Manolin and others will worry about his extended absence, as the Coast Guard and search planes later indicate (see 124:16); that is, Santiago is part of a larger community, both social and biological—a part of all the life on the ocean.

115:12 **I went too far out:** An admission, perhaps a confession, of his Nietzschean daring, of his striving, of his human compulsion to achieve. One of the eight times Hemingway repeats the "too far out" phrase. Two more will occur at 116:16 and 120:15.

115:14–15 **You do not have that spear on your head for nothing:** The marlin's spear is a good defensive weapon against predators such as sharks. Billfish have also been known to pierce through the sides of boats with their spears, in one case out of anger for a mate who had just been gaffed on board by a fisherman.

116:5 **pain of life:** We are given life through the birth pangs of our mothers, and, when we age, the pain of creaky joints reminds us that we are alive. But more particularly, several earlier lines coalesce in this image of life born from pain and death. This passage refers back to the moment when Santiago harpoons the marlin (93–94), and Hemingway writes, "Then the fish came alive, with his death in him" (94:6). It also looks forward to the image of pain, death, and life contained in Santiago's one syllable cry of "*Ay*, . . . a noise such as a man might make, involuntarily, feeling the nail go through his hands and into the wood" (107:5–8). Both Romantic concepts of the heroic and Christian ones undergird this paradoxical understanding that life, death, pain, and struggle are part of the mystery that is life, natural and eternal.

116:10 **But I am too tired to say them now:** Less a comment on Santiago's lack of religious feeling or obligation than a statement of his complete exhaustion and physical depletion.

116:15–16 **You violated your luck when you went out too far outside:** This sentence is part of a larger reflection on "luck" on 116–17. Indeed, it is part of a much larger trope woven into the whole work. Almost as soon as this thought is entertained, Santiago says aloud, "Don't be silly" (116:17). Santiago is still ready to buy luck, "if there is any place they sell it" (116:19). Given the context of its utterance, the sentence above does not contradict Nietzschean readings of *The Old Man and the Sea*. It does not call Santiago back from his movement "too far outside." The idea of living a small life is entertained and rejected as "silly." Santiago continues to seek (buy, negotiate for) better luck and has not rejected the *orishas* who have blessed him with the luck that landed the marlin.

117:1 **They nearly sold it to you:** We come back to the mysterious "they," forces in the universe that one can propitiate by prayer, which Santiago tries to do, or sacrifice, which he also does. It is tied in with luck, as the next line in the book indicates, and about which we have had many entries, from entries at 10:20 and 10:24 on. Santiago has fished eighty-four days without a marketable fish; he is due for a change in luck, but only if the universe is fair, and Hemingway's universe is never fair; it is replete with disasters to measure the character of the individual to which they befall (see entry 124.4). Playwright Tom Stoppard investigated the same phenomenon, more comically, in *Rosencrantz and Guildenstern Are Dead,* where a tossed coin, instead of coming up roughly equal numbers of heads and tails, constantly comes up heads. Says Guildenstern, "A weaker man might be moved to re-examine his faith, if in nothing else at least in the law of probability" (I, p. 12). Significantly—and Stoppard was a fan and imitator of Hemingway early in his career—they announce the number of consecutive heads at eighty-five: "[E]ighty-five times, one after another. . . . Eighty-five in a row" (14), and this is the eighty-fifth time Santiago has gone out to catch a large fish. He does hook the fish and kill it, after extreme exertion, seemingly proving that his luck has changed for the better; and then the sharks strip him of it, as happens in Hemingway's malignant universe (and Rosencrantz and Guildenstern are killed in theirs). Santiago is destroyed but not defeated, and we admire him—and human courage, to endure and strive.

117:2 **I must not think nonsense:** With this reflection, Santiago confirms the silliness of his previous doubt about the wisdom of sailing far outside the usual limits and confirms his status as an *Übermensch,* as *El Campeón.*

117:18–19 **They will probably hit me again:** "They" are the sharks.

118:4 **their phosphorescence:** See note for 78:18–19.

119:4–5 **It was coppery and sweet . . . for a moment:** Santiago has spit up blood, a minor hemorrhage, thus causing many critics to believe in his soon-to-be-death. See 125:20–21. Carlos Baker (*Writer as Artist* 319) likens the blood taste to vinegar on the sponge given to Jesus as he hung on the cross (Matt. 32:49).

PAGES 120 THROUGH 127

120:15 **I went out too far:** The last of the eight times Hemingway repeats this allusion to Nietzsche and the human need to exceed boundaries.

121.3–9 **the depth of his tiredness:** These lines bring together a doubling of Christ images—the fish (*Ichthys*) and Santiago. Both are presented in extremis. Santiago mirrors Jesus's walk up the hill to Golgotha and his crucifixion. There is mystery, irony, and paradox in the phrase "the depth of his tiredness," since it is from the depths the marlin has come in all its glory providing Santiago with a grand epiphany of pure harmony. In "the depth of his tiredness," the harmony is destroyed. The grand marlin has been reduced to bones.

121:4 **looked back:** Santiago rows facing forward (compare entry 25:16), looking at the challenges ahead. Except in memory, he does not look back, but here he does, looking to see if the skeleton of the marlin is still there, to reconfirm, in his exhaustion, that he really did catch this gigantic fish, that it was not all a painful dream. It is a moment of weakness and lack of confidence, and, in looking back, Santiago is like Orpheus, looking back to see if Eurydice is still following him, thus losing her; and like Lot's wife (Gen. 9), who looks back at Sodom and is transformed into a pillar of salt. The passage also recalls entry 28:3: "No man, having put his hand to the plough, and looking back, is fit for the kingdom of God" (Luke 9:62).

121:10–11 **at the top he fell . . . mast across his shoulder:** Santiago's journey up the hill with the boat's mast on his shoulder recalls Christ's journey to Mount Calvary, bearing the cross to which he would be nailed. During Christ's journey, he too fell a number of times.

121:19 **He had to sit down five times:** This sentence continues to emphasize the physical toll the struggle with the fish has taken on the old man. He is exhausted nearly to the point of collapse. Still, with rests, he summons strength to continue. There are parallels here with Christ's journey to Golgotha as depicted in the Stations of the Cross. Historically, between one and seven falls are attributed to Christ, although the Gospels mention no falls. Today, the Stations of the Cross typically depict three, at the third, seventh, and ninth stations.

122:2–3 **he slept face down on the newspapers . . . the palms of his hands up:** Some critics (e.g., Strauch 198) have suggested that the old man's contact with the papers over the bed springs are a reminder of the daily imperfections of the shore world that Santiago has suffered for in order to keep the flawed human community in contact with nature's eternal values. The posture of the old man resembles that of crucifixion. In addition, his prone position indicates resignation and defeat. Since his hands have been cut and hurt, lying with them palm up would be natural; however, in a small shack like Santiago's *bohio*, one room in its description (15:19), one would expect the bed to be against a wall, not in the middle of the room where there are a table, chair, and cooking area (15:22); thus, lying with his arms straight out would be impossible. Once again, Hemingway is taking fictional license to emphasize Santiago's similarity to Christ.

122:21–22 **He did not care that they saw him crying:** In many societies, crying by males is seen as a sign of weakness; Manolin's free display of emotion would be especially damning in Cuba since machismo is so deeply ingrained in Latin American culture. Obviously, the young man's grief for the old man is profound enough to have overwhelmed any self-consciousness he may have had.

123:12 **Do you want a drink of any kind:** That is, something strong and alcoholic to dull the grief that the proprietor can see has so profoundly affected Manolin. Such a solution would be more macho than tears (see previous entry). This offer of an alcoholic drink also confirms that Manolin is not a ten-year-old boy but a man of twenty-two (see entry 22:11–13).

123:22–23 **to borrow some wood to heat the coffee:** Very few rural dwellings possessed a stove of any kind in prerevolutionary Cuba. Most households cooked on open fires of charcoal or wood. And the fire would have been on the bare, dirt floor of Santiago's *bohio*, the smoke going out the doorless entry and windows, if any. This is another reason that it is unlikely that Santiago would have a bed in the middle of his shack.

124:4 **They beat me:** "They," in Santiago's mind, are the sharks. But, for Hemingway, the universe is malevolent, frequently taking back any prize it has given. This is perhaps best expressed by the title he gave a collection of short stories, *Winner Take Nothing*, and by two passages in his *A Farewell to Arms*:

If people bring so much courage to this world the world has to kill them to break them, so of course it kills them. The world breaks every one and afterward many are strong at the broken places. But those that will not break it kills. (249)

You did not know what it was about. You never had time to learn. They threw you in and told you the rules and the first time they caught you off base they killed you. . . . Stay around and they would kill you. (327)

As in *The Old Man and the Sea,* the same unidentified but malevolent "they" appears to be a force of nature or the universe. Compare 117:1.

124:8 Pedrico: Another unseen friend and supporter of Santiago's like Rogelio (12:8–9), Perico (17:6), and Martin at La Terraza (20:6). The names Perico and Pedrico are both derivatives of Pedro, Peter, a fisherman saint like Saint Iago, Saint James. Pedrico gets the head, a relic, to chop up and use as bait (124:10), to gather more fish, as Saint Peter became a fisher of more men. There is, of course, the possibility, that Hemingway intended Pedrico and Perico to be the same character and misspelled one name. (See entry 17:6, first entry), for, as Jeffrey Herlihy-Mera, writes, in Cuban Spanish, "postvocalic and intervocalic d are often silent" ("He Was Sort of a Joke" 98, fn. 10).

124:11 **the spear:** Santiago gives the spear to Manolin, who "wants it" (124:13). Significantly, this relic of the fish is not a "bill" or a "sword," as in billfish or swordfish, but a "spear." Thus, Manolin becomes the new champion, in the Grail myth story, the inheritor of the spear that Perceval/Parzival saw in the Grail Castle, a white lance, with blood running down it. Behind these objects is the fertility myth where the lance enters the Grail cup, a symbol of human procreation and fertility. Beegel likens Manolin's inheriting the spear as "the passage not only of Santiago's prowess as a fisherman but of a legacy of war from one generation to the next" ("Monster of Cojimar" 31). But if Manolin uses the marlin's spear as the point of his harpoon in the future to dispatch fish or the sharks that prey on his catch, he will continue the paradoxical means of using violence to connect between the human community and mother sea, male penetrating female and creating fruition, perpetuation.

124:15–16 **"Did they search for me? . . . with planes":** We are reminded that Santiago is a part of a community that cares about him, a part of a social group, like the lions he will dream about, and also part of a larger biological one.

125:2 **together again:** This is the beginning of Manolin's revival of Santiago's lost faith in the champion's obligation to nature. It also underscores Manolin's identification as Gawain/Percival/Parzival in this parallel to the Fisher King story. See

Friar and Brinnin 473–75; Sylvester, "Cuban Context" 258, 262; and Sylvester, "They Went through This Fiction," throughout.

125:3 **I am not lucky:** Santiago's declaration of defeat in the play of the universe prepares the way for luck to be revitalized, for harmony to be restored, in community. He has fought long, hard, and alone for three days and come up empty in all senses of the word. The turn from *salao*, the worst kind of bad luck, to luck comes in the lines that follow, as Santiago returns to land and to community, to the boy who has followed him as disciple and initiate, and to the fishing community that values and supports him. "One man alone" (*THHN*) cannot restore luck, but in community, and with the help of the *orishas*, luck and psychic harmony (25:15) can be restored.

125:4–5 **I'll bring the luck with me:** After his long fight with the great fish, as he touches land and begins his trek up the hill toward his shack, furled sail on his shoulder, Santiago loses his grip on that special harmony achieved during his struggle. He and the fish are emptied out. We are at the nadir of *salao*—the lack of all harmony. A revival of luck, harmony and hope begins with this line. It begs a question: what will the boy bring to restore luck? First, himself. Another answer begins four lines down (125:9): "we must get a killing lance," probably a suggestion of the Grail lance and the Crucifixion. The turn of luck is not presented through Christian images of resurrection. The Christian saga in the novella ends with Jesus on the way to Golgotha. The turn of luck is imagined through a disciple and an object and a place associated with Santeria, a religion designed to return good luck. The object: the steel spring leaf blade (125:10–13) that they will prepare—the blade calls up the sword or double-headed axe associated with Oggun, the *orisha* of masculinity and power. His presence will assure the restoration of harmony. The place: Guanabacoa, a center of Santeria practice and the present home of the Guanabacoa Museum: Cult to the Orishas.

125:7 **I do not care:** Manolin is asserting himself, his willingness to defy his biological father and align himself with his spiritual father and mentor, Santiago. It thus marks a sign of maturity and independence for the young man.

125:10–11 **You can make the blade from a spring leaf from an old Ford:** Usually referred to as a "leaf spring," this device predates the coil springs commonly used in cars today. It is made of one or more flat strips of metal, three to five feet in length, a few inches wide, and approximately one-half to one-and-a-half inches thick, which are curved slightly up and clamped together, one above the other. (See Figure 14.) They are heat-treated for strength after being formed.

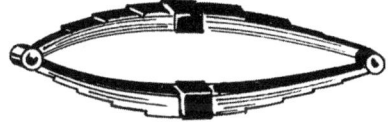

Fig. 14. Leaf spring.

125:11 **We can grind it in Guanabacoa:** Guanabacoa is a city three miles east of Havana, with a population of thirty thousand in 1952, the closest city with services to Cojimar. At that time, it was a manufacturing center with a stone quarry. According to Rene Villarreal, the matador Luis Miguel Dominguin asked Hemingway to direct him to a Santeria priest. Villarreal says Hemingway sent the bullfighter to Guanabacoa because it was an Afro-Cuban religious center. Given that the *orisha* Oggun presides over all things iron, and over knives in particular, it may matter that Santiago wants to grind the lance in Guanabacoa. (Email, Raúl and Rene Villarreal, 1 July 2008).

125:12 **not tempered so it will break:** Tempering steel involves heating it to a certain temperature and then cooling it quickly. Depending on the method and amount of heat used, the process imparts varying degrees of hardness and resilience. Tempering steel actually reduces brittleness, so "not tempering" it would mean that it more likely would break, the opposite meaning Santiago is indicating. This is again an example of purposefully awkward syntax, much like the earlier "The great Sisler's father was never poor and he, the father, was playing in the Big Leagues when he was my age" (22:11–13). Hemingway is again urging readers to look beneath the surface, here, to see the blacksmithing act as a metaphor for experience: to be tempered in life is to experience much and, thus, to be less brittle, to withstand much without breaking, as Santiago has done. Compare *A Farewell to Arms*: "The world breaks every one and afterward many are strong at the broken places" (249).

125:20–21 **my chest was broken:** On 119:3, Santiago could "hardly breathe." In the next line, he tastes his own blood, "coppery and sweet," like the brassy taste that Pilar likens to the smell of death (*FWBT* 252). Some critics have seen as the unstated subject of this dialogue Santiago's belief that he has been fatally injured and that his and Manolin's plan to fish together is parallel to their opening fiction of the nonexistent cast net and food that the two "went through . . . every day" (16:17 and corresponding entry 16:17–18). See Sylvester, "They Went through This Fiction," throughout. Dr. Ronald E. Drusin writes that Santiago's dehydration reduced his blood volume, resulting in a concentration of red blood cells making his blood more viscous and thus more likely to clot, a thrombosis. The combination of spitting up blood and feeling "something in [his] chest was broken" after the fierce battle with the sharks is, according to Dr. Drusin,

> compatible with a man experiencing a myocardial infarction or heart attack. With enough damage to the left ventricle, the main pumping chamber of the heart, to produce acute congestive heart failure, pulmonary edema, in which the heart cannot empty efficiently, the non-ejected blood raises blood pressure in the left ventricle, left atrium, and lungs. The capillary pressure may be so high that some capillar-

ies may rupture yielding small amounts of blood into the alveoli. The patient feels suddenly very short of breath with blood stained foamy material rising into the mouth. As the acute phase diminished, this fluid may be reabsorbed and go away. The heart, however, remains damaged and the patient may experience shortness of breath with walking and other exertion. His need to stop as he walks home carrying the mast may be "stations of the cross" but may be explained by his exhaustion and shortness of breath. Arrhythmias may produce falling/fainting as happened as he began to walk home from the boat. As the marlin died from the harpoon to his heart, I believe the ordeal had injured Santiago's heart, an injury from which he was unlikely to recover and would have prevented him from fishing again. His death in a few days or weeks would be likely. (email of July 2002)

Of course, for a dehydrated man in his seventies who has slept little for the last three days and has just undergone a day and a night of extreme physical exertion, falling several times while carrying a mast would be quite likely, even without a heart attack. While Dr. Drusin provides an excellent medical analysis for Santiago's condition and probable outcomes, readers must remember also that Santiago is *El Campeón* and has in the past, at least as he remembers it, accomplished superhuman feasts. Santiago, as *El Campeón,* may fish again and land an ever-bigger fish. Philip Young writes that Santiago, at the novella's end, "falls asleep to fish again another day" (123); Joseph Waldmeir feels that the "immanence of death for the sacrificer [Santiago] as well as for the sacrificed [the marlin] . . . are made clear at the climax of the struggle" (quoted in Weeks 167); Bickford Sylvester writes that "Santiago's crucifixion must end as did Christ's—in death" ("They Went through This Fiction" 476), and "He will die. That is why the boy is 'crying again'" ("Hemingway's Extended Vision" 135); Baker indicates that Santiago "falls into the deep sleep of renewal, of diurnal resurrection" (*Writer as Artist* 320). Even with all these critical reactions, readers must determine for themselves whether Santiago's "We must get a good killing lance" and "We can grind it at Guanabacoa" are statements of shared purpose of two who will fish again or a polite fiction. Again, Hemingway provides the clues and leaves interpretation to the aware reader.

126:22–23 **just garbage:** Both literal and ironic, for the skeleton has proven Santiago's prowess and re-established his status among his friends and with the other Cojimar fishermen. The bones are indeed relics of his struggle and, as such, connect to the relics of that other Saint Iago, Saint James, seaborne and buried at Compostela, Spain, and other Christian relics, including the seaborne statue of the Virgin, at Santiago, Cuba, visited by Pope Francis in September 2015.

In Afro-Cuban religion, after a blood sacrifice is offered, the animal is passed over the body of the person seeking cleansing and balance; then, the carcass of the sacrificed animal must be discarded. The most common place of discard is a garbage can. The debris in the water next to the Terrace serves that role. The sacrifice that has restored Santiago's balance and luck has been completed, the carcass disposed. (See Grimes, *Hemingway's Religious Odyssey* 160.)

126:23 **the tide:** The second line of the novella mentions the Gulf Stream, which flows in a great circle from Africa to North America and back again (see Figure 5). Santiago sails north from Cojimar, is pulled northwest by the marlin until it tires, then east with the current, and finally southwest back to home, describing an irregular circle. The tide flows in and out at regular intervals. Santiago has sailed out of Cojimar and back for years of his life, more circles and cycles. All these patterns, together with life and death, success and failure, youth and age, are represented in this work and anticipated by the image in Hemingway's short story "Indian Camp," where young Nick, who has just witnessed birth and death, sees a bass making a circle in the water (*SS* 95).

127:1 **Tiburon:** Spanish for shark. The head has been cut off and given to Pedrico and the spear to Manolin, leaving only the skeleton of the ribs and tail, adding to the tourist's misperception. The reader's awareness of the tourist's ignorance, especially that sharks have no ribs, comes from having been introduced throughout the novella to Santiago and his plight; and, through sharing these, the reader comes to share his values and disappointment in those that do not, like the unadventurous man with whom Manolin fishes, his commercially minded parents, and the equally commercially minded young fishermen. Thus, Hemingway ends the novella on an ironic note that separates the knowledgeable from the ignorant, the biologically aware craftsman from those commercially minded, the informed reader from all others.

WORKS CITED

Acevedo-Guttierez, Alejandro. Biologist, Western Washington University. E-mail to Peter L. Hays, 9 Apr. 2015.
Almeida, León Ismael. Cuban journalist. E-mails to Hays, 2015, 2016, and 2017.
Apseloff, Lynn Susan. "Another Inconsistency in *OMS*." *The Hemingway Newsletter*, no.22, June 1991.
Backman, Melvin. "The Matador and the Crucified." *Modern Fiction Studies*, vol. 1, no. 3, Aug. 1955, pp. 1–10; reprinted in Baker, *Critiques*, 135–43.
Baker, Carlos. *Ernest Hemingway: Critiques of Four Major Novels*. Scribner's, 1962.
———. *Ernest Hemingway: A Life Story*. Scribner's, 1969.
———. *Hemingway: The Writer as Artist*. 1952. Scribner's, 1969.
Barbour, James, and Robert Sattelmeyer. "Baseball and Baseball Talk in *The Old Man and the Sea*." *Fitzgerald-Hemingway Annual 1975*, edited by Matthew Broccoli and C. E. Frazer Clark, Microcard Edition Books, 1976, pp. 281–87.
Beegel, Susan. "Eye and Heart: Hemingway's Education as a Naturalist." Wagner-Martin, *Historical Guide*, pp. 353–92.
———. "A Guide to the Marine Life in Ernest Hemingway's *The Old Man and the Sea*." *Resources for American Literary Study*, vol. 30, 2006, pp. 236–315.
———. "The Monster of Cojimar: A Meditation on Hemingway, Sharks, and War." *The Hemingway Review*, vol. 34, no. 2, Spring 2015, pp. 9–35.
———. "Santiago and the Eternal Feminine: Gendering La Mar in *The Old Man and the Sea*." Broer and Holland, pp.131–56.
———. "Thor Heyerdahl's *Kon-Tiki* and Hemingway's Return to Primitivism in *The Old Man and the Sea*." Wagner-Martin, *Eight Decades*, pp. 514–51.
Bellegarde-Smith, Patrick, editor. *Fragments of Bone: Neo-African Religions in a New World*. U Illinois P, 2005.
Bender, Bert. *Sea Brothers: The Tradition of American Sea Fiction from* Moby Dick *to the Present*. U of Pennsylvania P, 1988.
Bergson, Henri. *Matter and Memory*. Translated by N. M. Paul and W. S. Palmer. Zone Books, 1988.
Bianchi, Martha Dickinson, and Alfred Leete Hampson, editors. *Emily Dickinson*. Little and Brown, 1952.
Bingham, Brian. Biologist, Shannon Point Marine Center, Western Washington University. E-mail to Bickford Sylvester, July 2002.
Brandon, George. *Santeria from Africa to the New World: The Dead Sell Memories*. Indiana UP, 1993.

Brasch, James D., and Joseph Sigman. *Hemingway's Library: A Composite Record.* Garland, 1981.

Brenner, Gerry. *The Old Man and the Sea: The Story of a Common Man.* Twayne, 1991.

Broadus, R. N. "The New Record Set by Hemingway's Old Man." *N&Q,* vol. 10, April 1963, pp. 152–53.

Broecker, Wallace. Newberry Professor of Geology, Lamont-Doherty Earth Observatory, Columbia University. Email to Sylvester, July 1999.

Broer, Lawrence R., and Gloria Holland, editors. *Hemingway and Women: Female Critics and the Female Voice.* U Alabama P, 2002.

Burhans, Clinton. "The Old Man and the Sea: Hemingway's Tragic Vision of Man." *American Literature,* vol. 31, Jan. 1960, pp. 446–55; reprinted in Baker, *Critiques,* pp. 150–55, and Jobes, pp.72–80.

Burns, Ken, and Geoffrey Ward. *Baseball: An Illustrated History.* Knopf, 1994.

Burwell, Rose Marie. *Hemingway: The Postwar Years and the Posthumous Novels.* Cambridge UP, 1966.

Cain, William. "Death Sentences: Rereading *The Old Man and the Sea.*" *The Sewanee Review,* vol. 114, no.1, 2006, pp. 112–25; reprinted in Wagner-Martin, *Eight Decades,* pp. 553–67.

Castro, José I. *The Sharks of North America.* Oxford UP, 2011.

Churchill, Dean. Assistant professor of meteorology, University of Washington; formerly meteorologist, NOAA, Miami. E-mails to Sylvester, Aug. 2002.

Cirino, Mark, and Mark Ott, editors. *Ernest Hemingway and the Geography of Memory.* Kent State UP, 2010.

Conrad, Joseph. "Youth." *The Portable Conrad,* edited by Morton Dauwen Zabel, Viking Press, 1963.

Cox, William. President, International Arm Wrestling Federation. E-mail to Sylvester, July 2002.

Cruz, Mary. *Cuba y hemingway en gran río de azul.* Unión de Escritores y Artistes de Cuba, 1981. Translation of excerpts in text by Mary Delpino.

De Espinosa, Alonzo. *The Guanches of Tenerife: The Holy Image of Our Lady of Candelaria and the Spanish Conquest and Settlement.* Kraus Reprint, 1972. (Seville edition, 1594, translated and published by the Hukluyt Society, 1907. Reproduced by permission of the Hakluyt Society.)

de Pourtalès, Guy. *Nietzsche en Italie.* Grasset, 1929.

DeRojas, Alma. "'I am not religious . . . But . . .': The Virgin of Cobre and Cuban Catholicism *a mi propria manera.*" Grimes and Sylvester, pp. 133–49.

DeVanas, Andrew. Meteorologist, NOAA, Key West. E-mail to Sylvester, Sept. 2002.

Donaldson, Scott. *By Force of Will: The Life and Art of Ernest Hemingway.* Viking, 1977.

Drusin, Ronald E. M. D. Cardiologist, Rolf H. Scholdager Professor, and associate dean of education, Columbia School of Medicine; chief cardiologist, Heart Transplant Unit, Columbia Presbyterian Hospital. E-mail to Sylvester, July 2002.

Dudzinski, Kathleen. Biologist, Dolphin Communication Project. E-mail to Hays, 10 Apr. 2015.

Eckert, Scott. Senior research biologist, Hubbs Seaworld Research Institute. E-mail to Sylvester, Mar. 2000.

Ellis, Richard. *The Empty Ocean: Plundering the World's Marine Life.* Island Press/Shearwater Books, 2003.

Erdman, Donald S. "Spawning Cycle, Sex Ratio and Weights of Blue Marlin off Puerto Rico and the Virgin Islands." *Transactions of the American Fisheries Society,* vol. 97, 1968, pp. 31–137.

Fangue, Nann A. Associate professor and master adviser, Department of Wildlife, Fish and Conservation Biology, University of California Davis. E-mail to Hays, 25 July 2015.

Farrington, S. Kip, Jr. *Fishing with Hemingway and Glassell*. David McKay, 1971.

Faulkner, William. "The Bear." *Go Down, Moses*. Modern Library, 1955, pp. 191–331.

———. "Review of *The Old Man and the Sea*." *Shenandoah*, vol. 3, Autumn 1952, p. 55.

Fergusson, Erna. *Cuba*. Alfred Knopf, 1946.

Fiedler, Leslie. *An End to Innocence: Essays on Culture and Politics*. Beacon Press, 1952.

———. *Waiting for the End: The American Literary Scene from Hemingway to Baldwin*. Stein & Day, 1964.

Flora, Joseph, M. *Reading Hemingway's* Men without Women. Kent State UP, 2008.

Flores-Pena, Ysanur, and Roberta J. Evanchuk. *Santeria Garments and Altars*. UP of Mississippi, 1994.

Friar, Kimon, and John Malcolm Brinnin, editors. *Modern Poetry: American and British*. Appleton-Century-Crofts, 1951.

Friedman, Norman. *Form and Meaning in Fiction*. U of Georgia P, 1975.

Gomez de la Maza, Federico. "Peces cubanos de corzo." *Revista de Agricultura, La Habana*, vol. 19, no. 4, 1936, pp. 51–61.

Gomez de la Maza, Federico, and Mario Sánchez Roig. "Las agujas y su pesca en nuestros mares." *Mar y Pesca*, April 1957, pp. 22–24.

Gonzalez-Wippler, Migene. *Santeria: African Magic in Latin America*. Julian Press., 1973.

Grimes, Larry E. E-mails to Sylvester, Apr. 2002–Apr. 2003.

———. "'Bad Luck or No Luck at All': Religion, Magic and Chance." Knott, pp. 201–11.

———. "Hemingway's Religious Odyssey: The Afro-Cuban Connection in Two Stories and *The Old Man and the Sea*." Grimes and Sylvester, pp. 150–64.

———. "Lions on the Beach: Dream, Place and Memory in *The Old Man and the Sea*." Cirino and Ott, pp. 57–66.

Grimes, Larry E., and Bickford Sylvester, editors. *Hemingway, Cuba, and the Cuban Works*. Kent State UP, 2014.

Gurko, Leo. "The Heroic Impulse in the Old Man and the Sea." *English Journal*, vol. 44, no. 7 1955, pp. 11–15; reprinted in Jobes, pp. 64–71.

Hamilton, Edith. 1940. *Mythology*. Mentor, 1969.

Hays, Peter. "Exchange Between Rivals: Faulkner's Influence on *The Old Man and the Sea*." Nagel, pp. 147–164.

Hemingway, Ernest. *Across the River and into the Trees*. New York: Scribner's, 1950

———. *By-Line: Ernest Hemingway*. Edited by William White. Scribner's, 1967. Hereafter *BL*.

———. Correspondence with Robert Morgan Brown, 14 July 1954. Collection at the Humanities Research Center, University of Texas, Austin.

———. *Death in the Afternoon*. Scribner's, 1932.

———. *Ernest Hemingway: Selected Letters, 1917–1961*. Edited by Carlos Baker. Scribner's, 1981.

———. *A Farewell to Arms*. Scribner's, 1929.

———. Fishing Log, the Hemingway Collection, box 88, John F. Kennedy Library, Boston.

———. *The Garden of Eden*. Scribner's, 1986.

———. "The Great Blue River." *Holiday*, July 1949, pp. 60–63, 95–97; reprinted in *BL*, pp. 403–16.

———. *Green Hills of Africa*. Scribner's, 1935.

———. "Interview." *Writers at Work: The* Paris Review *Interviews, Second Series*, edited and interviewed by George Plimpton, Viking Press, 1963, pp. 214–39.

———. *Islands in the Stream.* Scribner's, 1970.

———. "Marlin off Cuba." *American Big-Game Fishing,* edited by Eugene V. Connett, Derrydale, 1993, pp. 55–81.

———. "Marlin off the Morro: A Cuban Letter." *Esquire,* Autumn 1933, pp. 8+; reprinted in *BL,* pp. 137–43.

———. *A Moveable Feast.* Scribner's, 1964.

———. Nobel Prize acceptance speech, 10 Dec. 1954. nobelprize.org/nobel_prizes/literature/laureates/1954/hemingway-speech.html. Accessed 11 Aug. 2017.

———. "On Being Shot Again: A Gulf Stream Letter," *Esquire,* June 1935, pp. 25, 156–57; reprinted in *BL,* pp. 198–204.

———. "On the Blue Water: A Gulf Stream Letter. *Esquire,* Apr. 1936, pp. 31, 184–85; reprinted in *BL,* pp. 236–44.

———. *The Old Man and the Sea.* 1952. Scribner's, 1995.

———. "The Old Man and the Sea," manuscript, the Hemingway Collection, box 90, John F. Kennedy Library, Boston.

———. "Out in the Stream: A Cuban Letter." *Esquire,* Aug. 1934, pp. 19, 156, 158; reprinted in *BL,* 172–78.

———. *The Short Stories of Ernest Hemingway.* 1938. Scribner's, 1995.

———. "The Snows of Kilimanjaro." *The Short Stories,* pp. 52–77.

———. *The Sun Also Rises.* Scribner's, 1926.

———. "There She Breaches! Or Moby Dick off the Morro." *Esquire,* May 1936, pp. 35, 203–5; reprinted in *BL,* pp. 245–56.

———. *To Have and Have Not.* Scribner's, 1937.

Hemingway, Gregory H. *Papa: A Personal Memoir.* Houghton Mifflin, 1976.

Herbermann, Charles George, et al., editors. *The Catholic Encyclopedia IV.* Appleton, 1907–12, p. 516.

Herlihy[-Mera], Jeffrey. "'Eyes the Same Color as the Sea': Santiago's Expatriation from Spain and Ethnic Otherness in *The Old Man and the Sea.*" *The Hemingway Review,* vol. 28, no. 2, 2009, pp. 25–44.

Herlihy-Mera, Jeffrey "'He Was Sort of a Joke, In Fact': Ernest Hemingway in Spain." *The Hemingway Review* 31, no. 2, 2012, pp. 84–100.

———. "Hemingway's Cuban English." *Lingua Franca* [blog]. *The Chronicle of Higher Education,* 17 July 2017. http://www.chronicle.com/blogs/linguafranca/2017/07/20/hemingways-cuban-english/. Accessed 21 Aug. 2017.

Hicks, David. World champion arm-wrestler. Communication with Sylvester, July 2002.

Highet, Gilbert. Review of *The Old Man and the Sea. Harper's,* Oct. 1952: 102+.

Hobbs, Ronald, M.D. E-mails to Sylvester, June 2002.

Hotchner, A. E. *Papa Hemingway: A Personal Memoir.* Random House, 1966.

Hovey, Richard. *Hemingway: The Inward Terrain.* U of Washington P, 1968.

Huntley, Paula. *The Hemingway Book Club of Kosovo.* Tarcher/Putnam, 2003.

Hurley, C. Harold. *Hemingway's Debt to Baseball in* The Old Man and the Sea. Mellon, 1992.

Jobes, Katharine T., editor. *Twentieth-Century Interpretations of* The Old Man and the Sea: *A Collection of Critical Essays.* Prentice Hall, 1968.

Johnson, Kenneth G. "The Star in Hemingway's *The Old Man and the Sea.*" *American Literature,* vol. 42, no. 3, 1970, pp. 388–91.

Keltner, John. Ophthalmology Department at UC Davis Medical Center. 10 and 11 Aug. 2015, email to Hays.

Killinger, John. *Hemingway and the Dead Gods: A Study in Existentialism*. U of Kentucky P, 1960.

Kim, Esther. Ophthalmology Department at UC Davis Medical Center. E-mails to Hays, 23 and 25 Feb. 2016.

Kipling, Rudyard. *Rewards and Fairies*. Macmillan, 1910.

Kirkconnell, A., G. E. Wallace, and O. H. Garrido. "Notes on the Status and Distribution of the Swainson's Warbler in Cuba." *The Wilson Bulletin*, no. 108, pp.175–78.

Klimley, A. Peter. *The Biology of Sharks and Rays*. U of Chicago P, 2013.

Knott, Toni D., editor. *One Man Alone: Hemingway and* To Have and Have Not. UP of America, 1999.

Larson, Kelli. "Trolling the Deep Waters: Hemingway's Cuban Fiction and the Critics." Grimes and Sylvester, pp. 263–354.

Lech, Raymond B. *All the Drowned Sailors: Cover-Up of America's Greatest Wartime Disaster at Sea, Sinking of the Indianapolis with the Loss of 880 Lives because of the Incompetence of Admirals, Officers, and Gentlemen*. Stein and Day, 1982.

Longmire, Samuel E. "Hemingway's Praise of Dick Sisler in *The Old Man and the Sea*." *American Literature*, vol. 42, 1970, pp. 96–98.

Losada, Luis A. "George Sisler, Manolin's Age, and Hemingway's Use of Baseball." *Hemingway Review*, vol. 14, no. 1, 1994, pp. 79–83.

Losch, Paul S. Operations librarian for the Latin American Collection, Smathers Library, University of Florida. E-mail to Hays, 19 Aug. 2016.

Love, Glen A. "Hemingway's Indian Virtues: An Ecological Consideration." *Western American Literature*, vol. 22, 1987, pp. 202–13.

Lynn, Kenneth S. *Hemingway*. Simon and Schuster, 1987.

MacDonald, Dwight. "Ernest Hemingway." *Encounter*, Jan. 1962; reprinted in *Against the American Grain*, Random House, 1962, 167–78.

Mandel, Miriam B. "A Lifetime of Flower Narratives: Letting the Silenced Voice Speak." Broer and Holland, pp. 239–55, n. 313–15.

———. *Reading Ernest Hemingway: The Facts in the Fictions*. Scarecrow Press, 1995.

Mather. Charles O. *Billfish: Marlin, Broadbill, Sailfish*. Saltaire Publishing, 1976.

Melville, Herman. *Moby-Dick, or the Whale*, edited by Alfred Kazin, Houghton Mifflin, 1956.

Meyers, Jeffrey. *Hemingway: A Biography*. Harper & Row, 1985.

———. *Hemingway: The Critical Heritage*. Routledge & Kegan Paul, 1982.

Muir, Edwin. "Review of *The Old Man and the Sea*." *The Observer*, 7 Sept. 1952, p. 7.

Murphy, Joseph M. *Santeria: African Spirits in America*. Beacon Press, 1993.

Myers, Ransom A., and Boris Worm. "Rapid Depletion of Predator Fish Communities." *Nature*, 15 May 2003, pp. 280–83.

Nagel, James, editor. *Ernest Hemingway: The Writer in Context*. U Wisconsin P, 1984.

Nelson, Lowry. *Rural Cuba*. Octagon, 1970.

Nickel, Matthew. *Hemingway's Dark Night: Catholic Influences and Intertextualities in Work of Ernest Hemingway*. New Street Communications, 2013.

Nietzsche, Friedrich. *The Birth of Tragedy* and *The Genealogy of Morals*, translated by Francis Golffing, Doubleday Anchor, 1956.

Nordel, Roberto, and Miguel "Willie" Ramos, "Let the Power Flow: Ebo as Healing Mechanism in Lukimi Orisha Worship." Bellegarde-Smith, pp. 167–86.

O'Hara, Dr. Mary. Ophthalmology Department of UC Davis Medical Center. E-mail to Hays, 11 Aug. 2015.

Oldsey, Bernard. *Hemingway's Hidden Craft: The Writing of* A Farewell to Arms. Pennsylvania State UP, 1979.

Ott, Mark. *A Sea of Change: Ernest Hemingway and the Gulf Stream, a Contextual Biography.* Kent State UP, 2008.

Park, Susanna. Ophthalmology Department of UC Davis Medical Center. E-mail to Hays, 11 Aug. 2015.

Peel, Ellen. President, Billfish Foundation. E-mail to Sylvester, July 2002.

Pinkney, Rick. President, Nova Scotia Arm Wrestling Association. E-mail to Sylvester, July 2002.

Prince, Eric. Chief, Migratory Fishing Biology Branch, NOAA, U. S. Dept. of Commerce, Miami. E-mail to Sylvester, Oct. 2002.

Quammen, David. *Monsters of God: The Man-eating Predator in the Jungles of History and the Mind.* Hutchinson, 2004.

Quirk, Father Kevin. Canon lawyer for the Catholic Diocese of West Virginia. E-mail to Sylvester, July 2002 and Feb. 2003.

Reynolds, Michael S. *Hemingway: The Final Years.* Norton, 1999.

———. *Hemingway's Reading, 1910–1940: An Inventory.* Princeton UP, 1981.

———. *The Young Hemingway.* Basil Blackwell, 1986.

Richert, Scott P. "The Five Types of Prayers." *ThoughtCo.* 29 May 2017. http://catholicism.about.com/od/prayers/tp/Types_of_Prayer.htm. Accessed 11 Aug. 2017.

Rosenfield, Claire. "New Worlds, Old Myths." Jobes, pp. 41–55.

Ross, Lillian. *Portrait of Hemingway.* Simon and Schuster, 1961. "Afterword" available only on Kindle.

Roth, James. Curator, the Hemingway Collection, JFK Library. E-mail to Sylvester, Aug. 2003.

"Saintes Maries de la Mer, France." https://sacredsites.com/europe/france/saintes_marie_de_la_mer.html. Accessed 11 Aug. 2017.

Schatman, Ron. Atlantic blue marlin record holder, Miami charter company owner. E-mail to Sylvester, June 1992, July 2002, Aug. 2003.

Schorer, Mark. "With Grace under Pressure." *New Republic,* Oct. 6, 1952, pp. 19–20.

Schratwieser, Jason. International Gamefish Association. E-mail to Hays, 10 July 2015.

Schwab, Ivan R. Ophthalmology Department of UC Davis Medical Center. E-mail to Hays, 11 Aug. 2015.

Sisler, Dick. Letters to Sylvester, Oct. 1989, Nov. 1992.

Skorupa, Joseph. "Debunking Hemingway's Marlin Theories." *Popular Mechanics,* Oct. 1989, p. 44.

Smith, Chuck. Technical consultant, Samson Rope Technologies. E-mail to Sylvester, May 2002.

Starkie, Walter. *The Road to Santiago.* U of California P, 1965.

Steinessen, Sarah. Biologist, NOAA. E-mail to Hays, 13 Apr. 2015.

Stephens, Robert O., editor. *Ernest Hemingway: The Critical Reception.* Burt Franklin, 1977.

Stewart, Robert H. Professor of oceanography, Texas A and M Univ. E-mail to Sylvester, Aug. 2002.

Stoneback, H. R. "Hemingway and the Camargue: Van Gogh's Bedroom, the "Gypsy" Pilgrimage, Saint-Louis, the Holy Marys, Mireio, Mistral, Mithra, and Montherlant." *North Dakota Quarterly*, vol. 66, no. 2, 1999, pp. 164–95.

———. "In the Nominal Country of the Bogus: Hemingway's Catholicism and the Biographies." *Hemingway: Essays of Reassessment,* edited by Frank Scafella, Oxford UP, 1991, pp. 105–40.

———. "'You Know the Name Is No Accident': Hemingway and the Matter of Santiago." Grimes and Sylvester, pp. 165–79.

Stoppard, Tom. *Rosencrantz and Guildenstern Are Dead.* Grove Press, 1967.

Strauch, Eduard. *Beyond Literary Theory: Literature as a Search for the Meaning of Human Destiny.* UP of America, 2001.

Sylvester, Bickford. "The Cuban Context of *The Old Man and the Sea.*" *The Cambridge Companion to Hemingway,* edited by Scott Donaldson, Cambridge UP, 1996, pp. 243–68.

———. "Hemingway's Extended Vision: *The Old Man and the Sea.*" *PMLA,* vol. 81, no. 1, 1966, pp. 130–38; reprinted in Jobes, 81–96.

———. "Hemingway's Italian Waste Land: The Complex Unity of 'Out of Season.'" *Hemingway's Neglected Short Fiction: New Perspectives,* edited by Susan Beegel, UMI Research P, 1989, pp. 75–98.

———. "'They Went through This Fiction Every Day': Informed Illusion in *The Old Man and the Sea.*" *Modern Fiction Studies,* vol. 12, no. 4, 1966, pp. 473–76.

Taylor, Charles. *The Old Man and the Sea:* A Nietzschean Tragedy." *The Dalhousie Review,* vol. 61, no. 4, 1981, pp. 631–43.

Thompson, Robert Farris. *Flash of the Spirit: African and Afro-American Art and Philosophy.* Vintage, 1984.

Thompson, Stith. *Motif Index to Folk Literature: A Classification of Narrative Elements in Folktales, Ballads, Myths, Fables, Mediaeval Romances, Exempla, Fabliaux, Jestbooks, and Local Legends.* Indiana UP, 1989.

Thoreau, Henry David. *A Week on the Concord and Merrimac Rivers.* U of Michigan Library, 2009.

Toynbee, Phillip. "*The Old Man and the Sea.*" *Encounter,* 17 Oct. 1961, p. 87.

Tricas, Timothy C., et al. *Sharks and Rays.* Weldon Owen, 1977.

Tyack, Peter. Senior scientist, Woods Hole Oceanographic Institute. E-mail to Hays, 10 Apr. 2015.

Tyler, Lisa. *Student Companion to Ernest Hemingway.* Greenwood Press, 2002.

Ulanski, Stan. *The Billfish Story.* U of Georgia P, 2013.

Unterecker, John. *A Reader's Guide to William Butler Yeats.* Noonday Press, 1959.

Valenti, Patricia. *Understanding* The Old Man and the Sea: *A Student Casebook to Issues, Sources, and Historical Documents.* Greenwood Press, 2002.

Vergano, Dan. "'No Place to Hide': Damage to Large Species Might Be Permanent." *USA Today,* 15 May 2003, p.12D.

Villarreal, Raúl. E-mail LG, 17 Oct. 2015.

Villarreal, Raúl, and Rene Villarreal. E-mail to Sylvester, 1 July 2008.

Villarreal, Rene. E-mail to Grimes, 1 July 2008.

["The Virgin of Cobre."] *Enciclopedia Universal Ilustrada: Europeo Americana,* vol. 13. Espasa-Calpe, S.A., 1908, p. 1090.

Wagner-Martin, Linda, editor. *A Historical Guide to Ernest Hemingway.* Oxford UP, 2000.

———. *Hemingway: Eight Decades of Criticism.* Michigan State UP, 2009.

Weeks, Robert P. "Fakery in *The Old Man and the Sea*." *College English,* vol. 24, 1962, pp. 188–92.

Wells, Arvin R. "A Ritual of Transfiguration: *The Old Man and the Sea.*" *The University Review,* vol. 30, 1963, pp. 95–101.

Wilkes, R. Jeffrey. Professor of physics, University of Washington. E-mail to Sylvester, June 2002.

Williams, Wirt. *The Tragic Art of Ernest Hemingway.* Louisiana State UP, 1981.

Wood, James R., and Fern E Wood. "Reproductive Biology of Captive Green Sea Turtles *Chelonia mydas.*" *American Zoology,* vol. 20, 1980, pp. 499–505.

Wooster, Dana. Senior feline keeper, Woodland Park Zoological Gardens, Seattle, WA. E-mail to Sylvester, Mar. 2000.

Wrobel, David, et al. *Pacific Coast Pelagic Invertebrates: A Guide to the Common Gelatinous Animals.* Sea Challengers, 1998.

Young, Philip. *Ernest Hemingway: A Reconsideration.* Harcourt, Brace and World, 1952, 1966.

Zug, George R. "Penial Morphology and the Relationships of Cryptodiran Turtles." *Occasional Papers of the Museum of Zoology: University of Michigan,* no. 647, 1966, pp. 1–24.

———. E-mail to Sylvester, Mar. 2000.

INDEX

Page numbers in italics refer to illustrations.

Aberdeen Bestiary, 77–78
Acevedo, Alejandro, 65
Achilles, xviii
Adams, Nick, 66, 118
Africa, x, 3, 29, 35, 38, 39, 58, 72, 118; dreams of, 37; smell of, 38
Afro-Cubans, ix, 12, 20, 55, 74, 76, 97, 100, 108, 109, 116, 117
Ahab, 73, 84, 89
allegory, Christian, 20, 80, 93
Almeida, Ismael Léon, xi, 61, 82–83, 92, 99, 105
American Big Game Fishing, 62, 66
American Indian (Native American), 11, 12, 59
Amfortas, 91
Andreson, Ole, 40
Anita (boat), xiv, xv, xvi, xxiii, 66
anthropomorphizing, 46, 49, 75, 100
Apostles, 26
Arion (poet), 65
arm wrestling, 79–80, 82
Ascension, 4, 97
Ashley, Lady Brett, 73, 89; Jake and, 99
ay, implications of, 104

Backman, Melvin, xxii, 69
Bahamas, 3
bait, 14, 50, 52, 63; seizing, 62, 65–66
bait fish, 10, 60, 61, 62
Baker, Carlos: *Ernest Hemingway: Critiques of Four Major Novels*, xxii; *Ernest Hemingway: A Life Story*, xvi, 43, 64, 73, 84; *Hemingway: The Writer as Artist*, xxi, 16–17, 33, 38, 42, 52, 99, 111, 117; on Santiago, 117
Barbour, James, 31
Barnes, Jake, 7, 89; Brett and, 99

baseball, 27, 30, 33, 35, 36, 41, 363; Santiago and, 10, 23–24, 25, 31–32
Beach, Sylvia, 68
beaches, x, 110; lions on, 35, 37, 39, 94; whiteness and, 38
"Bear, The" (Faulkner), 11, 48; Boon, 93
Beard, Captain, 38, 42
Beegel, Susan: "Eye and Heart: Hemingway's Education as a Naturalist," 45; "Guide to the Marine Life in Ernest Hemingway's *The Old Man and the Sea*, A," 9, 55, 56, 62, 82, 83, 105; "Monster of Cojimar, The," 9, 95, 106–7, 114; "Santiago and the Eternal Feminine: Gendering La Mar in *The Old Man and the Sea*," 9, 11, 22, 49, 50, 55, 74, 80, 83, 108; "Thor Heyerdahl's *Kon-Tiki* and Hemingway's Return to Primitivism in *The Old Man and the Sea*," 20, 48, 102
before the mast, explained, 35
Being-Itself, xviii, 87
Benedict XV, Pope, 21
benevolent, described, 6
Berenson, Bernard, xxi
Berg Library, 18
Bergson, Henri, 38, 39
Bible, versions of, xvii, 94
billfish, 51, 98; spear of, 110, 114
Billfish, Marlin, Broadbill, Sailfish (Mather), 62
Billfish Story, The (Ulanski), 51
Bimini, xvii, 4, 6
birds, 14, 45, 46, 53, 71, 75, 79, 100; migrating, 72
Birth of Tragedy, The (Nietzsche), 67
black spots, 90, 94
blackness, 53
bladders, 58, 69–70, 88

Blake, William, 12
blindness, 14, 53, 90, 94
blood, 11, 69, 72, 92, 107–8, 117; life/death pulse of, 80; offering of, 88, 109; plankton and, 94; presentation of, 81; as sports reference, 79–80; taste of, 82, 111, 116; yin/yang in, 80
blood pressure, 116
blood trope, 11–12, 69, 72–73, 80–82, 94, 107–8
Boca Ciega, 110
bodega, described, 26
bohio, 20, 113
bone spurs, 78, 83
Boon. *See under* "Bear, The" (Faulkner)
brains, shark, 97, 99, 100, 107
Brasch, James D., 68, 88
breeze, xix, 13, 38, 72, 75
Brennan, Jack, 40, 99
Brenner, Gerry, xxiv–xxvi, 49, 58
Brinnin, John Malcolm, 115
broadbill, 69, 100
Broadus, R. N., 4
Brown, Robert Morgan, xxi
Browning, Robert, 89
bullfighters, 42, 43
bulls, 71, 73–74
buoyancy, 69–70, 88, 95
buoys, 46–47, 61
Burhans, Clinton, xxii, 41
"Burnt Norton" (Eliot), 38
Burwell, Rose Marie, xvi, xvii
Busch Stadium, 32
Buske, Morris, ix

Cabanas, xiii, xvi
Cadwalader, Charles, xiv
Cain, William, 103
Cain and Abel, xxv
Calvary, 86, 104, 112
Cambridge Companion to Ernest Hemingway (Donaldson), ix
Camus, Albert, xxiii
Canary Islands, x, 3, 37, 38, 58, 61, 76, 77, 94
cancer, skin, 6, 84
"Canticle of the Sun" (St. Francis), 76
Casa Blanca, 79
cast nets, 11, 22
Castro, Fidel, 8, 23
Castro, José: sharks and, 104–5, 106
Catalan, 18, 69
Catholicism, 20, 30, 72, 74, 76, 77, 101–2

Caxton, William, 21
Céspedes, Carlos Manuel de, 27
Cézanne, Paul, xxi
Charles Scribner's Sons, 3, 33
Christ, 4, 7, 20, 26, 28, 55, 65, 77, 78, 103; birth of, 84; crucifixion of, 56, 64, 69, 79, 90, 93, 104, 111, 112, 117; disciples and, 7–8; Greek acronym for, 93, 94; leprosy and, 86; Passion of, ix, 64, 73, 84, 86, 87–88, 100, 104, 108, 112–13, 115; resurrection of, 77, 90, 94; Saint Peter and, 101; suffering of, 69, 90, 104; symbolism of, 97
Christianity, x, 7, 12, 26, 64
Churchill, Dean, 13, 54, 74
Cienfuegos, 79
climate, indicators of, 28–29
clouds, *74, 75,* 97, 103
Cobre, 28
cod liver oil, 9, 48
Cojimar, 8, 9, 10, 13, 14, 34, 43, 46, 47, 48, 61, 64, 82, 91, 96, 106, 116, 117–18
commercialism, 24, 47
community, 20, 40, 110, 114
Compleat Angler (Walton), xvii
Compostela, 7, 21
Conrad, Joseph, 38, 42
consciousness, cognitive, 87
Cosmopolitan, xvi
craftsmanship, 14, 35, 47, 52, 53, 118
cramps, 73, 106–7, 107–8; preventing, 108–9
Creator, 79
Critical Heritage (Meyers), xx
Cross, carrying, 86
cross-trees, described, 82
crucifixion, 56, 64, 69, 90, 93, 94, 104, 111, 112, 113, 115, 117
Cruz, Mary, xiii
ctenophores, 55
Cuban Revolution, 23
Cult to the Orishas, 115
culture: Christian, 12; Cuban, 24; fishing, 47; Native American, 59
Cummins, D. Duane, xi, *xxiv*
current, 12–13, 53, 61, 78

Daily Mail, 97
Dana, Richard Henry, 35
David (*Garden of Eden*), pole of, 87
David (*Islands in the Stream*), 68, 100
Davis, Roger (*Islands in the Stream*), xvii

death, xviii, 89, 95; acknowledgment of, 74; life and, 103; natural order and, 93; resistance to, 99–100
deep wells, fishing in, 50
dehydration, 73, 85, 90, 96, 106, 116, 117
Delpino, Mary, xiii
depth: literal/symbolic importance of, 51; one-mile, 61
DeRojas, Alma, 22
destiny, xxii, 8, 26, 54, 67; self-professed, 61
Diario de la Marina, 24
Digital Library of the Caribbean (University of Florida), 24, 25
DiMaggio, Joe, xvii, 24, 27, 32, 33, 36, 40, 102; bone spur of, 31, 83; career of, 27; faith in, 25, 30–31; resurgence of, 26, 28
disciples, 7–9
dolphinfish, 46, 54, 80, 83, 87; color of, 82; gutting, 82; playing/joking by, 65
Dominguan, Luis Miguel, 116
Donaldson, Scott, ix
dorado, 54, 82, 83
dreams, 29, 37, 39, 40–42, 87, 114
dressed out, described, 23
Drusin, Ronald E.: on myocardial infarction/heart attack, 116–17
Dudzinski, Kathleen, 65
Durán, Gustavo, 27
Durocher, Leo, 36

easterly wave, 86–87, 103
Ebbets Field, 32
Eckert, Scott, 59
eighty-five (number), 22–23, 27
eighty-seven (number), 27–28
Eisenhower, Dwight D., 48
El Campeón, Santiago as, 4, 56, 68, 73, 79, 82, 87, 89, 111, 117
El Cid Campeador, 82
El Mundo, 24
Elijah, 4
Eliot, T. S., 6, 38, 39, 42
Emanuel, 63
End to Innocence (Fiedler), xx
endurance, 64, 76, 79
Ernest Hemingway: A Reconsideration (Young), xxi, xxiii
Eros, xxiii
Esquire, 71, 92, 99
eternal, xxii, 11, 27, 67, 94, 110, 113

Eucharist, 88, 103
Eurydice, 112
Evanchuk, Roberta J., 55
exceptionalism, xiii, 68
eyes, 23; cat, 78, 107; marlin's, 95; Santiago's problems with, 93–94; shark, 107

faith, 8, 17, 19, 23, 25, 30, 37, 44, 68, 101, 114
Fangue, Nann A., 92
Farrington, S. Kip, Jr., 6, 9, 46–47
Fathers, Sam, 48
Faulkner, William, 11, 39, 48, 93
feeding, 14, 50, 53, 54, 83, 92, 102, 104; migrations, 13
feminism, xxiv, 49
Fergusson, Erna, 30
Fiedler, Leslie, xx
Finca Vigía, xvi, 68, 108
Finito, 102
fish: big-game, 63; Christian sign of, 55; days without, 27–28; focus on, 76; Greek word for, 93; movement of, 61; raw, 72
Fisher King, ix, 6, 7, 34, 43, 89, 91, 114
fishermen, 10, 11, 101; commercial, xvi, 51; Cuban, 19; intimacy between, 7–8; successful, 9, 36; tricks of, 85
fishermen in May, described, 28
"fishers-of-men" allusion, 34
fishing: catch-and-release, xxv; commercial, 102; deep, 51; long-line, 46; shark, 9, 46; spring, 28; technique for, 63
fishing days, number of without a large catch, 4
fishing lines, 18–19, 72, 87–88, 90; cutting, 69; gaining, 82; hand-held, xxv, 4, 5, 18, 50, 51, 88; steady, 71
flag of permanent defeat, 5
Flash of the Spirit (Thompson), 91
Flora, Joseph M., 64
Flores-Pena, Ysanur, 55
Florida Current, 3, 12–13, 28, 54
Florida Straits, 3, 13, 28, 44, 62, 96
flying fish, 46, 54, 77
folk medicine, Cuban, 108–9
folk traditions, 74
formalized, described, 56
forty (number), application of, 4
Fowler, Henry, xiv
Francis, Pope, 117
Friar, Kimon, 115
Friedman, Norman, 47

frigate birds, 46, 53
Fuentes, Gregorio, *xxiv*

gaff, 5, 33, 78–79, 100
galanos, 104–5, 106, 107. *See also* whitetip sharks
Galilee, 7
gambling, 12, 36
Garcia, Manuel, 40, 99
Gawain, 114
gender terms, xxv, 23, 49, 66, 89, 100
Gilbert, Perry W., 9
God, 63, 65, 74, 79, 90, 101
Golffing, Francis, 67
Golgotha, 112–13, 115
Gomez de la Maza, Federico, 61
González, Miguel, 36
good and evil, acceptance of, 19–20
Gospels, 94, 113
Grail Castle, 114
Grail myth, ix, 89, 114, 115
Grand Banks, 51
Great Blue River, xiv, 55
great well, described, 45
green: as condition of fish, 11
Grey, Zane: fishing days and, 4
Grimes, Larry: "'Bad Luck or No Luck at All': Religion, Magic and Chance," 76; *Hemingway, Cuba, and the Cuban Works* (editor with Bickford Sylvester), ix; "Hemingway's Religious Odyssey: The Afro-Cuban Connection in Two Stories and *The Old Man and the Sea*," 21, 85, 91, 118; "Lions on the Beach: Dream, Place and Memory in *The Old Man and the Sea*," 39, 77
Guanabacoa, 115, 116, 117
Guanabo, 110
Guanche, 7
guano, 20
Guildenstern, 111
Gulf of Mexico, 3, 28, 44, 107
Gulf Stream, xiv, xxii, 3–4, 21, 28, 44, 45, 54, 55, 102, 109, 118; color of, 6; fishing in, xiii, xiv; map of, 2
Gulf weed, 44, 45, 56
Gurko, Leo, xxii–xxiii
Gutiérrez, Carlos, *xii*, xiv, xv, *xv*, xvi, xxiii, 50, 66; on Hemingway, xiii

Hail Marys, 74, 76
Hamilton, Edith, xviii

hand game, 79
handlining, 50–51
hands, ix, 11, 12, 80, 81; cramping, 73, 89, 106–7, 108; healing of, 18; personified, 89; sin and, 90; spastic, 10; traitorous, 82; weakened, 31; wounded, 69, 72, 89, 90, 104, 107–8, 109, 110, 113
hands-on-the-line method, xxv, 51
harbors, 8, 37, 65, 79
hard-braided line, ix, 18–19
harpoons, 33, 70, 76, 81, 110; described, 5; rope for, 98–99; using, 15, 72, 80, 97
Hatuey beer, 30
Havana, 8, 12, 13, 28, 32, 35, 36, 45, 64, 76, 79, 110, 116
hawks, 71, 72
Hays, Peter, ix, 11, 48
Hayward, Leland, xvi–xvii
healers, 90, 97
heart, 60, 97, 116–17; feeling, 95
Hemingway, Ernest, *xii*, xv; *Across the River and into the Trees*, xvi, xvii, xx; "Big Two-Hearted River," 66; "Clean, Well-Lighted Place, A," 109; Correspondence with Robert Morgan Brown, xxi; *Death in the Afternoon*, 84, 93; *Farewell to Arms, A*, xvii, 12, 42, 45, 87, 89, 113–14, 116; "Fifty Grand," 40, 99; Fishing Log, xiv, 50, 59, 62; *For Whom the Bell Tolls*, xx, 7, 71, 89, 99, 102, 116; *Garden of Eden, The*, 87; *Green Hills of Africa*, 3, 73; "Indian Camp," 118; "Interview" (*Writers at Work*), xvii, xxi; *Islands in the Stream*, xvii, 4, 54, 68, 100; "Killers, The," 40; "Marlin Off Cuba," 62, 66, 70, 77, 92; "Natural History of the Dead, The," 84; Nobel Prize, xx, xxi; Nobel Prize acceptance speech, 52; *Old Man and the Sea, The*, ix, xiii, xx, 4, 39, 41, 45, 48, 50, 54, 64, 87, 93, 94, 106, 107, 108, 109, 110, 114; "On Being Shot Again," 99; "On the Blue Water," xiii, 50; "Out of Season," 42; "Out in the Stream," 92; Pulitzer Prize for, xx; "Snows of Kilimanjaro," 15; style of, xxiv; suicide of, xxvi; *Sun Also Rises, The*, xvii, 3, 7, 40, 71, 73, 89, 96, 99; "There She Breaches! Or Moby Dick off the Morro," 71; "Today is Friday," 64, 76; *To Have and Have Not*, 4, 30, 59, 99, 115; "Undefeated, The," 99, 102; vision of, xxiii; *Winner Take Nothing*, 113
Hemingway, Gregory, xxvi

Hemingway, Patrick, xxvi, 48
Hemingway, Pauline, xxvi
Hemingway Collection, xix
Hemingway: The Inward Terrain (Hovey), xxiii
Hemingway: The Writer as Artist (Baker), xxi
Hemingway's Education: A Re-examination (Buske), ix
"Hemingway's Extended Vision" (Sylvester), xxiii
Henry, Frederic, 12, 42, 89
Herbermann, Charles George, 21
Herlihy-Mera, Jeffrey, 7, 9, 26, 27, 61, 73, 75, 82, 114
Hernández, Anselmo, xxiii
heroism, xxii, 41, 68, 110
Hesiod, xviii
holiness, 93, 95
Holy Land, 21
homosexuality, latent, xxiv
Honduras, 15
hooking, 62, 64, 100
hooks, 10, 71, 96
hope, 14, 47, 66, 81, 101, 110, 115; resolution and, 99
Hotchner, A. E., 6
Hovey, Richard, xxiii
Hudson, Thomas, 54
human agency, 90
human imperfection, 48
human potential, 30
humanity, 100; labor and, 42
humans, nature and, 71, 79
Hurley, Harold, 23–24, 26, 33
hurricanes, 9, 28, 75, 87
Hürtgen Forest, 106

iceberg theory, 17
Ichthys, 55, 88, 93, 108, 112
identity, 11, 38, 39, 41–42, 106
Iesous Christos Theou Yios Soter, 55–56, 93
"If-" (Kipling), 88
Iliad, Hemingway and, xviii
imagery, 6, 12, 69, 73, 81, 93
imagination, 12, 38, 39
International Gamefish Association, xiv
iridescence, 55, 56, 58
Ivancich, Adriana: arrival of, xvi

Jacob, 78
Jaws (movie), 106

Jehovah, 42
jellyfish, 55, 56, 57, 58, 67
Jesus Christ, Son of God, the Savior, 20, 55–56, 93
Jews, 29
Jobes, Katherine T., xxii, xxiii, 65
John Fitzgerald Kennedy Library and Museum, xix
John the Divine, 7
Johnson, Kenneth, 83
Jordan, Robert, 7, 89, 99
Joyce, James, 16
Judas, 73, 82

Keltner, John, 90
Key West, 4
killing, xxii, xxv, 47, 63, 66–67, 84, 92, 94, 115, 117; love and, 102
Killinger, John, xxiii
kingdom of God, 44
kinship, 6, 7, 47
Kipling, Rudyard, 88
Klimley, A. Peter, 104, 107, 109
knife, sheath, 69
knight of faith, xiv
Koje Island, 48
Kongo Cosmogram, 91, *91*
Korean War, 25, 48, 107

La Habana Elegante, Hemingway and, xiii
Lanham, C. T., 41
"Lapis Lazuli" (Yeats), 41
Larson, Kelli, xxvi
leaf springs, 115, *115*
Life, xvi, xx
light, exposure to, 52, 53
lions, 35; on the beach, 39; community and, 40; dreams of, 29, 39, 40–41, 42, 87, 114; identification with, 39, 41; natural features and, 40; power of, 77; presence of, 77
long-line fishing, 46–47
Longmire, Samuel E., 31
Lord's Prayer, 77
Losada, Luis A., 33
Lot's wife, 112
love, killing and, 102
Love, Glen, xxv–xxvi
luck, 44, 54, 99; bad, 108; buying, 110; dependence on, 51–52; lack of, 9; restoring, 115; violation of, 110–11

Luque, Adolfo, 36
Lynn, Kenneth, xxvi

MacDonald, Dwight, xx
Mack, Connie, 35
mahi-mahi, 54, 83
Major Leagues, 31, 33, 36, 116
mako sharks, *98,* 105; blood and, 72; death of, 100; feeding habit, 102; resistance by, 99–100; size of, 97–98; teeth of, 98; will of, 99–100
man-of-war, 56–57; immunity of, 57, 58
man-of-war bird, 46, 53
mandala, mystery of, 42
Mandel, Miriam B., 26, 50, 105
Manolin, xxv, 9, 14, 29, 30, 69, 104, 110, 113, 118; defiance by, 115; faith of, 68, 114; nature and, 47; Santiago and, xxv, 8, 30, 34, 41, 43, 48, 63, 65, 67, 72, 75, 88, 91, 114, 116; withholding name of, 42
Maria (*For Whom the Bell Tolls*), 89
marlin, xvi, xxiii, 9, 12; action of, 88; attacks by, 199; bait and, 60, 62; behavior of, 62, 66; bill of, 66; bleeding by, 72; blue, *xii,* 65, 91; brother, 75; colors of, 66, 91, 92; current and, 61; feeding by, 50, 55, 62; fishing for, 13, 14, 28, 45, 50, 51, 53, 63, 64, 67–68, 93; gender of, 65–66; hanging motionless, 96–97; killing of, 104; landing, 89, 91, 95, 96, 108; male/female, 66; mechanoreceptors of, 60–61; nobility, 75; older/larger, 62; sharks and, xvi, 10, 40, 48, 81, 88, 97; silver, *xv;* spear of, 110; spiritual detachment from, 95; spotting, 62; sympathy for, 100; tail of, 92; towing by, 63; weight of, 65; will of, 31; wounding of, 72
Martin, 26, 114; Santiago and, 29–30; stew from, 30; Terrace and, 29
mast, 64; carrying, 18, 112; stepping, 95
Mather, Charles O., 62
Mau Mau rebellions, 48
Mayo Clinic, 73
McCarthy, Senator Joe, 27
McGraw, John J. "Little Napoleon," 35, 36
Melville, Herman, xx, 73
memories, 37, 38, 41, 66; long-term, 35; visual, 39
Meyer, Wallace, xvii
Meyers, Jeffrey, xx, xxvi, 6
Meza, Ramón, xiii
Moby-Dick (Melville), xx, 73, 89
Modelo Beer Factory, 30
Modern Fiction Studies, ix

money, 7, 14, 48
moon, 85; gravitational pull of, 49; theory of, 50
moral maturity, 11
Morgan, Harry, 30, 99
morning, feeling, 45
Moses, 4
Mosquito Coast, 15
Mote Marine Laboratory, 9
Motif Index of Folk Literature, xviii
motorboats, 46–47, 48
Myers, Ransom A., 47
Myers, Wallace, xvi
mysteries, x, 12, 81
mysticism, 26, 49, 59–60
mythologies, 59, 83–84

nada, 109
narrative, 16, 19, 22; strategy, 45; third-person, 45
natural aristocracy, 30, 41
Natural History Museum, xiv
natural order, xxvi, 45, 75; life/death and, 93
natural world, understandings of, 87
nature, xxii, xxiii, 46; aristocracy of, 40–41; eternal values of, 113; force of, 114; heart of, 40; humans and, 71, 79; integration into, 45; oneness with, 47; paradoxes of, 57; struggle with, 79
Negro, 79, 82; as blood brother, 80
Nelson, Lowry, 34
Nereus, xviii
neuromasts, 61, 78
New Testament, 4, 64, 86, 101
New York Yankees, 24, 25, 26, 27, 28, 30, 31, 32
New Yorker, xvi
Nicaragua, 15
Nickel, Matthew, 109
Nietzsche, Friedrich, ix, xxiii, 67, 68, 81, 89, 90, 100, 102, 107; allusion to, 112
Nietzsche en Italie (Pourtalès), 68
Nietzscheism, Christianity and, x
Nixon, Richard, 48
Noah, 4
numerology, 26

oakum, 38
oars, 62, 85
Obeah, 62
objective correlative, 11, 25
ocean: color of, 54–55; as feminine entity, 46; gravitational pull on, 49. *See also* sea

ocean depths, 45, 62, 88
Ochun. *See* Oshún
odds, 79, 82, 109, 115, 116
Oedipal complex, xxiii
Oggun, 108
O'Hara, Mary, 90
old man, phrase, xviii
Old Man and the Sea: The Story of a Common Man, The (Brenner), xxiv
Oldsey, Bernard, xvii–xviii
Old Testament, xxv, 4, 101
olfactory function, shark, 97
One God, 20
Oriental Park, 35
Orion, 83, 101
orisha, 20, 21, 22, 44, 55, 108, 109, 111, 115; ocean, 108; river, 108
Orpheus, 112
Oshún, 20, 22, 28, 44, 55, 85, 108, 109; color of, 56, 72
Ott, Mark, xiv, xvi, 4, 45, 50, 62, 65, 66
Our Fathers, 76, 91
Our Lady of Charity, 21, 22. *See also* Virgin of Charity; Virgin of Cobre
Oxford Book of English Verse, The, xvii
Oxford English Dictionary, 56

pain, 88–89, 91, 93, 110
Palo Monte, 91, 108
Papa. A Personal Memoir (Gregory Hemingway), xxvi
Paris Review, The, xviii, xxi, 17
Park, Susanna, 23, 90
Partisan Review, The, xx
Parzival, 34, 42, 91, 114
Passion of Christ, ix, 64, 73, 76, 84, 86, 87–88, 90, 100, 104, 108, 112–13, 115
Pedrico, 26, 114, 118
Pedro, 26, 114
pensativo, 29
Perceval, 7, 114
Perico, 24, 26, 114
Perkins, Maxwell, xvi, 3
pesos, value of, 96
phosphorescence, 44, 71, 85, 86, 111
Pilar, 99, 116
Pilar (boat), xiv, xxiii, 4, 43
plankton, 56, 57, 58; blood and, 94; coloring of, 55; feeding on, 55, 60; red sifting of, 55
Plimpton, George, xvii, xxi

PMLA, ix
porpoises, 54, 65, 83, 87
Portrait (Ross), xvi, xxi
Portuguese man-of-war, 56, 57
Pourtalès, Guy de, 68
poverty, indicators of, 28–29, 37, 54
power, 77, 102
prayers, 65, 67, 74, 76–78, 94, 111; accidental, 79; nada, 109
pride, 101–2
Prince, Eric, 28
Prometheus, myth of, 67
Psalms, 74, 78
psychic harmony, 115
psychic integration, 42
psychic unity, 42
psychological survival, 60
ptomaine poisoning, 75
pull, described, 63

quartering, described, 109
quest, 21
questions, rhetorical, 37
Quint, 106

rainbow, 55, 56, 58
Ramos, Miguel "Willie," 97
Raver, Duane, xi, 92
Reading Hemingway (Mandel), 50
reality, 23, 51, 52, 53, 87
Regla Ocha, 108, 109
relics, 7, 20, 21, 22, 114, 117
religion, 103; Afro-Cuban, 77, 97, 100, 108, 109, 116, 117–18
remoras, 15, 16, 92
resolution, 22; hope and, 99
restoration, 21
resurrection, 77, 90, 93, 94
Reynolds, Michael, xvi, xviii, 68, 88
rhythm, poetic, 38
Richert, Scott P., 76
Rigel, 83
rituals, 11, 12, 66–67, 80, 100
RMS Nova Scotia, 106
robber birds, 46
Rogelio, 11, 26, 114
Roig, Sanchez, 61
Romans, 29
Romero, bulls and, 71, 73–74
Romero, Pedro, 40

ropes, 38, 98–99, 101
Rosencrantz, 111
Rosencrantz and Guildenstern Are Dead, 111
Rosenfield, Claire, 66
Ross, Lillian, xvi, xxi
Roth, James, 18
rowing, 44, 112
Russell, Joe, xiv, *xv*

Sacred Heart of Jesus, 20, 21, 80, 108
Saint Andrew, as fisherman, 8
St. Anselm of Canterbury, 88
Saint Francis of Assisi, xiv, 72, 76, 81
Saint Iago, 84, 117; as fisherman, 101, 114
Saint James, ix, xiv, 21, 67, 81, 102, 117; as fisherman, 8, 101, 114; Santiago and, 7
Saint John, as fisherman, 9
St. John of the Cross, 109
Saint Martin, ix, 29
Saint Peter, ix, 102; as fisherman, 8, 26, 101, 114
salao, 4, 108, 115
salmon, ix, 51
Samuelson, Arnold, xvi
San Pedro, 101
Sánchez Roig, Mario, 61
Santeria, ix, x, 62, 108, 115, 116
Santiago: agony of, 90, 93, 104, 113; antagonism of, 58; appearance of, 16; awareness of, 86, 103; balance of, 118; benefactor of, 29; champion, 60, 68, 73, 81–82; combat of, 107; confidence of, 44; craftsmanship of, 52, 84–85; deceit of, 67, 77; defeat of, 115; determination of, 106–7, 109; dreams of, 29, 39, 40–41, 41–42; effectiveness of, 42, 106; exceptionalism of, 48, 53, 68; exhaustion of, 81, 85, 93, 109, 110, 112–13, 117; expectation of, 54; health of, 96, 108–9; identity of, 38, 41–42; identification with marlin, 99, 100; isolation of, 63, 74; lamentation by, 81, 107; Manolin and, xxv, 30, 34, 43, 48, 63, 65, 67, 72, 76, 88, 114, 116; meditation by, 102–3; memories of, 35, 66; mind's eye of, 45; mortal imperfection of, 10, 73; new Cuba and, 47; observation by, 49, 50, 97; optimism of, 20, 101; pain, 110; paradoxical identity, 71, 83–84; past/present and, 42; pride of, 102; prowess of, 64, 65; psychic unity of, 42; reciprocative approach of, 49; renewal, 118; research on, 26; self-identity of, 68, 84; skin of, 60; social role of, 6, 72; spiritual role of, 6; strength of, 79; struggles of, 51, 55, 56, 79–80, 92; vision of, 12, 55, 71, 90, 93, 94; weather and, 14; weakness of, 112; wind and, 13; women of, 21, 22; wounding of, 31, 69, 111, 116
Santiago de Cuba, 117; pilgrimage to, 21
Santiago del Prado, 21
Santiago el Grande, 109
sardines, 10, 26
Sargasso weed, 22, 44, 56, 96
Sargassum weed. *See* Sargasso weed
Sartre, Jean-Paul, xxiii
Saunders, Edward "Bra": cramps for, 73
scavengers, 102, 106
Schorer, Mark, 51
Schratwieser, Jason, 92
Schwab, Ivan R., 90
Schwartz, Delmore, xx
Scribner, Charles, III, xvi; dedication to, 3
sea, *74;* color of, 6; healing by, 97; identification with, 6–7, 22, 49; rising of, 76; rolling of, 74; small, 76, 78; wounding by, 97. *See also* ocean
sea hawks, 53
sea life, communing with, 75
sea logs, xiv, xvi, xvii, 4, 50, 62, 71
Sea of Change, A (Ott), 4, 50
sea swallows, 45, 46
seaweed, 56
self-identity, 61, 67, 68, 84
Settelmeyer, Robert, 31
sexism, xxiv, xxv
Shakespeare, William, xvii
shark factory, 9, 10
shark liver, 48, 60
sharkfin soup, 105
sharks, xvi, 65, 82, 94, 97–98, *98, 105,* 118; attacks by, 81, 99, 106, 109, 111; bonnet-headed, 105; brains of, 97, 99, 100, 107; eyes of, 107; feeding by, 106; fighting, 100, 106, 114; fins of, 105, 106; great white, 106; hammerhead, 68; landing, *19;* marlins and, 10, 40, 48, 81, 88, 97; olfactory function of, 97; shovel-nosed, 105, 106; survival skills of, 100, 106; teeth of, 98, 99, 100, 109; warm-blooded, 98; whitetip, 104, 104–5, 106, 107, 109
Shaw, Robert, 106
sheath knife, described, 69
sheet, 106; described, 28, 101
Sigman, Joseph, 68, 88

Simonides-Quintillian tradition, 39
sin, 101; hands and, 90; pride and, 102
Sisler, Dick, xxiv, 31–32, 33, 116
Sisler, George, 32, 33, 116
Sisyphus, xiv
skiff, 4, 5, 64
skin, 6, 57, 58, 86, 92; weathered/scarred, 60
skin cancer, 6, 84
small sea, 76, 78
Smith, Chuck, 18
social conflict, 48
social dimension, 41, 47
social groups, 72, 114
Sodom, 112
sounding, 63, 64
Spanish Civil War, 27
spear, 5, 15, 93, 110, 114, 118
spiritual perspective, restricted, 14
spiritual survival, 60
spoon, described, 96
Sportsman's Park, 32
spurs, 31, 78–79, 83
Starkie, Walter, 21
stars, 83, 85; as distant friends, 83–84
stations of the cross, 112–13, 118
steel, tempered, 116
Steinessen, Sarah, 65
Stephens, Robert O., xx
stern, 44, 83; described, 19
stillness, 75, 95
stingrays, 100, *101*
Stoneback, H. R., 58
Stoppard, Tom, 111
strangeness, 15, 16, 56, 59, 77, 78, 96–97; defined, 14
Strauch, Eduard, 49, 113
strength, xxiii, 11, 29, 64, 68, 76, 77, 79, 81, 87, 88, 102, 112
sucking fish, 15, 16, 92
sunlight, 52; fish activity and, 83
superstition, 62
survival skills, 100, 106
swamping, 94–95
swordfish, 69, 98, 114
Sylvester, Bickford, ix, 91; "Cuban Context of *The Old Man and the Sea*, The," 18, 20, 26, 34, 43, 115; *Hemingway, Cuba, and the Cuban Works* (editor with Larry Grimes), ix; "Hemingway's Extended Vision: The Old Man and the Sea," xxiii, 57, 65, 67, 78, 117;

"'They Went through This Fiction Every Day': Informed Illusion in *The Old Man and the Sea*," 99, 115, 116, 117
symbolism, xxi, 11, 18, 69; Christian, xxii, 55, 87, 90, 97

Taino Indians, 21
Taylor, Charles, 68
teeth, shark, 98, 99, 100, 109
terminal, described, 27
terns, 46
Terrace restaurant (La Terraza), xxv, 8, 29, 31, 43, 114, 118
Theogony (Hesiod), xviii
theology, Catholic, 76–77, 101–2
thole pins, 44, 62
Thompson, Charles, 71
Thompson, Robert Farris, 91
Thompson, Stith, xviii
Thoreau, Henry David, 68
three-hook rig, xxv, 46, 47
Thus Spoke Zarathustra (Nietzsche), 68
Tiburon, 118
tiller, 106, 109
too far out, xviii, xix, 68, 81, 82, 92, 110, 111, 112
Toynbee, Phillip, xx
trade winds, 13–14, 72, 91, 96, 103
treachery, using, 67
Tricas, Timothy C., et al., 104
trickery, 15, 16, 17, 57, 64, 67, 77, 85, 92, 108
trolling, 4, 50, 51
Tropical Park, 31
tuna: bait fish and, 61; raw, 73
turtles: eggs of, 60; green, 59; harvesting, 14–15; hawksbill, 59; heart of, 60, 95; hunting, 15, 16; loggerhead, xvi; myths about, 59–60; sea, 59; sex life of, xvi; veneration of, 59
Twentieth-Century Interpretation of The Old Man and the Sea (Jobes), xxii
Two Years before the Mast (Dana), 35
Tyack, Peter, 65
Tyler, Lisa, 49, 50

Übermensch, xiv, 81, 111
Ulanski, Stan, 51, 61, 66, 78, 91
"Ultimate Billfish, The" (Ulanski), 91
universe, xxii, xxiii, 20, 58, 73, 82, 111, 113, 115; force of, 114
USS *Indianapolis*, 106

Van Guilder, Gene, 84
Vergano, Dan, 47
Villarreal, Raúl, xi, 108, 109, 116
Villarreal, René, 108, 116
Virgin Mary, 55; Afro-Cuban manifestation of, 20–21; statue of, 21, 117
Virgin of Charity, 28. *See also* Our Lady of Charity; Virgin of Cobre
Virgin of Cobre, 20, 27, 108; described, 21–22; manifestation of, 55; pilgrimage to, 76; presence of, 55. *See also* Our Lady of Charity; Virgin of Charity
vision, 16, 17, 23, 38, 71, 78, 97; constricted, 93–94

Wagner-Martin, Linda, 103
Waiting for the End (Fiedler), xx
Waldmeir, Joseph, 117
Walton, Isaak, xvii
warblers, 71, 100
Waste Land, The (Eliot), 6
weather, 4, 9, 75, 103; bad, 86–87; patterns, 13–14

Wells, Arvin R., 40
whitetip sharks, 104, *105,* 106; diet of, 109; eyes of, 107; teeth of, 109
whore, described, 57
Williams, Wirt, xxi
Wood, James R., and Fern E., 59
Wooster, Dana, 39, 41
World War II, 25, 48, 60, 95, 106
Worm, Boris, 47
Wrobel, David, 55

Yeats, W. B., 16, 41
yellow, 22, 44, 55, 56
Yemaya, 55, 108, 109
Yoruba, 109
Young, Philip, xxi, xxiii–xxiv, 33, 117
Youth (Conrad), 38, 42

Zeus, 67
Zug, George R., 59